Wakefield Press

# A VIEW FROM THE HORIZON
## MY LIFE IN POLITICS AND BEYOND

Peter Duncan was the Attorney-General in Don Dunstan's reforming Labor Government in South Australia in the 1970s and a minister and parliamentary secretary in both the Hawke and Keating governments. He initiated many pieces of social reform legislation, including the abolition of capital punishment, the recognition of de facto couples, making rape in marriage a crime (the first in the English-speaking world) and equal employment opportunity. Perhaps his most notable personal achievement was his Private Members' Bill on homosexual law reform, passed into law in 1975. He was one of the very few politicians to serve in a state parliament and in the federal parliament.

# A View from the Horizon
## My Life in Politics and Beyond

# Peter Duncan

Wakefield Press

Wakefield Press
16 Rose Street
Mile End
South Australia 5031
www.wakefieldpress.com.au

First published 2024

Copyright © Peter Duncan, 2024

All rights reserved. This book is copyright. Apart from any fair dealing for the purposes of private study, research, criticism or review, as permitted under the Copyright Act, no part may be reproduced without written permission. Enquiries should be addressed to the publisher.

Edited by Penelope Curtin
Designed and typeset by Clinton Ellicott, Wakefield Press

ISBN 978 1 92304 251 3

A catalogue record for this book is available from the National Library of Australia

Cover images

*Front, top left to bottom right:*
With Puspa and the Australian Consul-General in Bali at Australian Government-sponsored tourism seminar
With my friend José Ramos-Horta in Dili, Timor Leste
With Nick Xenophon at Taman Unique Hotel, Lombok
Friends of the Earth poster advertising Peter Duncan as speaker
With Don Dunstan and daughter Georgia, 1987
With Paul Keating
With Paul Noack, and sons Jock and Macgregor, campaigning for a nuclear-free Elizabeth, 1981

*Back, left to right:*
Lynn Arnold, Brian Medlin and Peter Duncan addressing other draftees and anti-Vietnam war protesters outside Keswick Barracks on the day Peter was called up
Swearing-in of Sir Douglas Nichols as the first First Nations person as Governor
Marriage to Julie, 1979
With lifelong friend and comrade David Wilson, circa 1971, anti-Vietnam war march. The mass media portrayed those opposed to the war as 'scruffy long-haired gits', prompting Peter and David to wear suits

This publication has been assisted by the History Trust of South Australia–Wakefield Press History Initiative.

# Contents

| | |
|---|---|
| Foreword | vii |
| Dedication | ix |
| CHAPTER ONE  The beginning of my political consciousness | 1 |
| CHAPTER TWO  Pre-parliamentary life | 20 |
| CHAPTER THREE  Married life and a parliamentary career | 30 |
| CHAPTER FOUR  The Member for Elizabeth | 35 |
| CHAPTER FIVE  Homosexual law reform | 44 |
| CHAPTER SIX  The Dunstan Government | 53 |
| CHAPTER SEVEN  Dunstan's Attorney-General | 64 |
| CHAPTER EIGHT  Tragedy and change | 80 |
| CHAPTER NINE  The Corcoran Government and marriage to Julie | 97 |
| CHAPTER TEN  The Bannon Opposition | 110 |
| CHAPTER ELEVEN  The Hawke Government | 130 |
| CHAPTER TWELVE  Change continues | 144 |
| CHAPTER THIRTEEN  The Keating ascendancy | 156 |
| CHAPTER FOURTEEN  The 1993 federal election | 170 |
| CHAPTER FIFTEEN  Post-parliament | 179 |
| CHAPTER SIXTEEN  Lombok and Julie's death | 204 |
| CHAPTER SEVENTEEN  A new life | 217 |
| CHAPTER EIGHTEEN  A lawyer once again | 228 |
| Timeline: Peter Duncan | 250 |
| Legislative and Attempted Reforms at a Glance | 254 |
| Acknowledgements | 262 |

# Foreword

During the 1970s Peter Duncan was the reforming Attorney-General to the equally reforming South Australian Premier Don Dunstan. He was a minister in the Hawke Government and parliamentary secretary to the Attorney-General in the Keating Government; he was therefore one of the very few politicians in Australian history to successfully move from the state legislature to federal parliament and to occupy ministerial positions in both jurisdictions.

The book begins with his political awakening and takes us to the end of Peter's parliamentary career to the defeat of the Keating Government, along the way providing a ringside seat to politics in both the South Australian and Australian parliaments. It is up-front and personal and forthrightly illuminates the personalities of successive premiers and prime ministers and describes the action behind closed doors.

Perhaps Peter's most notable and memorable achievement was his Private Member's Bill in the South Australian Parliament (1973–75), the first in the Westminster system, worldwide, to treat homosexuals and heterosexuals equally, prompting the former High Court Judge, Justice Michael Kirby, to later describe him as 'the father of homosexual law reform in Australia'. He reformed not only laws but legal practice and agencies. An activist minister and local member, Peter was involved in early environmental law reform, including the victory over the damming of the Franklin River in Tasmania. A lawyer himself, he set up a successful legal practice in Adelaide, which still bears his name. He played an important role in saving the youngest of the Bali Nine (the teenage drug mule Scott Rush) from the firing squad.

History requires that Peter be acknowledged, his contributions to progressive change recorded for posterity. The work of this reforming legislator in removing the yolk of discrimination from the necks of gay men and from women, consumers, tenants and vagrants, along with abolishing hanging and making rape in marriage a crime (the first in the English-speaking world), was not only pioneering but transformative. Much of what we now understand as modern Australian law, including recognition of de facto couples, equal employment opportunity, the protection of the disabled, the criminalising of discrimination on the grounds of race and public interest disclosure – the list goes on – can be traced to his pioneering work. If Peter believed in something, he was prepared to cross the floor of parliament (as he did over the privatisation of the Commonwealth Bank).

Against this reformist backdrop, a brutally honest autobiography emerges, painting a portrait of an imperfect man and setting Peter's memoir apart from so many others. Gone is the self-congratulatory and smug tone usually associated with the memoirs or autobiographies of past politicians, who, as they attempt to assure their place in history, airbrush their transgressions, their flaws and their mistakes from the pages of their personal record and the public account.

The memoir also covers Peter's remarkable post-parliamentary life and starkly reveals that the flame of his political passion has not been extinguished, despite the impact of Parkinson's Disease and old age.

His has been a tumultuous life, marked by the loss of his beloved wife Julie from cancer at a relatively young age, his attempted suicide, his business successes and failures, and even criminal charges, in September 2007, of which he was acquitted. It has also been a life of joy and renewal, with his partner Puspa, his children and grandchildren, and friends and comrades over a long life, a distant horizon from which he may view his life's journey: a rich life to be celebrated. His autobiography is funny, sad, insightful, totally honest, idiosyncratically Australian and unambiguously authentic.

Hon. Rev. Dr Lynn Arnold AO

# Dedication

*A View From the Horizon: My life in politics and beyond* is dedicated to Julie Duncan, my partner in life, who was aged only 52 (five years younger than my father) when she succumbed to cancer, in 2005. The writing of this autobiography would have been much improved by her wise counsel, her style and her skilful editing. The story of my life and of people I have encountered should have been a joint effort with her. Julie would have softened some judgements, edited the more controversial pieces and turned the knife more adroitly in a few instances.

Andy Williams's version of 'Days of wine and roses', the music by Henry Mancini and lyrics by Johnny Mercer, was my mother's favourite song, remaining so until her dying days, and we played it at her funeral in 1991. It witnessed another surge in family popularity when Julie first read the lyrics and discovered the connection to English poet and writer Ernest Dowson. But first, let us turn to the lyrics by Johnny Mercer:

> The days of wine and roses laugh and run away like a child at play,
> Through the meadow land toward a closing door,
> A door marked 'never more', that wasn't there before,
> The lonely night discloses, just a passing breeze filled with memories,
> Of the golden smile that introduced me to,
> The days of wine and roses, and you.
> The days of wine and roses …

It was Julie's sunny and welcoming smile that first attracted me to her when we met at lunch in Hobart in 1978. Later, the lyrics seemed to be a direct reference to our love and the generally sad theme we well understood. But it was the connection to Ernest Dowson, the originator of the phrase 'The days of wine and roses' that we found the most charming.

Ernest Dowson was a poet associated with the so-called 'decadent' movement, a concept inherently attractive to us in the 1980s. However, the correct words were: 'They are not long, the days of wine and roses' – and how true that tragically proved to be in our case. Incidentally, he also coined the phrase, 'Gone with the wind'.

In Julie's self-penned obituary, she wrote:

> Peter had already been branded – even before I met him. He was on the agenda as a passionate radical – oooh dangerous – and for passing some of the best legislation the country has ever seen. Things that cost so little, like laws for gays, women, consumers, tenants, used car buyers, vagrants, laws that abolished hanging, made rape a crime in marriage and forced the advertised average of 50 matches into a box. Legislation which left him forever labelled as dangerous, but which was never seriously changed, and which was broadly adopted nationally relatively quickly, I could only admire.

From that first meeting to this day, I miss her every day. I know Julie would have enjoyed this reminisce.

*A View From the Horizon* is also dedicated to Puspa (Wiwik Puspa Rini), who has been my loving partner and constant companion as my days matured from autumn to the winter of old age. I credit Puspa, a tall Indonesian woman from Java and who is younger than me and beautiful, with opening my eyes to the natural world in which we live and to respecting all living things. She did so as we embarked on our favourite pastime of bushwalking and discovering every corner of Lombok. Our daily morning hill climb near our home in Senggigi covers about four kilometres and has done wonders in slowing down the progress of Parkinson's Disease, from which I suffer, keeping us fit and ensuring our mutual love of nature is experienced joyfully every day.

Peter J. Duncan

CHAPTER ONE
# The Beginning of my Political Consciousness

My first political engagement, at least as far as I can remember, occurred in 1965 following my enrolment in law at the University of Adelaide. It happened that I turned 20 on the first day of 1965, when the death lottery – conscription for the Vietnam War – was introduced. I was called up but was automatically granted a deferment being a student. To that point, I had given little thought to conscription and the Vietnam War, but in retrospect I realise I had been a pacifist by nature since childhood. I believed that settling disputes physically was inherently wrong.

I have a vivid recollection of a memorable fight one day in primary school between me and the school bully, Roger Benz, who was always picking on other boys. Although I can't recall the reason for the fight, I can remember being terrified. We were on the bitumen schoolyard rolling around, when suddenly I found myself on top of Roger, and in my fright, I grabbed him by the neck and started banging his head onto the hard bitumen ground. Before long a teacher had rescued Roger. And the other students rescued me, explaining to the teacher that bully Benz had started it. As there was no real damage, there were no repercussions, except that Roger left me alone after that. In my later, pacifist, life, I often joked that I had only ever been involved in one fight, which I had won, and so I quit while I was ahead. At university, I soon became a conscientious objector to military service.

I took full advantage of orientation week – even to the extent of joining the uni rowing club, my only attempt to get involved in sport at university. Although I didn't realise it then, I attended university during an amazing period. It was quite possibly *the* time of the century – the remarkable 1960s – to be on campus. I joined the Labor Club and became a tutor for ABSCOL, the Aboriginal scholarship and tutor scheme, my interest in this role having been sparked by Bob Ellis – not the late well-known scribe of the same name – but the Bob Ellis staffing the Labor

Club booth when I enrolled as a member. Bob, who had just been elected as the national convenor of ABSCOL, and I started a conversation about politics more generally. After he had explained the scheme to me, I happily agreed to become a tutor.

My recruitment occurred just after the freedom ride to western New South Wales, led by the late Charles Perkins, an event that had attracted a great deal of media coverage, especially in that it revealed the disgraceful conditions of Aboriginal people living in regional Australia. A week or so later, Bob organised a meeting of the half a dozen people who were the ABSCOL group, including Baden Teague, later a Liberal Party Senator. Despite our enthusiasm, we achieved little – after all, we were only young non-Indigenous university students with no real expertise in mentoring and tutoring, although we did organise some useful fundraising. I now realise that our group was confronting many of the problems I also faced throughout my adult life when dealing with Aboriginal policy issues.

The year 1964 was a great example of my successfully managing lots of activities simultaneously. Good experience for being a super-busy government minister later in life. I studied hard for my matriculation in Sydney and, having matriculated, applied for university entrance at the University of Adelaide, as my father had transferred to Adelaide with the Commonwealth Bank.

More than 100 students were enrolled in first year law. Males while on campus were expected to wear a sportscoat (houndstooth) and a Law School tie, while the fewer than 20 women in our year were not burdened with a prescribed dress code, neat casual being all that was required. I had a few cheap suits which I had worn as a junior printing executive at John Sands in Sydney, and they became my standard dress in first and second years. Given that I still couldn't believe that I was a law student, the phrase 'a grin in a suit' comes to mind. By second or third year, the authorities requiring law students to wear ties and coats had lost the argument. The lecturers wore academic gowns, at least to lectures, including the dashing Brian Grieves, whom I later appointed as a judge when I was Attorney-General.

During first year I was living at home with my parents, first in Stonyfell, and later in Linden Park. In August of that year, on my father's birthday, the family went to a well-known Adelaide French restaurant, Chateau Fort, owned by an eccentric French chef, Monsieur Vigor. We arrived and were shown to our table, and drinks soon arrived. The menu was presented, and food ordered. My father ordered a steak, 'well done'. The waiter advised that the steak was best not overcooked. My father insisted. Next, the French chef arrived with a similar explanation. Nonetheless, my father, possibly having somewhat unsophisticated tastes, prevailed. Exasperated, the chef–owner withdrew to the kitchen. When the food arrived, my father's steak was burnt to a cinder. Being my father and conflict-adverse, he drowned the cinders in sauce and ate his main course, determined not to let this issue ruin the night.

We were then offered dessert and my father was told by the waiter that Monsieur Vigor was preparing a special dessert for Dad, 'on the house'. My father surmised that the gratis dessert was to compensate for the steak fiasco. When the dessert arrived, my father was presented with a plate on which sat a large scoop of ice cream with cigarette butts protruding like spikes, with the chef commenting that 'Here is a dessert that should well satisfy your taste in food monsieur'. My normally restrained father advised the assembled family that we were leaving without paying. We did, and as far as I know, there were no repercussions. What a pity that episode occurred before smartphone cameras and social media. Notably, many Adelaide people of a certain age have a 'Chateau Fort story'.

Recently I recalled this incident, prompting me to speculate on the events and people that had shaped my father. The Depression struck as Dad was entering adult life. His father, my grandfather, Walter Duncan, had a financially turbulent life. A Nationalist Party Senator for most of the 1920s, he earlier had paid positions in the trade union movement.*
He was on the staff of Billy Hughes, the party-swapping (he was expelled from three) seventh Australian prime minister, during the First World War. My paternal grandmother died when my father and his brothers were young children and during their childhood they were constantly uprooted and moved to various locations around Sydney. I remember in the early 1960s, when we were living in Sydney – I was a teenager at the time – we would be driving along and my father would say, 'Oh, there is [name] street where we used to live'. For a while when growing up, my father went to a private boys school but at other times there was barely enough food on the table. He managed to get a job in the Commonwealth Bank in the early 1930s and perhaps this job came with a little help from his father, Senator Walter Leslie Duncan (1883–1947), Senator for New South Wales,

---

\* The Nationalist Party, also known as the National Party, was an Australian political party. It was formed in February 1917 from a merger between the Liberal Party and the National Labor Party, the latter formed by Prime Minister Billy Hughes and his supporters after the 1916 Labor Party split over First World War conscription.

1920–45 (Nationalist Party), or his uncle Edward (Ted) Riley, 1859–1943, an ALP member of the House of Representatives.

I believe that the combination of an unstable childhood and the conditions of the Depression scarred him for life. Although my father was politically a radical, he was very cautious in his personal life, which seems to have influenced his views on religion, social life and finances.

My first recollection of social life in the Law School was its class divisions. Male students from St Peters College and Prince Alfred College and women from private non-Catholic schools formed a distinct group and tended to socialise together. The male or female students from Catholic schools comprised another group, while students from high schools and lesser private schools made up the also-rans group. I soon made friends with people from this group, including Chris Townsend, Arwed Turon, my lifelong friend Peter Kellett, Greg Holland, George Ozolins, Ian Bidmeade and others. Coming to terms with this class division was quite a shock, although these barriers soon disintegrated as those of us who passed first year moved into second year. Social life then became more a case of law students being a clique, a group within the wider student body. The university rowing club turned out to be equally riven with class distinction and displayed little interest in rowing with a student from Sydney, and before long I had abandoned the rowing club altogether.

A few weeks after moving to Adelaide, I purchased a cream 1960 Volkswagen Beetle using the money from the sale of a 1957 Jaguar I had bought very cheaply a few years earlier. Apart from its relatively low price, it was a remarkable magnet, never failing to attract desirable young women. The VW was to become my personal transport for the next six years and was a great car for that period of my life. On reflection, I now see it as a metaphor for how I was also changing. In Sydney, my Jaguar, which I'd bought on an instalment plan – and it had consumed about two-thirds of my wages – symbolised my priorities at that time in my life. In Adelaide, I bought what I could afford – the VW. I was happy with it and to have it unencumbered.

Financially surviving at university soon became an issue, one to which I had given insufficient thought. My father paid the fees and gave me a small allowance, which was not nearly enough for even my reasonably modest requirements. In first year, I struggled through, working as a builder's labourer in the first and second term vacations. It was hard work but paid well. While working in this job, I joined the Builders Labourers Federation, my second union membership after the Printers Union, the latter I'd joined in Sydney while working for John Sands before we moved to Adelaide.

In the second term holidays, I was working on the extensions to St Aloysius Catholic College in Wakefield Street, Adelaide. Next door was Frank J. Siebert Funeral Directors. My job, under the supervision of the foreman, was to dig the trenching for the plumbing, after which the plumbers would install the piping. The next task for me was to backfill the trenches and then hose them to ensure that the soil was well settled. However, water, as they say, always finds its level. I was duly undertaking this work when a black-suited man came running on to the site yelling loudly, and all hell broke loose. The foreman was quickly informed that the water had somehow entered the basement of the funeral parlour and was threatening to give the coffins a new lease of life as small boats. The foreman saw this as confirmation of his belief that 'eggheads' (a term used for intellectuals or people out of touch with ordinary people and known as 'nerds' these days) were idiots, and, probably to assuage the anger of the man from the funeral parlour, sacked me on the spot.

I went home without my pay, with three days remaining before the job was supposed to finish, following which I would return to uni for third term. My father, having enjoyed a laugh at this incident, advised me to pay a visit to the union. The union officials were terrific. Not only did they extract the backpay due for work already done, but also some pro rata holiday pay and pay for the three days I should have worked had not the 'illegal' termination occurred. The union attitude was that the foreman had failed in his duty of supervision and that any fault lay with him not me. In due course, the cheque arrived, and I was set to financially survive until Christmas.

Exams had finished for me in about the middle of November and on the day of the last exam, I headed for Sydney in my Volkswagen for the 1965–66 holidays. Once there, I called at John Sands to see some of my old workmates, thinking that I might be able to get temporary work during the busy Christmas period. One of my former workmates gave me a copy of the most recent printing trades newspaper, which included an advertisement for a full-time printing salesman at the *Land* (a newspaper catering predominantly to a rural readership). I applied and was employed the next day at a very attractive salary and commission for sales made.

The five weeks until Christmas were hard work but the people at the *Land* loved my work, which made me worry about how I was would terminate my 'permanent' employment. My twenty-first birthday fell on

1 January and my parents were organising a birthday party for 25 February, when I was supposed to be back in Adelaide to enrol for second year law. Happily, sometime in the middle of February, my boss came in one morning in a cranky mood and criticised some minor aspect of my work. Seeing an opportunity, I raised the stakes and told him that if he wasn't happy, I would resign, and I did. I was paid out and left on relatively good terms, with no one at the *Land* ever realising that I was a full-time university student in Adelaide.

Around the time I turned 21, I think I was becoming more interested in political issues. I clearly remember being disappointed by the 1961 Australian election outcome, which Labor lost by a knife edge, my perspective influenced, no doubt, by my father's disappointment with the result. The assassination of the US President, John Kennedy, in 1963 also loomed large. It is easy to forget just how alarmed the entire world had become during the Cold War, but the Cuban missile crisis had just been resolved and when Kennedy was killed it was widely believed that 'the Russians had done it'. Nothing much has changed. It is likely that a similar response would occur today.

My political education initially came from my father, who instilled in me the Australian ethos of a 'fair go', which simply required applying a fairness test to any issue. My position on pacifism, which I'd held from childhood, developed some coherence and sophistication at university and has stood me in good stead ever since – personally, physically and philosophically. At university and since, I have been a lifelong peace activist. I was a conscientious objector to the Vietnam War and opposed the war itself throughout the entire time of Australia's involvement, which ended with the election of the Whitlam Labor Government. I was a foundation trustee of the Graham Smith Peace Trust in Adelaide. Later, when a member of the Australian Parliament, I was one of only six members of the House of Representatives to vote against the Hawke Labor Government's decision to involve Australia in the first Gulf War. I also opposed the Indonesian invasion of East Timor and supported the independence of Timor Leste, through all those long 25 years of Indonesian occupation. I have been on the right side of history, on these matters, throughout my adult life.

In first year university, I studied politics under Neal Blewett and Bob Hetherington; Politics I with Bob Hetherington was an important influence on my political development. Any prior understanding I had of politics was little more than an unstructured disorganised collection of ideas. Now the ideas were structured into a coherent format, which included the makeup of parliaments, elections and electoral systems; the political parties and what they stood for; the idea of collective action versus individual action; and freedom versus authoritarian ideologies, although the latter was not explored in detail, as it was a subject for study in second year.

I had some vague idea at the time that Bob Heatherington might have been a Labor Party supporter, but when questioned specifically, he was careful not to admit to any such affiliations. I presume he subscribed to the (in my view) nonsense view of a values-free lecturer. I later discovered that he was married to the daughter of the Labor state education minister, Ron Loveday, and was a member of the Labor Party. He and I both worked on the unsuccessful campaign to elect Keith Le Page as the Labor Member for Sturt in 1966. Bob later moved to Perth, where he worked as a lecturer at the University of Western Australia, before obtaining preselection for a Western Australian Legislative Council seat, which he won. He remained in the WA Parliament until 1989.

Sometime in the late 1980s I met Bob again, at an ALP National Conference. He was at that time part of the Right faction delegation from WA, and I was from the SA Left. When I challenged him about being in the Right faction, his unexpected response was, 'We Catholics know where home is!' He also explained his reasons for having moved to WA. He felt that his Labor orientation would mean that he would find promotion difficult, as the politics department at Adelaide University, under the new head, Professor Graham Duncan (no relation), was pursuing a New Left political agenda. I was pleased to catch up with Bob, and to have the opportunity to thank him for the role he had played in my political development.

I was a student of Neal Blewett in the third term of Politics 1 and attended an engaging lecture given by him: 'From the Playford Government to the Dunstan Labor Government – a study in the politics of change'. I must say I found studying politics fascinating and much more interesting than the dry law subjects that seemed to have no connection to life, as I then knew it. Neal Blewett became the Member for Bonython in 1977 and an excellent Minister for Health in the Hawke Labor Government. Years later Neal made a joke purportedly at my expense:

'My god! Was I responsible for Duncan?' [laughter]
'No Neal. If you were responsible, I would be with you and your Centre
    Left faction, reintroducing tertiary education fees and student loans!',
    I responded.

By 1966, Professor Graham Duncan had recruited several young radical lecturers and tutors, including Brian Abby, R.W. Connell and, at the time, the New Left-supporting Bob Catley, before his conversion to extreme conservatism and the Right of the Labor Party. Students for Democratic Action did not really emerge until late in 1966 or 1967, but the issues the New Left brought into focus were surfacing. White Australia, and the appalling treatment of Aboriginal Australians (not counted in the census until the 1967 referendum); the influence of the US civil rights movement; and the campaign against the Vietnam War and conscription were radicalising the campus. I was committed to reform through the ALP, but the emerging New Left had a big influence.

Big questions started to exercise my mind. Why was society so hierarchical? Why couldn't we have a more egalitarian society? The structures of society seemed to need changing. It was not simply a case of choosing between rich and poor. Just because people were good at business did not seem to be reason enough to give them the right to a greater say in public policy. Why couldn't society provide enough food, shelter and medicine for everybody? I could really understand the New Left argument that simply raising the standard of living but keeping people subordinate to others wasn't a solution.

Prior to 1965, the Law School staffing had been largely reliant on part-time lecturers and tutors from the Adelaide legal profession. In 1965, Professor Arthur Rogerson, an English academic, was appointed as the Dean of the Law School. He recruited a group of full-time lecturers who were young, interesting, and reasonably radical for lawyers: Brent Fisse, John Keeler, Brian Greaves and later the criminologist Alan Perry, from New York. Margaret Doyle was appointed as a tutor, a first for the Law School in terms of full-time appointments.

Brian Greaves had a sort of 'take no prisoners' style, dictating his lectures and occasionally including the punctuation and spelling! He treated first year students with a degree of contempt, telling us in one lecture that, 'First year law isn't so much about legal education as a gate-keeping exercise, as about one-third of you won't be in the Law School next year'.

His prediction proved to be largely true. On one occasion, a female student arrived late to his lecture. Greaves invited her to walk down to the front of the lecture theatre and when she did, he then invited her to walk across the lecture theatre in front of him. Finally, he told her to walk up to the back of the lecture theatre and out the door and to come back for the next lecture on time. When I was Attorney-General, I appointed Brian as a judge of the District Court, and he became a thoroughly excellent judge.

I first met Don Dunstan, if not in Orientation Week 1965, then soon after, when he came to the campus to address a student meeting on the Barr Smith lawns. Not long after this address, I was invited – I think by David Combe, the ALP's organiser in SA – to Don's house in George Street, Norwood, for a Young Labor Contingent (YLC) meeting. I had joined Young Labor and the Labor Party in April 1965. At the time, membership of the ALP was a prerequisite for becoming a member of Young Labor. Don and his wife Gretel's house was a hub of activity for the young enthusiastic Labor acolytes of the time. Don had a very important influence on me, convincing me early in my university life that the Labor Party could achieve real change, real reform. Don became one of my mentors, the other being Lionel Murphy. Don and I didn't always agree, but, with the exception of issues associated with casinos and poker machines in 1973 and uranium in the late 1970s, we got on very well.

Holding residential seminars at Graham's Castle in Goolwa was one significant activity of the Young Labor Contingent. Scheduled three times a year, the seminars were very popular and well attended, with the accommodation almost always booked out. The format comprised a combination of a significant (usually interstate) Labor MP as the guest speaker and small group discussions on prominent issues of the day. Gough Whitlam came on several occasions, as did Lance Barnard (later prime minister and deputy prime minister respectively), Senator Lionel Murphy, Clyde Cameron, Senator Sam Cohen, Victorian Opposition Leader Clyde Holding, Tom Uren and Jim Cairns. The seminars were usually attended by Mick Young and/or David Combe, as ALP party officials, to ensure that the proceedings were reasonably orderly and not generating negative headlines. We learned a great deal about politics and political issues through these seminars and in my opinion it is a great pity that residential seminars such as these are no longer held as political education activities for young people. In retrospect, it is also a great pity that more young trade unionists did not participate or were not more enthusiastically encouraged to do so.

I was exposed to these interesting, I thought at the time, ideas at university. I became radicalised and much more concerned with the politics of making the world a better place. A debate flourished in the Left in the university about 'the path to socialism' and whether the Labor Party provided any solution to the problems of South Australia, Australia and the world, or whether a more radical framework was desirable, such as the Communist Party. By late in my second year of university, the New

Left was emerging on the Adelaide campus. Two of my friends in first year law, Peter O'Brien and Rob Durbridge, had left the Law School and had become radicalised, establishing and leading Students for Democratic Action (SDA), branches of which were established on other university campuses around Australia.

O'Brien, Durbridge and others had rented a large flat in an old traditional house in Lefevre Terrace, North Adelaide, where they produced the SDA weekly newsletter *Grass Roots*; ran 'Party schools' (generally group discussions on theory and political practice and campaign organising); and partied in the more traditional sense of the word. I participated in much of this activity and enjoyed the socialising. The house was owned by David St Ledger Kelly of the Kelly clan, which is part of the Adelaide legal establishment. St Ledger Kelly was my Elements of Law lecturer in first year and I recall thinking at the time that he was a fairly dour character, although my opinion of him changed in later years. On one occasion, I had been partying with the SDA people at Lefevre Terrace and had fallen asleep. I woke up in the morning and needed the bathroom urgently but encountered a locked bathroom door, the only option then available to me being the back garden. In the middle of obtaining the desired relief, I suddenly heard St Ledger Kelly's clipped tones behind me:

> Mr Duncan. I hope you would know by now from your legal studies that a tenant and his guests might have the right to party on until unreasonable hours, but they certainly do not have the right to murder the petunias in the landlord's garden.

I murmured some apology and departed.

Many of those active in the university Labor Club at the time went on to play prominent roles in politics and society in South Australia and the nation, and included John Waters, the secretary of the Young Labor Contingent, who was later a long-term member of the National Conference representing the Northern Territory; David Combe, who later became the ALP National Secretary; and John Bannon who went on to become premier of South Australia. Anne Summers, a leading feminist writer and columnist, editor and publisher, headed the Office of the Status of Women in the Department of Prime Minister and Cabinet and advised prime ministers Hawke and Keating on issues relating to women, while her then husband John Summers became a professor at Flinders University. Also among the group were my friend and lifelong confidant David Wilson; Graham Maguire, subsequently a Labor senator; and

Les Wright, later an economist of note, as well as Julien Miles and Phyl Mahony, Robyn Layton, Julie and Bob Ellis, and many others.

Almost concurrent with my arrival in South Australia was the great struggle for a Labor victory in the 1965 state election. Although the election was basically over by the time I had settled into university life, it had generated an aura of excitement, which lingered on during the year, with the *Advertiser* adopting 'the end is nigh' tone, breathlessly announcing daily initiatives from the new government.

It is almost impossible from this distance to appreciate the upheaval in South Australian life that the 1965 election represented. Although the new Labor Government was yet to start implementing its programs, the overturning of the comfortable power structures of the previous 32 years must have seemed like a revolution to the bureaucracy and business establishment. For those of us on the Left, it was an exciting time. Given its three decades of conservative government, the state was viewed elsewhere as boring and as a very, very ordinary and dreary place. The Walsh Labor Government radically transformed South Australia with many reforms, both major and minor.

Later that year, the Menzies Government announced that Australia would send a battalion of combat troops to Vietnam, provoking an eruption of protest both on campus and in the city. I attended the first of my many anti-Vietnam War demos sometime in the middle of 1965. By the time of the federal election in 1966 – the Vietnam election – I was fully engaged in ALP politics. I was the vice-president of the University Labor Club and on the campaign committee for the candidate for Sturt, Keith Le Page.

We worked hard every weekend, door-knocked most of the electorate and were justifiably indignant about the Vietnam War and conscription. Although we were completely optimistic about the election outcome and Keith Le Page's chances, the election was a catastrophe, with Labor losing in a landslide, and in Sturt, despite all of our efforts, Labor went backwards. I learned two valuable lessons from this election: first, the opinion polls were mostly right; and second, an overly enthusiastic Labor base can lead to a degree of blindness towards reality.

At the end of 1966, I obtained a holiday job with the Commonwealth Railways, initially as a 'silver boy', in other words, a dishwasher, dish pig or slushy. Later, I was promoted to a conductor second-class. It was a great job: once you were employed, you could be rostered for a trip or not, as you pleased. The passenger trains on which I was working ran from

Port Pirie to Parkston (Kalgoorlie) and Alice Springs. The Alice Springs–Darwin line had not been built and the connection of standard gauge between Kalgoorlie and Perth was under construction. On my first rostered trip, I arrived in Port Pirie just before Christmas to find that the Commonwealth Railways paymaster in Port Augusta was sick, and as a result Christmas holiday pay would be paid four days late.

The relevant union, the Australian Workers Union (AWU), declared our train to Perth 'black'. It was a 'double header'; in other words, a double-size train, with all the passengers about to arrive from Adelaide on the SA Government railways connecting train. Although the union was concerned about my not being a member, as soon as I indicated my support and my preparedness to join the union, I was issued with an AWU ticket, which I paid for a couple of trips later. The 'blacking' of the train had the desired effect. ComRail announced that additional accounting staff had been recruited from Adelaide and that all those who urgently required pay would be paid the next day. Our train was de-blacked and departed only four hours late, the passengers able to sleep on the train as planned.

During the 1966 Christmas vacation, I attended the Student Labor Federation conference in Melbourne and was surprised to find that it was not simply a gathering of ALP-aligned Labor clubs but a gathering of a very broad group of Left organisations and individuals. Maoists such as Albert Langer from Monash University, Brian Jones from Students for a Democratic Society at Sydney University, and Brian Laver and Mitch Thompson of Students (later Society) for Democratic Action at the University of Queensland. I think John Bannon was in Melbourne, mainly attending a National Union of Australian University Students (NUAUS) meeting, of which he became president. Others who attended included Jim Spigelman (later a judge and Chief Justice of New South Wales); Geoffrey Robertson (later an international jurist, human rights lawyer, academic, author and broadcaster); and Darce Cassidy (campaigner for social justice and alternative media and one of the 'freedom riders', along with Charles Perkins). The conference eventually disintegrated into turmoil. Following that experience, the next Student Labor Conference I attended was exclusively for groups supporting, if not affiliated with, the Labor Party.

While in Melbourne at that conference, I met Richard Walsh, one of the editors of the satirical *Oz* magazine. *Oz* was looking for a distributor in Adelaide and because I was always short of money as a student, I jumped at the opportunity. I went back to Adelaide and conferred with my friend

George Ozolins, who by then was an arts student. We agreed to become *Oz*'s Adelaide distributors, not a simple matter, because *Oz* was always, it seemed to us, being sued or charged for various alleged civil or criminal legal breaches. As distributors in South Australia, we would potentially be liable. Despite these concerns, the prospect of income prevailed, and we became the distributors, a job that involved collecting the magazines from Adelaide Airport and distributing a few copies to various delicatessens around the city.

All the newsagents were tied into a restrictive trade practice with Gordon and Gotch and would only sell publications distributed by that large wholesaler. This restrictive trade practice had to wait for Lionel Murphy's Trade Practices Act in the 1970s to be rendered illegal. Until then *Oz* magazine was excluded from newsagent distribution. At the height of our work, we were receiving 1500 copies from Sydney. George and I were getting about $75 each per month, which at the time was very good money. Incidentally, Richard Walsh still owes us $23, the amount we had to pay the airline for the last issue, which was never sent to Adelaide. Years later, I was told by Richard that they didn't send any copies to Adelaide because the last issue had quickly become a collector's item.

In early 1967, my father was moved by the Commonwealth Bank back to Melbourne and I was required to find my own accommodation. I found a flat at 54 Buxton Street, North Adelaide, which I rented from December 1966. The premises consisted of an old house divided into three flats. I became friendly with the owner, a Bulgarian woman, and I soon ascertained that she had a large mortgage and was stressed by her experience as a landlady dealing with tenants. I offered to rent the whole premises at a rent marginally more than her mortgage payment. I then found tenants for the other two flats at a rental amount that covered my payment to her. In other words, I had the small rear flat gratis. This arrangement worked very well until November 1969, when I discovered that the group of students who had rented the large front flat had done a runner. That they didn't owe much rent wasn't the problem: the major issue for me was that they had pulled up the floorboards and beams in the main living room and used them for firewood. The carpet that they'd subsequently laid on the bare earth floor had rotted.

I telephoned the owner's agent, who had been appointed in the middle of 1969. I had intended to come clean and admit the problem, but before I could describe my predicament, the agent explained that he had been meaning to contact me because the owner had sold the premises to a developer who was proposing to build flats on the site. He informed me that all of us had to be out by Christmas because the building was to be demolished. I was greatly relieved. I heard nothing about the missing floor but the experience taught me that both landlords and tenants can act reprehensively. That was a lesson I applied when designing the Residential Tenancies Act a decade later.

By the end of 1966, I had decided to seek election to the Student Representative Council (SRC), as one of the two Law School representatives. My election campaign and strategy were designed to limit my negative appeal (dangerous Left wing radical) and focus on my positives. Running as a Labor candidate in the Law School would have guaranteed defeat. My anti-conscription stand was popular amongst male law students, most of whom faced the death lottery and potentially military service at the end of their university life. However, while opposition to conscription was popular, opposition to the Vietnam War would not have drawn wide support in the Law School. I decided to try to attract votes from the new group of first years by hosting a welcoming party for them in the backyard of my new flat in North Adelaide. My proposal, in the absence of other options, was welcomed by the organising committee. On the night, I introduced myself to the first years and handed out a pamphlet with nothing much more on it than 'Vote Peter Duncan for Student Representative Council', and the sub-slogan 'Gives good parties'. As often happens, this vacuous election campaign was successful, and I was elected to the SRC.

That year, 1967, was an exciting time to be on the SRC. Peter O'Brien and Julian Disney were the editors of *On Dit*, the student newspaper, and were continually causing distress to some group or other. The SRC was the nominal publisher and would have been bankrupted if the multitude of claimed defamations had been litigated. I was on the SRC *On Dit* committee, which dealt with these complaints. Mostly, they were settled with an apology in person, not even in print.

Towards the end of the year, the *On Dit* editor position for 1968 was advertised, prompting me and my friend Arwed Turon to nominate as co-editors, roles elected by the SRC itself. We considered we were well-suited candidates as co-editors: Arwed, with his irreverent sense of humour and deep interest in the arts, and I, consumed by political issues. I can't remember who the competition was, but we won by one vote. Apart from paying a stipend of $200 per month, which Arwed and I shared, the editorship of *On Dit* involved a scholarship, following graduation, to work as a cadet journalist at Adelaide's the *News*, the city's daily afternoon newspaper.

Fortunately for the *News* management, they never had to contend with me or Arwed as cadets. The law became our ultimate destination.

It was during this year also that the referendum was held to alter the Australian Constitution to ensure Aboriginal Australians were counted in the census. Prior to the passing of the referendum, not only had Aboriginal Australians not been counted in the census, but state or Commonwealth parliaments could restrict their civil rights and rights as citizens. ABSCOL played a part in campaigning for a 'yes' vote. When the referendum was carried overwhelmingly, there was a feeling of vindication, as if something had materially changed in the lives of Aboriginal and Torres Strait Islander citizens. Sadly, of course, that was not the case, although some legal constraints had been removed and the stage set for the important, but inadequate, improvements in the lives of Aboriginal and Torres Strait Islander people.

During my adult life, Aboriginal and Torres Strait Islander graduate numbers have moved from none to 25,000 at the time of the 2016 census. Although this number indicates a certain degree of Aboriginal advancement, it masks the reality confronted by most Aboriginal people. That said, as demonstrated in recent times, a large group of highly educated Aboriginal and Torres Strait Islander people now advocate on behalf of First Nations people.

In the context of the political Right on the Adelaide University campus during the late 1960s, a moribund Liberal club existed, but little else by way of conservative or reactionary activity. The Australian Security Intelligence Organisation (ASIO), the National Civic Council (NCC) and the Democratic Labor Party (DLP) were no doubt present. I can recall seeing the state secretary of the DLP, Mark Posa, at a Union Hall meeting in support of the 1967 referendum campaign. When identified, Posa was roundly booed for several minutes. I presume that the NCC operated through the Catholic clubs and societies on the campus but kept a decidedly low profile. As incoming *On Dit* editors, we had no idea that 1968 was going to be a politically tumultuous year, the first disaster being the defeat of the Dunstan Government, despite getting 54 per cent of the statewide vote. This election result broke our hearts and enraged many, and provided us with an ideal opportunity to publish a special edition. We had done as much as we could to support the Dunstan Government, but the impact of the gerrymander in the rural areas was deeply disheartening.

Beyond domestic politics, the Soviet invasion of Czechoslovakia occurred later in 1968, the event that finally divided the Communist Party of the Soviet Union from the Communist Party of Australia, the CPA. By 1967, the CPA had already become alienated from its counterpart in the Soviet Union and was following the direction of the European Communist parties. To somebody who held social reformist views on many matters, it looked like a much more attractive proposition than the Stalinist party, although I never really viewed the Communist Party as an option or as offering a solution to the problems confronting Australia and the world: I was too wedded to the ballot box and liberal democracy, which means, I suppose, that my path to the ALP represented an intellectual choice; I was not a recruit in the traditional sense.

The year 1968 was the year of student revolts in Europe (including the Paris Uprising) and the assassinations of Robert Kennedy and Martin Luther King Jr. After our final edition of *On Dit* had been published, Richard Nixon was elected as the US President. The time when we were editors certainly provided a smorgasbord of political events to keep any student editor fully occupied.

The SDA, with Peter O'Brien and Rob Durbridge leading the charge, was campaigning for student democracy – for far greater student involvement in university governance. Their demands included abolition of exams and substantial student representation on the University Council, committees and faculty boards. Geoffrey Badger, the Vice-Chancellor (VC), was inclined to see these demands as having some merit and believed that the issues could be resolved by reasonable discussions between representatives of the various parties, perhaps resulting in compromises by all. He invited 30 of the student leadership to a buffet dinner at his university-owned home in Springfield, Adelaide's most expensive suburb. Many from the SRC and the University Union were invited, the *On Dit* editors, and some radicals, including Rob Durbridge and Peter O'Brien.

This dinner turned out to be a bad tactical error. Two days later, SDA's newsletter, *Grass Roots*, published an edition condemning the university for providing the vice-chancellor with a 'mansion on millionaires row'. After little progress had been made for student representation on the University Council, the SDA organised an occupation of the vice-chancellor's office, a move seen as outrageous by the uptown media and the establishment. However, the Chancellor, John Bray, and the VC were inclined to weather the dispute to avoid heightening the drama. The outcome was that some progress was made on student representation on the University Council and formal exams were abolished in a few courses, a partial victory and mainly viewed as a sensible outcome.

At the beginning of 1968, the law students in my year who wished to use their law degree to practise law were required to take up Articles of Clerkship with a practising lawyer. I did not have any contacts within the legal fraternity and so put my name down on a general list of students seeking articles at the Law Society Office. Given the difficulty in finding articles, I was fortunate to be assigned to Bruce Roberts and Brebner, a small commercial firm mainly undertaking the preparation of real estate documents for Lensworth Finance, owned by Bruce Roberts and his brother Gwynn Roberts. It was an old-fashioned outfit, run very properly. The Roberts brothers were addressed as Mr Bruce and Mr Gwynn. I was to find out soon enough that in their political lexicon, the Liberal Party was a Left wing organisation. In fourth year, the rules required the clerk to be at the law practice from 9 am until 5 pm, unless attending lectures or tutorials, with an hour off for lunch. This was somewhat difficult for me as editor of *On Dit*, although thanks to the other partner in the firm, Charlie Brebner, a very decent person, I managed to reduce my tasks with the firm to a certain degree. Brebner could see no reason why I had to draft documents from scratch, when the firm already had similar documents in precedent files. So, when Mr Bruce gave me a document to draft, I simply took it to Charlie, who gave me the appropriate precedent, thus saving me hours of drafting time.

The other factor working in my favour was the drinking habit of Mr Gwynn Roberts, notionally the General Manager of Lensworth Finance, which shared premises with the law firm. Mr Gwynn would be inebriated by 10 am and I would offer to drive him home at lunchtime. He would happily agree, and after taking him home to Unley Park, I would use the afternoon to work on *On Dit*, back at the office. Unfortunately, on one occasion, when dealing with the second to last edition of the paper, Mr Bruce entered my office, and my double life was exposed. However, after I had completed fourth year, and in my final year of articles, I was quite productive for the firm at the starvation wages paid, so all was forgiven. I completed my articles and was admitted to the practice of law in 1970.

The loss of the 1968 state election was a devasting event in local politics and in the history of South Australia. How could Don Dunstan, a hugely popular state premier, lose an election? The answer of course was a rigged electoral system and the then-influential Adelaide *Advertiser*, which was vehemently opposed to the government. There was a widespread feeling of unfairness, not only amongst the political class, but more generally (a strong sense of 'we was robbed'). The incoming Hall Liberal

Country League Government had a smell of illegitimacy attached to its every move and *On Dit* played to this mood at every opportunity.

During this period, I had a notable run-in with Don Dunstan. He came to the campus for a meeting in April 1968 and *On Dit* reported on the meeting and his speech. His staff had handed out copies of the speech, which we published *verbatim*, including a note in parentheses: 'Refer David's notes'. We did it as a bit of undergraduate humour. Don didn't see it that way and considered it as very unprofessional behaviour, blah blah blah. I argued that, if a written copy of a speech was handed out and it had prompts in it, then we were entitled to run it; and that it was his staff's fault, not ours. This episode didn't much endear me to David Combe, who was the 'David' referred to in the notes to the speech.

In July 1968, I was interviewed by the *New Left Review*, along with several other student leaders and described as: 'Peter Duncan, aged 23, fourth Year Law Student at Adelaide University, editor of *On Dit*, member of the Student Representative Council, member of the Socialist Club, the ALP Club and Students for Democratic Action'. I don't remember being a member of a socialist club and the SDA had no formal membership, although I must plead guilty by association with the SDA. The other correction was that the ALP Club was in fact the Labor Club. When it was set up or reformed in the early 1960s, the Labor Party Secretary, Geoffrey Virgo, was strongly opposed to any campus organisation using the name of the ALP.

Towards the end of 1968, I attended the Student Editors' Conference in Brisbane. It was a great opportunity to meet the other student editors, and my only regret was that the conference was not held at the beginning of the year for incoming editors, which would have been more beneficial in terms of contacts made. As part of the conference, each student newspaper submitted what was regarded as its best edition of that year, to be judged by the editor of the *Courier-Mail*. *On Dit* was runner up to the University of New South Wales' paper *Tharunka*, the Aboriginal word for message stick.

In the middle of 1969, a federal by-election was held in Bendigo. The ALP candidate was a young schoolteacher, David Kennedy. Gough Whitlam was the Labor Party Leader, and the by-election was viewed at the time as an opportunity for Gough to make a mark. The Young Labor Contingent decided to hire a bus and take a group of young party members to Bendigo to assist with arrangements. The bus trip was extremely successful, both socially and politically. We door-knocked and helped in other ways for three days and, when David Kennedy was elected the following weekend as the Labor member, he was very generous in his praise of our efforts. I didn't appreciate the internal politics at the time. The Bill Hartley and George Crawford-led Victorian Central Executive of the ALP were not supportive of Whitlam and saw David Kennedy as a Whitlam supporter.

The most notable political event of 1969 was the federal election, which Labor, with Gough Whitlam as Leader, narrowly lost. I was very disappointed, almost depressed, by this result. With the loss in South Australia the previous year, followed by the Whitlam loss, I began to have doubts about whether the parliamentary road could produce a genuine path to reform. The one aspect of the 1969 election was that Norm Foster won Sturt for Labor, a particularly pleasing achievement, in that a wharfie had knocked off the blue blood, Ian 'curly boy' Wilson. Wilson's family had had a long history of Right wing political involvement in the state, and his father, Sir Keith Wilson, had, in effect, bequeathed the seat of Sturt to Ian Wilson.

At the beginning of 1969, Sally Morton – my girlfriend at the time and later to become my (first) wife – moved to Melbourne to undertake nursing midwifery studies for a year, which led to numerous trips to Melbourne. I would see Sally during her free time and my parents for the remainder of the weekend. By this time, my parents were very pleased and proud of what they saw as my achievements.

CHAPTER TWO
# Pre-parliamentary life

I graduated in 1969 and was admitted as a barrister and solicitor in South Australia in 1970. A friend from Law School, Chris Cocks, had been admitted to the Bar a short time before my admission and had bought a partnership in a one-person practice, Scoresby Shepherd and Co. Shepherd was suffering from stress and soon resigned from the practice and Chris invited me to join him in a partnership. We changed the name to Cocks, Duncan & Co., which proved to be a mistake, as it attracted the attention of the Law Society's Legal Practice Committee. The conservative members of the committee were horrified to find that a couple of newly admitted young lawyers were in practice without the supervision of a more experienced practitioner. They threatened to make our practising certificates provisional and deny us the right to practise without supervision. We discussed our options.

Our practice operated from offices in Cowra Chambers in Grenfell Street, Adelaide. Across the corridor was an elderly lawyer, Charles Wheatley Reeves, whom Chris had met in passing. We shared a kitchen, and, in a coffee-making moment, Chris described our predicament to Reeves, who immediately offered to discuss a merger on the basis that he would retire after a couple of years. We ultimately reached agreement, and the Law Society was off our backs. Reeves had told us that he was the lawyer for Harris Scarfe, a longstanding Adelaide department store, and we believed we were joining a financially stable partnership.

It soon became apparent that his only work for the retailer was debt collection. This was before the 1971 Springboks Rugby tour, which was opposed by Cocks and me because of the South African apartheid regime. In 1970, media coverage on the possibility of a race-based team led to a discussion and heated argument with Reeves. He was a former South African, who apparently, as a young lawyer in South Africa, had helped draft some of the most abhorrent apartheid laws, of which he was particularly proud. Chris Cocks and I agreed that we couldn't continue in practice with Reeves. We met with Reeves and informed him of this. His response was to request that we give him a month to wind up some files and he would retire. A perfect solution.

We left his name on the letterhead for a while, wary of attracting the attention of the Law Society again. Chris and I struggled, but gradually over the next year we increased our client base, and with assistance from a most generous barrister, Christopher Legoe and my legal friend Derrence Redford Stevenson, we managed to survive without getting into too much legal trouble. Derrence, an excellent lawyer, was flamboyant, upsetting the Law Society and the Supreme Court by striding from his chambers to court across Victoria Square in the full legal regalia of wig and gown, a practice viewed as touting for business and prohibited in those days, when lawyers were not allowed to advertise. Sadly, Derrence was murdered in 1979. His gay lover was convicted of the crime.

Chris Legoe, later a Supreme Court Judge whom I appointed when Attorney-General, was the barrister in a civil matter in which I was involved. The case was between my client, Michael Mazzeo, an Italian migrant who had won a lottery, and Brian Edward Warming, a leading Adelaide second-hand car dealer. Warming had set up a complicated fraud to relieve Michael of his assets and, disturbingly, had done so with the assistance of a lawyer. It took two years to unravel the civil fraud but eventually we won, restored Mazzeo's property and obtained orders for damages and costs.

That said, executing the court's judgements and orders against Warming was almost as complex as winning the case. Our bailiff, Sid Allen, was a master at serving legal documents and in the matter of serving Brian Warming, who lived in a villa in Beaumont, Sid borrowed a postman's uniform and a red pushbike from a mate and turned up at Warming's house with a large parcel. Sid successfully served the documents on Warming and, with his house in danger of sale under a court order, Warming backed down and paid the damages and costs. I think the $20,000 costs saved our firm from near bankruptcy, or at least paid off an out-of-control overdraft. Incidentally, this experience with Warming helped to guide my views on the need for consumer law reform when I was Attorney-General.

Although I had barely earned a reputation by this time, I was deeply committed to the principles of fairness and justice, to the point that I would fight like hell to see justice restored. Over the years, the law firm that we started in 1970, which now operates as Duncan Basheer Hannon, became immensely successful and the leading industrial law practice in South Australia. At its pinnacle, the firm employed about 50 staff.

This was still the time of conscription to national service. My personal battle against conscription was about to heat up. Once I had finished university and completed articles, I received a formal notification to attend at Keswick Barracks in Adelaide for two years military training. By this stage, I had spoken several times at anti-Vietnam protests and had attended many more demonstrations, and ASIO undoubtedly had an extensive file on my activities. At this point, the Vietnam War, to the extent that it involved Australian combat troops, was in its fifth year. It was a war in which South Australians had died or been injured and had suffered the effects of Agent Orange and what is now described as post-traumatic stress syndrome. In fact, the first Australian killed in the war was from South Australia.

I had absolutely no intention of aiding the Australian-supported US invasion of Vietnam in any way. Initially, I had been a member of the Campaign for Peace in Vietnam and, particularly during the 1969 federal election, had campaigned for the Labor candidates, all of whom opposed the war. That had made a significant difference. The swing to Labor in South Australia had been over 10 per cent and Labor won eight of the 12 House of Representatives seats. However, given the loss of the 1969 election, I didn't feel that we were making sufficient progress and I began to support the more radical Vietnam Moratorium Committee (VMC). My call-up notice arrived about three weeks prior to the first Adelaide Vietnam Moratorium, in May 1970. I participated in the two subsequent moratorium demonstrations, wearing National Liberation Front badges, in other words, supporting Australia's enemy.

The chair of the VMC was Lynn Arnold, later Labor premier of South Australia. On the day I was to report for military service, the VMC organised a protest at 8.30 am outside Keswick Barracks. Using a loud hailer, Lynn Arnold and I addressed around 100 protesters and approximately 40 people who had been called up. I symbolically burnt my 'draft card', although in one sense I regret its destruction, since it would have been an excellent piece of memorabilia for posterity. The few military police there that day maintained a low profile. I never again heard from the military. I have suspected since that time that by 1970 the bureaucrats organising the conscription process had become more sophisticated and recognised that conscripting articulate young lawyers opposed to the war and conscription might be more trouble than it was worth.

Although the next South Australian election hadn't been due until 1971, an election was suddenly called for May 1970, prompting the ALP to begin to preselect candidates. The Young Labor Contingent had been conducting a campaign to have ALP members retire at 70 years of age. Only one member was affected by this campaign, the longstanding Member for the state seat of Adelaide, Sam Lawn, aged 73. True to the Young Labor policy, I decided to challenge Sam Lawn. I nominated, which resulted in a meeting with Don Dunstan, then Leader of the Opposition, who asked me to withdraw my nomination. Don's argument was that Lawn was a long-term member of the Caucus, in good standing, and, that although he was getting a bit 'long in the tooth', his loyalty needed to be respected and rewarded, and that the whole Caucus was behind Lawn. Don said not only could I not win, but I would do myself some damage in the party; and, finally, that we were involved in a great struggle to win the election and didn't need the diversion of a contested preselection. I refused this pressure and at the Convention received about a third of the vote, a respectable outcome. I was surprised that I didn't receive support from the AWU and received no explanation except that, 'we don't knock off sitting members'.

My relations with the AWU temporarily soured when Sam Lawn died the following year. I lived in the Adelaide electorate and belonged to the Adelaide ALP sub-branch. I naively announced publicly that I was going to seek preselection to run as the ALP candidate in the subsequent by-election, having run for preselection a year earlier. Unknown to me, I was potentially about to make an enemy of Jack Wright, the AWU secretary, who was intending to become the Member for Adelaide. Apparently, Wright had been promised support for the seat earlier by the 'machine', who ran the ALP in South Australia at that time and they planned to install Wright without a preselection. I soon got the message about what steps I should take for my future political health. I went to see Wright and explained that I had announced my intention to run without being aware of his intentions. Knowing that he had the overwhelming numbers to win, he was pretty blasé, reminding me that everyone has the right to nominate. I responded that I would not campaign and would only use the preselection to draw attention to myself for the future.

I stuck firmly to this undertaking. I think I received about 1000 votes out of 100,000. Wright was happy and Clyde Cameron was impressed with the speech I made to the ALP Convention, commenting, 'If people had voted on the basis of the speeches given to the Convention, you should have won'. James Edward (Jim) Dunford, the incoming AWU

Secretary, was impressed that I had kept my word and had not campaigned against Wright. I became Jack Wright's campaign manager for the by-election, which he won handsomely, and all was forgiven. The upshot was that this episode improved my standing in the AWU and I became close to the AWU leadership under Secretary Dunford, with Cocks Duncan becoming one of the main suppliers of legal services to the AWU and its members.

Soon after I had become a lawyer, Sally Morton and I married. The wedding was held at her parents' house in Beaumont, with the Registrar of Births, Deaths and Marriages as the celebrant. Marriage by a celebrant (of which there was only one in South Australia at the time) was extremely rare. It raised a few eyebrows; however, a marriage in the garden was seen as very avant-garde and was consequently entirely agreeable to Sally's parents. In any event, it was a great social success. My friend Peter Kellett, who is mentioned throughout this autobiography, was my best man.

During 1972, Sally and I went to Singapore and Europe, our first overseas trip. It was cheap and basic, but great fun – a domestic flight to Perth, a Russian ship (the *Khabarovsk*) to Singapore and a very cheap flight to London and then after three great months, the same trip home, in reverse. We stayed in London with a cousin, Jill Duncan, in Notting Hill Gate and used that as a base to visit Scotland and Europe. While in Scotland, I discovered that the clan of my Scottish ancestors, the Duncans, were highlanders and that Sally's family, the Mortons, were lowlanders. This became a great family joke at the expense of my then mother-in-law, who loved all things Scottish and belonged to the Robbie Burns Society.

We drove a rented Volkswagen from the UK to France, Germany, Sweden and back. On the way from East Germany into West Berlin, we passed through the Brandenburg Gate. The East German border guard noticed that I had a poster on my suitcase showing Richard Nixon with a military-style cap with a swastika insignia. The bag and I were marched into a very warm office, despite its being freezing cold outside. The commander, after recognising that the poster was a joke against Nixon, produced a bottle of spirits and we shared a few shots and a conversation in broken English. Sally, freezing in the car for 20 minutes and seriously worried that she would never see me again, was thrilled when I emerged unharmed. When I told her what had happened, she was understandably unimpressed.

During my absence, Chris Cocks heroically attempted to manage my file load, with its inadequate notes and records. It became a joke in the firm that they should have known that I would end up as a politician, because even at that stage, I was averse to keeping notes. Nevertheless, Chris was happy with the amount of legal work we were receiving from my union contacts. I recall that by 1973 we had about 10 union clients and this was to increase over the next few years.

Across the years I had a long and fruitful, legal, political and personal relationship with the leadership of the South Australian branch of the Australian Workers Union, which had been under the general control of that politician without peer, Clyde Cameron, the Member for the House of Representatives seat of Hindmarsh from 1949. Clyde and his supporters were generally aligned with the Left and were opposed to the Groupers and the National Civic Council. The Catholic Social Studies Movement, commonly known as 'the Groupers', was established by B.A. Santamaria in 1941, with the principal aim of recruiting Catholic activists to oppose the spread of communism, particularly in the trade unions. At a national level, the AWU was controlled by the National Secretary, 'Big' Tom Dougherty, and the NSW Secretary, Charlie Oliver. Sometime in the 1960s, the Right wing national leadership attempted to take over or remove the Left wing leadership of the AWU in SA. Clyde's brother, Don, elected as a senator in 1969, was the state secretary at the time and the matter ended up in court. The SA branch won the case.

All full-time officials of the SA branch had been sacked when the national officials purported to take over the branch, but following the court victory, the state officials were reinstated. This experience left the state officials – among them Jack Wright, Jim Dunford, Dave McKee, Alan Begg, Reg Groth and Jim Doyle – somewhat radicalised and more Left wing than they might otherwise have been. Roma Mitchell, QC, the country's first female judge and appointed governor of the state in 1991, led the legal team for the SA branch, with Ted Mullighan, later a Supreme Court Justice, as Junior. I was largely unaware of this momentous struggle, but when I set up a law practice in 1970, the AWU showed sympathy to this young Left wing lawyer and started to send me some work. Jack Wright, later deputy premier of SA, was the AWU Secretary in 1970.

One of the veterans from that turbulent experience, Jim Doyle, died in 2020. I had last seen Jim with Frances Bedford when I was in Adelaide in January 2019. To accurately estimate his contribution to the union movement, the broader labour movement and the working class would be an impossible task. A shearer by trade and a lifelong member of the Australian Workers Union, Jim, an AWU official for decades, devoted his life to assisting others and fighting the battles of the working class. Jim was always a supporter of mine, handing out 'how to vote' pamphlets in the Makin election campaigns, while all the while lecturing me about how, in his view, the ALP had failed the working class. With his death, the real battlers of this world lost a genuine champion.

It is almost impossible now to comprehend the hard-drinking culture that pervaded the trade union movement, and much of the labour movement, in South Australia during the 1960s and 1970s. The various unions had their favourite watering holes. The main centre of socialising was the Trades Hall bar, in the basement of Trades Hall on South Terrace. Any person contemplating a political career or simply seeking to influence the policy or politics of the ALP, or the union movement, needed to spend a fair amount of time there enjoying the company of like-minded people. It was a favourite watering hole of Jim Dunford, AWU secretary from 1971 until 1975. He was a larger-than-life character with a great sense of humour. He entered the Legislative Council in 1975, with my support. Don Dunstan was appalled at the prospect of Dunford entering the Caucus but was unable to change the outcome.

Sometime during 1973, Mick Young, then federal secretary of the Australian Labor Party, convinced Jim to employ John Lewin, a young industrial officer who had worked for a short time as industrial officer for the NSW branch, under the control at the time of Left wing secretary Lew Macky. Unhappy about losing control of the AWU in the 1970s, Mick installed a Trojan horse in the union in the person of John Lewin. Lewin was ostensibly part of the inner workings of the Left but was in reality a sleeper for Mick and the Centre Left faction, with his actions resulting in the AWU becoming politically unstable and unreliable for the Left. John Lewin was rewarded by Mick Young for services rendered when he was appointed as an Industrial Relations Commissioner by the Hawke Government.

From the first time I heard Lewin's upper-class pronunciation of the word 'isyous' as opposed to the more common pronunciation 'ishues', I should have known better than to trust him. The political deal delivered the AWU to the Centre Left and elevated Lewin to the bench.

At this time, the main source of work for my law firm was the Miscellaneous Workers Union ('Missos') under Left wing secretary extraordinaire Barry Cavanagh. Barry, the son of the Whitlam Government Minister Senator Jim Cavanagh, had built the Miscellaneous Workers Union in SA from about 2,000 members to around 10,000. As a result of the work of the legendary national general secretary Ray Gietzelt, the 'Missos' had an extraordinarily wide constitutional coverage. Barry had an enthusiastic group of organisers, including the assistant secretary Don Egglington, Clive Brown and others and his team worked long hours and drank hard. They would gather at the Trades Hall bar from about 5 pm until around 7 pm, when they would all be dispatched to a school to sign up school cleaners, for whom the union had coverage. Eventually, the Miscellaneous Workers Union claimed to have signed up about 80 per cent of the school cleaners in the state as members.

State industrial law included preference for unionists. The Missos' method of recruitment was to approach cleaners nightly and explain the benefits of membership. Most happily signed up and paid their dues; however, a few felt that because they were in their own businesses (as contractors) they didn't need a union. These people were then advised that if they didn't join the union, they would lose their contract. Although most of these cleaners saw the value of membership, a few were obstinate and needed further convincing. Unfortunately for me, Barry Cavanagh preferred to have his personal solicitor on hand in case there were any difficulties during these organising sorties. Several nights a week I would spend time drinking at the Trades Hall bar, but fortunately I was only required on a few occasions to accompany him to a school. The presence of a lawyer seemed to be intimidating enough to do the trick for a positive recruitment outcome.

Sometime during 1972 the James North industrial glove-manufacturing factory at Whyalla became an issue for the union, in that it was scheduled for closure. The company, through its manager, J.E. (Heck) Larven, simply shut the factory one night and sacked the 20 female workers. Barry Cavanagh alerted me and, along with a couple of organisers, we drove to Whyalla, where the James North employees and the members of the Ship Painters' and Dockers and Seamen's unions in Whyalla were jointly picketing the factory, which was not actually owned by James North but by the South Australian Housing Trust. I subsequently helped to establish a cooperative and arranged some assistance from the state government. Predictably, the mainstream South Australian press attacked the women and their supporters, but the local *Whyalla News*, generally a conservative paper, ran a strongly supportive editorial. I also organised for the South Australian Government to order gloves and other products from the factory, guaranteeing one month's work and giving the women enough time to form the Whyalla Co-operative, which operated for some time, although it was eventually sold to another private company, which later closed the factory, with the workers losing their jobs again.

It was during this episode in Whyalla that I first met seaman Frank Blevins, who became a lifelong comrade and friend, and subsequently a minister in the Bannon Government and Deputy Premier and Treasurer in Premier Lynn Arnold's Government. Our friendship cooled when he was a minister in the Bannon Government but recovered later. The rift was provoked when Frank took the Health Department's side in a dispute with the Miscellaneous Workers Union and the Ambulance Union. His reputation in the union movement never recovered from that episode.

Sometime during this period, the Miscellaneous Workers Union and I, as its lawyer, became involved in a dispute at the South Australian Rubber Mills (Uniroyal), a manufacturer of tyres and other rubber products. Bill Lean, the Commissioner of the Industrial Commission dealing with the matter, was causing the union considerable difficulty in wage negotiations. One of the shop stewards in the factory reported to the organiser that a set of car tyres was being made as a special order for Commissioner Lean.

Some little time later, when Commissioner Lean appeared to be deciding against the interests of the union members, Barry Cavanagh was quick to remind the commissioner that he was in the pocket of SA Rubber and, in public, announced that Commissioner Lean had received the specially ordered set of tyres from SA Rubber. Barry didn't actually say that the tyres had been gratis but this was the implication. Commissioner Lean then ordered Barry, and whoever was representing the company, from the hearing into Chambers. The person representing the employer refused to meet in Chambers on the basis that they intended to take the accusation of bias against the commissioner to the president of the commission. Barry and I dutifully attended Chambers, where Bill Lean asked Barry why he had broadcast the issue of the tyres, explaining to Barry that he was welcome to visit him at any time for a chat. Barry responded by enquiring about the wage increase for his members, suggesting a figure, to which Commissioner Lean agreed.

The commission had been adjourned until after lunch and when Lean came back onto the bench, he ignored the matter that had been resolved earlier in the day and gave a brief judgement ordering an increase of a lesser amount, but backdated. Barry immediately accused the commissioner of treachery and put on the transcript that we had met with Lean in his Chambers without the employers and that Lean had indicated there that his order would be an amount more than that he subsequently ordered. All hell broke loose. Bill Lean adjourned the hearing and referred the whole matter to the president of the commission.

Unfortunately, two unions covered SA Rubber Mills – the Miscellaneous Workers Union, which had 90 per cent of the members, and the Rubber Workers Union, a small Right wing outfit that covered the remaining workers. The upshot of these events was that the management of SA Rubber Mills contacted Ray Gietzelt, the national secretary of the Miscellaneous Workers Union, and declared that, if Barry Cavanagh remained secretary of the union in SA, the company would not cooperate with the Miscellaneous Workers Union and would ensure that all the union members in the plant joined the Rubber Workers Union rather than the Miscellaneous Workers Union. Consequently, the national executive of the Miscellaneous Workers Union removed Barry Cavanagh as SA secretary, bringing Barry Cavanagh's illustrious career to a sad end. He had been an outstanding union secretary, working seven days a week for his members for years.

In 1971, my father was diagnosed with terminal liver cancer; he died later that year and was cremated at Springvale Crematorium in Melbourne. I was not particularly close to my father, but looking back on his life, I recognise that I was extraordinarily lucky to have had him as a father. He had experienced a tough upbringing, his mother dying when he was about seven or eight. His father was in the Senate at the time and Dad and his two brothers were largely raised by Aunty Annie, my grandmother's aunt. In many respects, my father and I were direct opposites. His caution versus my brave recklessness. No doubt both approaches suited the personalities involved. He must have been very disappointed when I was 'departed' (the word 'expelled' never entered the school lexicon) from Homebush High but he helped me to find a job, and his financial backing enabled me to go to university at a time when such a privilege was mainly available only to the wealthy and the few with Commonwealth Scholarships. His support meant sacrifices for the family. Sadly, because of his early death at only 57, my father was never aware of my political career and achievements. What he would have made of it, I can only speculate.

CHAPTER THREE

# Married life and a parliamentary career

During most of this period, and prior to moving to Brougham Place, North Adelaide, I was living in a flat in Kent Town with my lifelong friend, Peter Kellett. Peter and I had met at Law School and became immediate friends, although he was behind me in political development. When we met in first year law, he was a Liberal-voting conservative. Using a legacy from his father, Peter had bought an MG TF, which gave him high status in first year. His girlfriend, Valmai Williams, was the daughter of Judge Williams.

By second year, Peter (known as PK) had decided that law was not for him and enrolled in an arts degree. Before long he had dispensed with his Liberal views and become a 'Greenie' and was moving towards what was to become his passion in life – outdoor education. Sometime during this period, he undertook an outdoor education university course in Eugene, Oregon, and I visited him there. On a later occasion, once I had entered parliament, PK gave me a copy of the so-called Oregon Bottle Bill. On returning to SA, I gave a copy of the Oregon Act to my parliamentary colleague Environment Minister Glen Broomhill, who embraced the concept; it subsequently became the basis of the SA Container Deposit legislation.

Before I was married, and afterwards, PK and I regularly went on 'wood chop BBQs'. These consisted of a few friends meeting at a suitable place in the Adelaide Hills, collecting a boot load of wood and then spending the remainder of the day walking, lighting a fire on the ground (self-chopped wood warms twice) and having a barbecue of a few steaks and snags and some rough red from a flagon. D'Arenberg Red Stripe was the order of the day. Great fun.

In the early 1970s, I started to think about my relationship with alcohol. I had been living a life where alcohol was central to my social existence and while I wasn't overly concerned, I felt that a few alcohol-related rules would be a good idea. I decided to have one day per week alcohol-free and to have September off the grog. Why September? Well, it only has 30 days so requires less abstinence than the months with 31 days. Then why not February with even fewer days? Well, February is summer in hot Adelaide, so refraining from a cold beer or a wine in February seemed a step too far. In addition to this measure, I attempted to drink only after 5 pm, which was not always easy. I was fortunate in that I have never had much enthusiasm for spirits or spirit-based cocktails, which I considered to be US drinks when I was a student. I was never a tobacco user and although I have tried other drugs, I have settled on alcohol as the drug of choice. Fortunately, although restricted, it is legal.

Upon returning from overseas in mid-1972, Sally and I obtained a Housing Trust flat in Elizabeth, and after the 1973 election bought a house in Mackenzie Road, Elizabeth Downs, which became the first home to our son, Macgregor (Mac) Duncan, an event that prompted much rejoicing and celebration.

By the early 1970s, I had pretty much developed the architecture of my belief system and philosophy in life. I had a firm attitude to religion, which had been developed in my teenage years. As I matured, my atheism was only strengthened. I am not anti-religion in terms of other people's beliefs. I simply believe in the 'live and let live' approach. In politics, I saw myself as Left Labor, a description I have not needed to change throughout my adult life.

So, what beliefs do I generally hold? Well, women should have the same rights as men, should get equal pay and be treated equally. Maybe now that sounds like a statement of the obvious, but it wasn't in the 1970s. LGBTIQ+ people should have equal rights and should not be discriminated against. Racism at large, which is probably more widespread than generally recognised – and against Aboriginal people particularly – is abhorrent and should be vigorously opposed. I believe in collective action to ensure that society takes care of its weakest members. Where we can prevent suffering, we should do so. Neglecting the aged, the sick, those with a disability and needy children has no place in Australia, but addressing these issues will necessarily involve a struggle. Housing and healthcare are rights, full stop. Education should be free, universal and readily available countrywide. Underprivileged children should have special support. Taxation should be progressive, and the tax system should be simple and targeted to ensure that avoidance is far more difficult. We should all pay tax based on our capacity to pay. Businesses should pay wages that ensure employees, and their families, can live a decent life. Inevitably, when the profit motive is involved, society needs consumer protection legislation and business ethics rules, enforced by government. Finally, of course, we must protect our environment. My 'list', first compiled over 50 years ago, has barely changed since then, although today, global warming and sustainability would be my number one priority. Nonetheless, it was as a good basis then as it is now. In retrospect I realise I was struggling to give effect to these beliefs. Then, in 1972, the Whitlam Labor Government was elected.

Sometime in 1972, with a state election due in 1973, the ALP Member for Elizabeth, Jack Clarke, announced his retirement at the forthcoming election. I had little or no connection with Elizabeth at the time but was considering the idea of becoming the Labor candidate. The preselection attracted a Melbourne Cup field, all of whom had some support from within the ALP Convention. Ray Roe, a member of the Postal Workers' Union and an Elizabeth City councillor, had the backing of his union and other postal/communications unions, while Terry Hemmings, a member of the Metal Workers Union and an Elizabeth City councillor, had his union's support. Brian Chatterton, a Barossa Valley vigneron, was favoured by Don Dunstan, who wanted Brian's rural experience in the Caucus, and Joyce Henriett, the electorate secretary to Bonython Member Martin Nicholls, had support from Senator Jim Toohey. There were others, now forgotten. That said, this large field of potential candidates advantaged me: the party machine, which usually controlled preselection, could not agree on a 'pea', meaning that the preselection was wide open. I received support from the AWU, the 'Missos' and a couple of small unions and several sub-branch delegates. The voting system was preferential.

I quickly learnt that large voting blocks of unions had already committed their first preferences, so I visited most union secretaries and asked for their second preference support. When asked for a small favour, believing it to be of no consequence, most people prefer to say 'yes' rather than to deliver a disappointment – even hard-nosed union secretaries. Most of the secretaries were dismissive but agreed to give me their second preferences. I started off with about 25,000 first preference votes from a possible 130,000. As the count continued, using the preference system, my numbers continued to accumulate as candidates with fewer votes were eliminated and the promised second preferences continued to grow, and I ultimately won, with 86,000 votes. After the preselection, there was some unhappiness and loose talk about overturning the result, which came to nothing.

Once preselected, I quickly got to work campaigning in Elizabeth, which was a very safe seat. Having an activist candidate was most welcome amongst the ALP branch members in Elizabeth and I soon realised that with a good campaign, Labor might also win seats in the Legislative Council district of Midlands, which covered Elizabeth, Salisbury, Gawler and some rural areas. Labor had never won seats in the Legislative Council outside the metropolitan area, defined for these purposes as north of Gepps Cross. Voting for the Legislative Council was voluntary, as was enrolment, but the elections were held on the same day. If we could dramatically increase the Legislative Council enrolment of Labor voters, we might win the two seats up for election. Instead of simply campaigning for Elizabeth, I had my team also enrol voters from the strongest Labor areas for the Legislative Council. We dramatically increased enrolment by more than 7,000 voters.

One minor problem was that one of our candidates for Midlands, Cec Creedon, Gawler's Mayor, believed that his best chance of election was to enrol voters in Gawler and induce them to vote Labor. I tried to explain that this wasn't a sensible strategy because the Labor vote in Gawler was, at best, a little above 50 per cent and enrolling people there inevitably involved enrolling some Liberals. But he was set in his ways. The outcome was that with the large enrolment increase in Elizabeth and a high voter turnout due to compulsory voting for the House of Assembly, Labor's candidates were elected. This was a tremendous shock for the Liberals. If Labor had pursued the policy of only enrolling Legislative Council voters in Labor-leaning areas, Labor could possibly have taken control of the Legislative Council 12 members to eight after two more elections.

Premier Dunstan was delighted, in fact thrilled, with this outcome. It enabled the government to introduce electoral reform for the Legislative Council, backed by the threat that if the legislation was not passed, Labor would win four more seats at the next election – two more in Midlands and two from Northern, which covered Whyalla, Port Pirie and Port Augusta. That result would have split the 20-member chamber and given Labor a real chance of obtaining a 12 to eight majority at the subsequent election, around 1979. The city-based Liberals understood the threat and supported the legislation, but there was one minor hiccup. The Liberals insisted that the Legislative Council be enshrined in the SA constitution.

Labor had a longstanding policy of abolishing the Legislative Council. The premier, understandably, wanted to implement reform to enable the Upper House to be reformed after the next election. I felt that if we waited, we could win the Legislative Council for the long term and then have it abolished. Don was having none of it. The Caucus approved the entrenching clause, and the party modified its platform in relation to abolishing the Legislative Council. Sometime later, when I was Attorney-General, Don and I agreed that retaining a bicameral parliament in a small state – an economic burden – could hardly be justified. I stress that this discussion was merely conceptual, as the government was not contemplating undertaking any steps in this direction. However, Premier Dunstan acknowledged that the constitutional entrenching of the Legislative Council did not apply to the Legislative Assembly and expressed the view that whichever chamber existed was immaterial; that is to say, if the House of Assembly was abolished and a single member electorate voting system established for the Legislative Council prior to the abolition of the Lower House, then the implication was that a unicameral parliament would be achieved.

On Saturday 2 December 1972, a Labor Government, which in three whirlwind years modernised Australia, was elected, with Gough Whitlam becoming Australia's twenty-first prime minister. The Whitlam policy program was as broad as it was radical. My minor 'problem' of being conscripted into military service was swept away with the ending of conscription in December 1972 by the first two-person Whitlam Government (a duumvirate of Whitlam and Deputy Prime Minister, Lance Barnard).

Like a dyke breaking, reports of an avalanche of decisions hit the front pages of newspapers around the country. The atmosphere was positive – almost euphoric. Australia was about to become a modern, tolerant, civilised nation. It seemed that everything was almost too good to last. Nationally, Whitlam seemed set for a generation in government. In South Australia, we had the Dunstan Government, with a comfortable Lower House majority and high prospects for re-election in 1973, and I was a candidate for the safe seat of Elizabeth. It could not get any better.

CHAPTER FOUR
# The Member for Elizabeth

At the 1973 election I had won the seat of Elizabeth for the ALP with more than 70 per cent of the vote. When the parliament met, I was sworn in and became one of only three new members of the Labor Caucus, Brian Chatterton and Cec Creedon in the Upper House being the other two. At the swearing-in, I began my lifelong practice in parliament of affirming, rather than swearing an oath on the bible or other religious text.

I looked forward to establishing an electorate office and playing a role in the Labor Government. The Elizabeth Labor Party sub-branch was full of wonderful, decent, committed members and comrades. We soon increased the membership to over 200 members, with more than 50 people attending monthly meetings. I enthusiastically welcomed the opportunity to be a very active local member in Elizabeth, which was a low-socioeconomic, working-class area. I soon found that the people of Elizabeth were, as they say, the salt of the earth. Plenty of locals sought my assistance, and almost to a person I found that their problems or complaints were real, justified and of substance. That was not always the case when I represented more affluent areas as a member of the Australian Parliament.

At the first Caucus meeting after the 1973 election, I was lauded by Premier Dunstan for helping to win the two seats in the Legislative Council. The Legislative Council enrolment drive in Elizabeth had played a key role in the election of Chatterton and Creedon. The Midlands electorate, which covered Elizabeth and Salisbury and adjacent rural areas to the north, had always been held by the conservative side of politics. The Labor victory was the beginning of the end of the 16 to four Liberal domination of the Upper House.

From 1973 until the end of 1975, we had numerous visits from Whitlam Government ministers, most of whom I was meeting for the first time. Bill Hayden, Charlie Jones, Les Johnston and Lionel Murphy, who was then the Australian Attorney-General, come to mind. Murphy's visit was the first time I had encountered him since Young Labor events in the 1960s, and we became firm family friends. Along with Dunstan, he became my mentor. Typical of Lionel, he immediately offered to have me stay with him in Sydney or Canberra when I was 'passing through'.

The Labor Party had significant representation on the Elizabeth Council – Ray Roe, Terry Hemmings, Martyn Evans, Peter Dewhurst, Lee Berry, David Whiting, Martin Mackowski and, earlier, Brin Whiting. There was a great deal of cooperation between the Elizabeth City Council and the state government, at both the political and bureaucratic levels, to the benefit of the community. I was friends with Dale Hassam, the son of the town clerk of Elizabeth, Oscar Hassam. Oscar and I soon developed an excellent working relationship. My first term coincided with the beginning of the Whitlam Government and funds were flowing to local government and the states, so cooperation was vital, both to get projects agreed and then to have the work progressed. In my electorate, road works, an Australian Legal Aid office, environmental improvements, a dramatic increase in Housing Trust building, school buildings and improvements were all occurring concurrently with myriad smaller projects and proposals.

Munno Para District Council was the other local government in the Elizabeth electorate. Unfortunately, it was still very much dominated by the old rural establishment that had held sway since settlement. In 1973, Munno Para Council had no Labor-supporting councillors, while the ward boundaries were gerrymandered to favour the rural interests. Elizabeth West and Elizabeth Fields, with perhaps 8,000 people, had two councillors; One Tree Hill, with maybe 500 people, likewise had two councillors, with the rigged boundaries having a direct negative effect on the residents' lives. If a constituent in Elizabeth city was doing it tough and needed rate relief, it was almost always granted. Not so Munno Para. 'People shouldn't buy houses if they can't afford to pay the rates' was the refrain.

In Munno Para, the council largely neglected the needs of the ratepayers in the built-up areas, while doing favours for the rural ratepayers, as the following anecdote indicates. The council had authorised the expenditure of funds for the in-house road-building gang to bituminise Craigmore Road, from Main North Road to One Tree Hill. In an extraordinary example of maladministration – or even blatant corruption – the work gang began to seal Medlow Road, which ran parallel to Craigmore Road. Fortunately, this 'mistake' was discovered after about a kilometre of bitumen had been laid, such that it had reached the entrance of the rural property of the council chairman. The council gang then began to 'correctly' seal Craigmore Road from about a kilometre in and onto One Tree Hill. The kilometre of dirt road remained unsealed for around two years. I set out to change this situation, and at the next council election we replaced the rural Tories representing Smithfield Plains and the Elizabeth West/Fields wards. Eventually, progressives became the majority and the council started acting in the interests of the ratepayers in the built-up areas. One of the new councillors was Jack McViety, an Australian Manufacturing Workers Union (AMWU) member, who later became the Chairman of Munno Para Council.

Once I became the Member for Elizabeth, I began to receive visits from constituents about their problems and I soon realised that many had minor legal issues that for political reasons were difficult for me to handle; for example, domestic or neighbour disputes – the sort of disputes the local member can't win by getting involved. I talked to the law students' association at Adelaide University, and they happily agreed to set up a free legal advice centre, operating from my electorate office, one night a week, on a roster basis. This service was widely welcomed by the community and continued to operate for some years before it was eventually incorporated into the Legal Services Commission, which I established in 1977, with an office in Elizabeth.

As the Member for Elizabeth in 1973, before the neoliberals/conservatives gutted public housing in Australia from 1980 on, it was important to have a close working relationship with the SA Housing Trust. Up to half of the constituents of the Elizabeth electorate were Housing Trust tenants and another 20 per cent were living as private residents in trust-built homes. The trust had an excellent arrangement for dealing with members of parliament and the complaints and queries their activities inevitably generated. One of the officers who dealt with state MPs was Jim Crighton, who was a senior officer in the trust and who had access to the general manager, the legendary Alex Ramsay. Jim Crighton was not bound by any of the general policies of the trust. He could make decisions based on the justice and fairness of the constituent's case or according to the best interests of the trust. These two things were not necessarily in conflict. He was able to make decisions, mostly without the need to refer matters upstairs. If a tenant was out of work and couldn't pay the rent, Jim would give them a month to see if they got a job; if a woman and kids were suffering domestic violence, Jim would allocate a new house. Jim Crighton was effectively the Housing Trust Ombudsman, but with power not just to enquire, but to make and implement decisions. Overall, a great system that should be replicated today.

Early on, I became involved in an issue involving the Housing Trust and the Munno Para Council. When building the Smithfield Plains subdivision, the Housing Trust, or its sub-contractor, had generated a large amount of mainly topsoil from the earthworks associated with the build. The soil had been dumped on land owned by the trust, to the west of Smithfield Plains. The pile was about 20 metres high and about 600 metres wide and was known as 'Mount Smithfield'. In the summer, when the soil had dried out and the prevailing wind was from the west, the Smithfield Plains houses would be blanketed in dust. This was a very serious issue for residents and therefore me. The trust claimed that it would eventually require the soil for filling in some yet-to-be-developed area and would not move the mountain. For me, as the local MP, this was a matter of great concern.

I spoke unsuccessfully with Jim Crighton and then then sought an appointment with Alex Ramsay. I had always liked Alex but, on this occasion, I became enraged when he quoted a figure for the cost of removal of Mount Smithfield and how many fewer houses they could build as a result. My anger did the trick. Jim Crighton phoned me later that day to say the trust had a solution. They would contract a private landscape gardener to plant fast-growing ground cover on the mountain of earth and would continue to water it. I was a bit sceptical about this solution but agreed to give it a go. Overall, it worked quite well, and Mount Smithfield became a green feature on what was otherwise a pretty barren landscape. When the soil was removed later in the decade, I had some complaints that the landscape had deteriorated!

Being a local member involved a great deal of showmanship. As somebody once said, all retail politics is a stage. During this period, I was fully occupied and consumed by the Elizabeth community. I was a member of several clubs, had a round of pubs in which I drank, and was always on the go. The longstanding Labor Member for Bonython in the Australian Parliament, Martin Nicholls, and I became friendly enough. As an old-style trade unionist, Martin didn't like Whitlam. I think that he initially saw me as a bloody nuisance, young and enthusiastic, as opposed to his own persona, which was exactly the opposite. Furthermore, in 1973, my shoulder-length hair meant that I certainly didn't look anything like most people's idea of an MP.

The majority of the publicans in Elizabeth were at least superficially Labor supporters. A few were strong supporters and could be relied upon to financially support my later campaigns. Murray Horlin-Smith from the Kariwarra and his family have been friends and supporters ever since. The police sergeant in Elizabeth, King O'Malley, also drank at the Kariwarra. He was an old-style cop who preferred to 'kick arse' rather than bother with the courts. He had spent most of his early police service in the country and had been named by his Irish parents after the Federation Labor politician best known for promoting the establishment of the Commonwealth Bank. I didn't have much time for the police in those days. I didn't trust them and still don't. But they fulfil an important role. However, King was a good cop and we worked very well together in Elizabeth, often getting just outcomes for constituents involved with police matters.

As a local MP, I was often called upon to help with desperate and urgent financial requests, such as no money for food to feed the children. People in middle-class areas have no understanding of the financial pressures constantly weighing on most working-class people. Members of parliament receive an electorate allowance to be spent at the members' discretion. In well-to-do suburbs, members spend these funds on buying raffle tickets, memberships of clubs and so on. In Elizabeth, I was always helping people in distressed circumstances with cash. I soon learned that I needed a few rules about spending this cash, and not particularly the sort of rules that accountants like. Mostly, people were either not good at managing their limited social welfare funds or had suffered a financial shock, such as the loss of a job, or a husband who had decamped with the family's meagre funds. The state community welfare department and some charities had schemes to help such people, but they were bureaucratic and often restricted to office hours. One rule was that I only helped people who were prepared to sign up for Anglicare's free short course in managing money. Soon, and sadly, I learned to offer cash only once. Later, as an anti-smoking advocate, I wouldn't give cash to smokers. My office kept a cash book of these payments and in 1974 I had paid out $1900.

During my early days as a politician, Medibank was non-existent and poor people were always under threat of bankruptcy arising from some health crisis confronting them. Constituents were frequently seeking my assistance with a myriad of health-related problems. In my electorate I had a young doctor of Indian descent, who was building up his practice. I referred many paying patients to him and on a quid pro quo basis he would see people unable to pay. This informal arrangement worked very well: he built up his practice with paying and non-paying (pro bono) patients. In addition, he had a right to practise at the Lyell McEwin Hospital and was often able to arrange hospital-based procedures at no cost. That doctor subsequently became a close family friend and was a member of the Royal

South Australian College of Urologists. Unfortunately, I was unsuccessful in organising the one large dental practice in Elizabeth to provide services to poor people. Even those in urgent need because of pain were interrogated about their capacity to pay and were required to borrow money in advance of treatment. Profit over people in pain. Absolutely disgraceful.

As the Member for Elizabeth, I conceived of the idea of establishing the Elizabeth West Food Cooperative – what is now known as a food bank. I organised a meeting at the Working Men's Club, assembling community representatives, Anglicare representatives, market gardeners from Penfield Gardens and the owner of the local Foodland supermarket, Horace [Horrie] Knight. My plan was to collect fruit and vegetables from the local growers and almost out-of-date groceries from the supermarkets. The idea seemed viable, and the meeting was supportive. We formed a committee, and the co-op was launched. We obtained support from the Meat Workers Union officers, who introduced us to some smallgoods factory owners and they donated their products. The co-op was successful beyond my expectations. Apart from some minor pilfering, it was capably run by volunteers for many years. The amount of fruit and vegetables donated also meant that the diet of many local people was improved.

The coordination of the fruit and vegetable supply was organised by our friend and Labor Party stalwart, Irene Krastev, and her brother, Stephen Oulianoff. Irene had to come to South Australia from Bulgaria after the Second World War, accompanied by her baby brother Stephen, with their mother joining them later. I first met them through the Elizabeth Labor Party branch when they were tenant market gardeners. They couldn't make any financial progress as tenants and wanted to buy the small farm. Although the owner of the farm was prepared to sell, Irene and Stephen were unable to raise the deposit required by the bank before approval of a loan. I arranged a meeting between the owner and Stephen and Irene at the property and explained that, if the owner increased his price by say 15 per cent, and then at settlement only received his original asking price, the numbers would comply with the bank's deposit requirements. Everything went smoothly, and long before they needed to, they had repaid the loan. An excellent outcome. Irene also arranged for her neighbours to donate large amounts of mainly vegetables regularly to the co-op. A side benefit of the co-op was that some of the volunteers worked as pickers on the farms at harvest time.

I had received something of a shock when I became the Member for Elizabeth. I had understood intellectually, and further learnt through regular contact, the daily struggle endured by many of my constituents. I was shocked however by the attitude of my parliamentary colleagues towards working-class people. It was difficult to convince even some Labor colleagues of their needs and suffering. Many of the Labor members had an 'only assist the deserving poor' attitude and were inclined to view poor people as victims of their own attitudes rather than of the circumstance of their birth or of their having been dealt a bad hand in life. Many Liberals showed little capacity to put themselves in the shoes of less fortunate citizens or to relate to them.

In October 1973, I greatly disappointed Premier Dunstan over my attitude to a Bill to allow for the establishment of casinos in South Australia. Don saw casinos as a generator of funds for the Treasury and a boost to SA's tourist credentials. I saw it differently. I was never enthusiastic about gambling in general and I particularly disliked the idea of introducing poker machines into South Australia. I had seen the impact of the 'one armed bandits' in NSW clubs, whereby the lives of working-class families were often destroyed. I knew people who spent their non-working/sleeping hours at the clubs and on the pokies.

Don finally persuaded me to vote for the Bill if my vote was going to be the difference between the Bill passing or failing. Of course, in accord with the Labor Party rules, a Bill to allow casinos was the subject of a conscience vote. Fortunately for me, the Bill was way short of the numbers necessary to pass the House of Assembly and I was not required to vote for it. I had resigned from the South Australian Parliament before the Bannon Government Bill that successfully established casinos and poker machines, so my moral stand against the poker machine scourge remained unblemished.

In the late 1980s a huge lobbying campaign was launched to introduce poker machines into licensed clubs in South Australia, a move opposed by the Australian Hotels Association for obvious reasons. The campaign was, however, successful, with an Act in 1991 enabling both clubs and hotels to have poker machines. Mick Young, the former Centre Left power-broker and long-time Labor Party operative, had resigned as the Member for Port Adelaide in the Australian Parliament, in April 1988. After his resignation, Young set up a lobbying consultancy based on his close ties with the Bannon Government and his similarly close ties with the Hawke Government. His business quickly became very successful. Among his large number of clients was Len Ainsworth, the founder, and at that time still the owner of Aristocrat Leisure, the largest poker machine manufacturer in Australia. Aristocrat paid Young to lobby for the introduction of poker machines to SA hotels and clubs. Young was provided with a very deep pocket to achieve the lobbying objective and made money available, or promises of money, to friendly MPs. He soon had a group of state Labor MPs enthusiastically supporting the introduction of poker machines.

Initially, John Bannon was ambivalent or lukewarm about the introduction of poker machines, but, as the lobbying continued and his Centre Left faction became more enthusiastic, he, as the state's Treasurer, could see rivers of gold. The ALP state secretary Terry Cameron (Clyde Cameron's nephew) was on board, as was the former Liquor Trades Union Secretary, Trevor Crothers, by then in the Legislative Council. I was unhappy about introducing poker machines into SA and attempted through the Left faction of the party to resist the pressure. However, it appeared that, with Premier Bannon committed, the Bill had momentum and would pass. Because the Bill was to be subject to the conscience vote, it wasn't possible to oppose poker machines via the ALP councils, where lobbing work had been done by the Left. Before he died, Bannon admitted that he deeply regretted allowing poker machines into South Australia.

It has often been claimed that members of parliament have the same status in the eyes of the community as corrupt bankers and used car salesmen. That may be generally the case, but often not so with individual members, whose standing amongst their constituents may be very high. During the 1970s, I was very popular in my Elizabeth electorate, as confirmed by numerous opinion polls. I was invited to many public functions and fundraisers, one of the more unusual invitations in 1974 being to present the prizes at the annual show of the Elizabeth Obedience Dog Club. The task involved placing ribbons around the necks of the assembled champion mutts. The grand champion most obedient dog was a German Shepherd. The marshal handed me the ribbon and the owner handled the dog. As I put the ribbon on the dog's neck, it lashed out and bit me on the wrist, drawing blood. The assembled Elizabeth Obedience Dog Club members were, of course, devastated. My quick response: 'This dog is probably very obedient, but the incident begs the question of what instructions the owner gave to the dog – perhaps this champion has been trained to smell out and attack politicians'.

In 1974, the federal Telecommunications Commission was planning to issue new radio station licences. A group of people, comprising me, Chris Hurford, the federal Member for Adelaide, and Bill Hayes, a former Lord Mayor and chairman of United Motors, met to discuss the possibility of forming a group to apply for a licence. Hurford's and my interest, at least initially, was to ensure that the licence went to an SA-based group and not to interstate interests. We soon came to the realisation that if we won the licence – which seemed likely – it had the potential, despite being commercial, to be more balanced in its public affairs coverage than that provided at the time by the existing stations. We convinced a number of the unions to become shareholders in the company we formed – Festival City Broadcasters P/L – and Chris and I became directors, looking after the interests of the ALP and union shareholders. Thus, was 5AA established, subsequently operating very successfully. Sadly, after about a decade of broadcasting, the majority commercial shareholders sold the business to a national group.

When I arrived as a newly elected member of the House of Assembly, I had some specific interests, one being civil liberties. Although not a very active member of the SA Council for Civil Liberties, I was a strong opponent of capital punishment and the use of corporal punishment. For all intents and purposes, the application of state-sanctioned corporal punishment had been abolished in South Australia. I also had an interest in rights to privacy and particularly in exploring the introduction of a tort of privacy. The government had earlier introduced privacy legislation, but it had not passed the Legislative Council. Most importantly, I was particularly appalled at the way gay people were treated and I was anxious to do something about this issue. Homosexual law reform consumed my parliamentary life for the whole of this period, as is elaborated in the following chapter.

I gave my maiden speech to the South Australian Parliament on 25 July 1973. As a young radical member, I was determined not to give the traditional maiden speech, in which, after thanking numerous people, the new member announces a shopping list of desired improvements, expressed in language replete with platitudes, and specifies the reforms he or she hopes to achieve during his or her parliamentary career. Instead, in the 1973 Address in Reply (the maiden speech), I chose to avoid a commitment to specific reforms and dealt in detail with industrial democracy and worker control or worker cooperatives, subjects with which I had been closely involved through the Whyalla Glove Factory Cooperative. Such matters have now dropped off the political agenda, but at the time they were high on Premier Dunstan's policy agenda. Looking back, I am very pleased that in my maiden speech I focused on an issue so crucial to the lives of working people.

Finally, to cap off a busy year, on 20 December 1973, my first son, Macgregor (Mac), was born.

CHAPTER FIVE
# Homosexual law reform

Between 1973 and late 1975, I was a young man with a passionate commitment to social justice, including a determination to pursue homosexual law reform. Less than a year before the 1973 election, Dr George Duncan, a lecturer in Law at Adelaide University (and no relation), had been drowned in the River Torrens, undoubtedly at the hands of South Australian Police Vice Squad members, conducting their so-called 'learn to swim campaign for poofters'. His death brought into sharp focus the persecution of homosexuals by the police and others.

For the small, enlightened element of the South Australian community, enough was enough. The appalling circumstances of this murder led, in late 1972, to the introduction by the Hon. Murray Hill, MLC, of a Bill for the reform of homosexual law. The Bill passed in a diluted form, with homosexual 'conduct' remaining illegal, but provided a defence if the accused could prove that the act was committed in private by two consenting adult males.

I found this new Act to be completely unsatisfactory for a number of reasons. Firstly, the criminal law should only be applied in circumstances where there is overwhelming public agreement and support. For example, over 99 per cent of the public agree that murder should be a crime. Criminalisation should not occur at the whim of one group or another, such as churches or employers. Secondly, homosexual behaviour between consenting adults was still a crime, enabling prosecution, persecution, blackmail, and public exposure to continue. Thirdly, under the normal criminal law, the burden of proof is on the prosecution. The Bill supported by Hill had effectively reversed the onus of proof. Finally, the legal position was completely unclear in circumstances involving more than two consenting adults. Apparently, three in a bed would still be illegal, which was ludicrous.

Looking back over nearly half a century, I can see how I was well placed to meet the challenging task of homosexual law reform. Elizabeth was and is a very safe Labor seat and those opposed to homosexual law reform could only have a marginal impact on my re-election prospects. When I first introduced the Homosexual Law Reform Bill in 1973, I was just 28 years old and full of youthful enthusiasm. I had studied criminal law at Adelaide University under Brent Fisse (now Professor Brent Fisse), who introduced me to the concept of victimless crimes, including homosexual conduct between consenting adults, crimes involving personal use of drugs, public drunkenness, loitering, prostitution, euthanasia and censorship.

Having accepted the concept of victimless crimes, I came to believe that, in relation to adults, the criminal law and the state should exercise a zero or a minimal role in these matters and I entered the parliament with a strong interest in reforming the law in these areas. Frankly, it appalled me that a class of otherwise law-abiding citizens should be subjected to the criminal law for behaviour that had no social impact except maybe to offend the sensibilities of some individuals. The events of the 1970s, and the circumstances and struggle leading to the passage of the Homosexual Law Reform Bill, are still fresh in my mind.

History is often concerned with perceptions of the past by the present generation, and it is fair to say that people now view the 1970s in Australia as a period of great social and political reform, reform widely supported by a radicalised community. Although it was most certainly true that it was a time of substantial reform, the notion of the influence of a radicalised community is simply not valid. Much of the electorate was politically cautious, best illustrated by the fact that at the height of national reform, the Whitlam Government never achieved anything more than a working majority in the House of Representatives. In response to the social repression of the 1950s, a noisy minority of young people emerged in the following decade, full of idealism and hope and with a desire to improve Australia. These people were collectivists at heart, some were radicalised, and many others were small 'l' liberals on social issues. This group was never much more than a minority, although its influence was much greater when its attitudes coincided with the wellbeing of a larger group, as it did on the issue of conscription to fight in Vietnam.

In South Australia, even with Don Dunstan dominating the political stage, and despite his adept political skills, Labor never managed a landslide in the Lower House. Don recognised that the forces of reaction were so powerful that the reform project would have been defeated if the government had simply relied on its traditional working-class base. What Don sought to do was to capture support from wider sections of the community to achieve an informal electoral cohort, one that consisted of not only the industrial working class, but also the Greek community, much of the Italian community and what I'll here call the intelligentsia – a small, educated elite, including the arts community. Don became accomplished in Greek dancing. He learned some Italian, which he polished subsequently, and did what came naturally to him: he became a great patron of the arts.

This coalition of political support provided a solid foundation and had the advantage, to some extent, of bullet-proofing the government from the influence of the *Advertiser* and the establishment, and enabled Labor in government to move ahead of community attitudes to a significant degree, although not at any time was there a majority of the population thirsty for social reform. This was the political situation in South Australia in 1973.

The powerful combination of the *Advertiser*, money as represented and symbolised by the Adelaide Club, and a Legislative Council dominated at the time by a majority of 14 Liberal members opposed to six Labor members (a majority perceived by many to be permanent) would have defeated even the political skills of Dunstan. Let me dispel the myth that reform was easy in the 1970s because of popular support. It wasn't. It was tough, grinding work, mostly unappreciated by the beneficiaries and mostly carried out against a huge barrage of reaction, finally destroying Dunstan's health and then the government.

Of course, the position of anyone who was not white, Anglo-Saxon, male and middle class was, to a greater or lesser extent, deplorable. The social disadvantage experienced by women and cultural minorities, Aboriginal people, people with disabilities was incomprehensible and the huge task involved in improving their position and circumstances was daunting. However, in 1973 I wanted to take on the challenge of improving the plight of the persecuted gay community.

A short time after my election in 1973, I received a letter from Don DeBats, Chair of the South Australian Council for Civil Liberties, of which I was a member, urging me to take action to alleviate the suffering and persecution of homosexual people. Soon after I received the letter, I drafted a Bill to decriminalise homosexual acts between consenting adults in private and introduced it into the parliament. I want to make the point that this was a Private Member's Bill, first introduced by me in 1973, long before I became Attorney-General. As such, it was not legislation of the Labor Government. The media, getting the details wrong, as usual, have in recent years reported that the reform was introduced by me as Attorney-General and as a government Bill. This is incorrect.

My Bill was also significantly different in content and effect from the Bill introduced by Murray Hill. The Hill Bill, which decriminalised homosexual acts in private, sought to do so by decriminalising specific defined acts that previously had been crimes. My Bill simply altered the law so that males and females, heterosexual or homosexual, were treated in relation to sexual behaviour without distinction. Importantly, it introduced a code of conduct applicable to all people, regardless of gender or sexual orientation. The latter was a world-first for South Australia and provided a model for reform, one that has now been copied in dozens of jurisdictions.

When I introduced the Bill in 1973, it passed the House of Assembly but was defeated in the Legislative Council. I again introduced the Bill, with a similar result, but the issues were widely debated in 1974. The problem was the rump of conservative Liberals in the Upper House. In 1974, it was generally believed in the community, even among people who were not at all enthusiastic about homosexual law reform, that the opportunity for prejudicial misbehaviour by the police persecuting homosexuals should be removed. Some of this attitude was reflected in the improving support for the reform in the Legislative Council.

The vote in both major parties was based on a so-called conscience vote. There were two gay or bi-sexual male members in the Legislative Council and both were members of the Liberal and Country League. One supported reform but the other was opposed. The opponent of the Bill had actually been seen on the beat in the South Park Lands. Early one morning, an old wardrobe appeared on the footpath in front of Parliament House with a sign reading: 'We have provided this closet so that [named legislative councillor] can come out as a gay person and support the Homosexual Law Reform Bill'. Parliament House security soon removed the cupboard and sign, but the damage was done. To this day I don't know who was responsible for this.

Premier Dunstan and I had numerous discussions about the Bill. At that time, I had no idea that Don was gay or bi-sexual. In the 1970s, you assumed people were straight unless there was strong evidence to the contrary. In addition, I was such a committed follower of Dunstan that I would not have believed it and would have attributed such allegations to Liberal smear. Don's influence in the debate was obviously of vital importance, although not necessarily in the way implied in some publications.

Earlier I mentioned his strategy of creating a coalition of electoral support from workers, Italians, Greeks and the intelligentsia. Without that support base, I think it unlikely that all the Labor members of the parliament would have been brave enough to support the measure, given the Bill's unpopularity. Opinion-polling at the time indicated that more than 60 per cent were in opposition, with only 17 per cent in support. Through his advocacy, Don had created a climate in which the Labor Caucus was more enlightened and reform-minded on social issues than it would otherwise have been. It is not true, however, that Don played any role in initiating the Bill, as some people have suggested. As I said, he gave it his enthusiastic support once the Bill had been announced and introduced.

During the course of the debate I had the following exchange with Tom Casey, the Labor Minister for Agriculture, a good Catholic, in a corridor in Parliament House:

> 'Peter, I don't know what makes a bloke like you tick. You seem to be a nice young fella, with plenty of opportunities ahead of you. Why would you want to take up the cause of the bum bandits?'
> 'Tom', I said, 'because I think everybody should be able to do what they like in the privacy of their own bedrooms'.
> 'Oh no', he said, 'the thought of it makes me puke'.

I reported the conversation to Don, who opined that, although it was a Private Member's Bill, it was serious business of the government to the extent that it reflected what the Labor Party was attempting to achieve in SA. Don spoke to Tom and later reported back to me that, if his vote was crucial, Tom had agreed to vote for the Bill.

I had not imagined just how difficult it would be to get the Bill through the parliament. Homosexual law reform (including the Hill Bill) in SA required four attempts before satisfactory legislation passed the parliament. On each occasion, the Lower House passed the Bill on the second reading. The Upper House, dominated by Liberals until after the 1975 election, was an entirely different matter. On the first occasion the Bill failed by one vote, when one of the Labor members (not Tom Casey) apparently did not hear the division bells and missed the division on the second reading. We attempted to recommit, but the numbers were not there to support a recommittal, an indication of just how delicate the support for the Bill really was, with some people just hoping 'the problem would go away'.

On the next occasion, in 1974, after a constitutional change gave the president of the Legislative Council a deliberative vote, the Bill failed after being the subject of a tied vote. Tom Casey voted against the Bill, claiming later that he thought the Bill had the numbers in support to pass. Finally, on the third occasion, in 1975, after the election of a reformed Legislative Council, which included my friend Frank Blevins, the Bill passed easily, with Tom Casey still opposed.

Controversial legislation does not exist in a vacuum and, as might be expected, this legislation was mired in intense public debate. For the record, I mention, in no particular order of importance, several public figures whom I believe played a role in the passage of the Bill. Firstly, was Sir Robert Helpmann. 'Bobby', as he was known, was the most famous South Australian of his generation – more so than Lord Howard Florey and Sir Mark Oliphant. He was the Artistic Director of the Adelaide Festival of Arts in 1970 and part of the programming committee for the 1968 festival. Bobby Helpmann was an important influence on what was, and still is, a small political class in Adelaide.

Another significant supporter was Des Colquhoun, the legendary editor of the pre-Rupert Murdoch *Advertiser* in the 1970s. He supported the Bill absolutely, by means of rational and logical editorials, positive news page coverage and a personal preparedness to stand up to its opponents, whether in the boardrooms or the front bars. The Catholic Archbishop, James Gleeson, also played an important role, with his refusal to issue a pastoral letter opposing the Homosexual Law Reform Bill being an important factor in its passage. He was under great pressure from conservative Catholics to do so. If a pastoral letter opposing the Bill had been issued, it would have put the then Attorney-General, Len King, the Deputy Premier, Des Corcoran, and other Catholics under great pressure. I remember him saying to me when we met, after the Bill's passage, that 'these poor souls will be under enough pressure come judgement day, without subjecting them to the temporal law'. Finally, the Bill's successful passage owes a great deal to then Associate Professor Roger Knight. He was the one gay activist with whom I communicated on a regular basis. Roger briefed Anne Levy, MLC, who, as a private member, had carriage of the Bill in the Upper House after the 1975 election.

I have not mentioned any homosexual law reform organisations or individuals associated therewith. This should not come as a shock. In the 1970s, homosexual males were persecuted and prosecuted by the police in a coordinated and vicious manner. At this time the Labor Government was unaware of the extent to which the police special branch collected files on thousands of homosexuals who were otherwise law-abiding citizens.

Known as 'pink files', they were subsequently used by the police in the surveillance of citizens or to limit their career prospects, the most notable incident occurring in 1967, when the police commissioner went to Premier Walsh with a file on John Jefferson Bray, who was in the process of being nominated as the Chief Justice of the Supreme Court of South Australia.

It is little wonder that, in the early 1970s, in this climate of repression and fear, only a small number of gay men, due to the risk of persecution and intimidation, were engaged in political action.

With the benefit of hindsight, I would observe today that a young, straight member of parliament, with a legal background and a safe seat to protect him from any electoral consequences, was exactly what was needed at the time. Reform did not occur because of a groundswell of support from the South Australian community or gay activists, although two groups — the Gay Activists Alliance Adelaide and CAMP (the Campaign Against Moral Persecution) — along with the Dr Duncan Revolution Bookshop, were active. I never met with representatives of these organisations. CAMP never sought to make representations, either in writing or in person. CAMP's only intervention in the debate, other than perhaps depositing the closet at the front of the parliament, was to suggest that it would send representatives into schools to explain the gay person's perspective. This suggestion was perceived by opponents of the Bill as homosexuals wishing to go into schools to proselytise homosexual lifestyles. This suggestion nearly sank the Bill, and I was forced to vigorously reject the proposal in the parliament in this second reading speech.

In this age of the Murdoch press's domination of the public discourse in Australia, the motives of politicians are nearly always questioned. 'What's in it for him or her?' the media screams. As far as I was concerned, I took up the cause of homosexual law reform for no other reason than it was the right and just course of action. Consequently, I was widely vilified by some in the Opposition in the front bars of the South Australia's drinking establishments and elsewhere. I wisely decided that any publicity reminding the voters of Elizabeth of my role in homosexual law reform would have been counterproductive, given the low base of community support for the initiative. The attitude of the community at large was sneering, sniggering opposition to homosexual people and reform of the law, an attitude exemplified by the comment in relation to the death of Dr George Duncan, 'He got what he deserved'.

The industrial working class, the core support base of the Dunstan Government, was basically opposed to decriminalisation, while the machine that ran the Labor Party in South Australia at the time was lukewarm at best. Homosexual law reform was not seen as a first-order issue of importance by most in the state Labor Government and Labor Party and was viewed by many supporters as a distraction. I do not want to see the historical memory of these events given a false gloss. It was the product of, and was only supported by, a small, enlightened elite. Homosexual people in an organised sense played a very limited role in the passage of the Bill and there was no organised mass pushing for reform. The tragic murder of Dr Duncan created a positive political climate for reform among the intellectual class, who were appalled by the murder. What followed, accompanied by a bit of luck and much perseverance, was the introduction and passage of the Bill. Dr George Duncan sacrificed his life for this reform. I hope that society will never forget that.

The Bill's passage had several consequences. Most importantly for individual gay men, it meant that their sexuality was immediately freed from the attention of the criminal law. Of course, unwanted attention from the police was another matter. Slowly, over time, police culture has changed, and homosexual men are no longer subjected to such widespread abuse.

Later, as Attorney-General, I appointed the first Commissioner for Equal Opportunity, Mary Beasley. Although the legislation supporting the appointment did not specifically apply to sexual orientation, from the time of her appointment Mary conciliated over complaints of discrimination against gay people and, over time and following later amendments, ensured that the position of homosexuals in the community was greatly improved.

The project of decriminalisation in South Australia, however, was not complete while some homosexual men still had criminal records for homosexual acts. This situation was belatedly resolved by Labor Government legislation introduced by the Weatherill Labor Government and passed in 2013. The *Spent Convictions (Decriminalise Offences) Act 2013* is now in force.

The passing of the South Australian Homosexual Law Reform Bill led to reform, over time, in all other Australian jurisdictions – in some cases, with regret for not moving faster – in New South Wales, Victoria and West Australia, and in Queensland and Tasmania, in the face of vicious rear-guard action.

The reforms had other consequences, unforeseen by me at the time. In the 1970s, I did not believe that changing the law had much impact on society's attitudes. Recent research has found that government policies regulating sexuality play a significant role in shaping citizens' attitudes towards sexual orientation and same-sex relationships. A survey published in 2014 found that policy-makers are more than just conduits for public opinion relating to sexuality. Rather, policy-makers, and the outcomes they produce, can play a powerful role in shaping public opinion on questions of LGBTIQ+ rights. This, in turn, seems to indicate that progressive LGBTIQ+ rights policies produce citizens with more tolerant attitudes. In other words, South Australia's reform of laws applying to homosexuals may have initiated a process that, across more than four decades, saw public opinion move from nearly 70 per cent in opposition, to the situation in Australia today, where support for marriage equality approaches 70 per cent. This is a revolution in attitudes during my lifetime. Of course, from the 1960s onwards, there has been remarkable progress across the world in society's attitudes to homosexuality.

I am still passionate about these issues. While change in Australian society's attitudes to homosexuals did occur, still more is needed in this country and, more importantly, internationally. A recent UN publication reported that at least 76 jurisdictions retain laws used to criminalise and harass people based on their sexual orientation. In Iran, Mauritania, Saudi Arabia, Sudan, Somalia and the Muslim north of Nigeria, consensual homosexual acts may still be punished by death. International shaming and ostracism of governments can be powerful tools. For example, Indonesia often responds positively (if reluctantly) to international criticism on human rights issues.

Great progress has been made in the past 45 years. It afforded me great personal satisfaction to witness the Homosexual Law Reform Bill pass into law and then after 45 years to see its successful outcomes. I am proud of the role I played and was delighted when I heard former High Court Justice Michael Kirby describe me as the 'father of homosexual law reform in Australia'. I have little regard for formal titles and honours, but that is a description I will carry with pride.

Dr George Duncan and his murder may fade from public consciousness (although I sincerely hope that doesn't occur) and Peter Duncan has grown old, but the outcomes of the events of more than 45 years ago endure and continue to positively impact on the lives of tens of thousands of, particularly, homosexual men. Acceptance won, the bigots were rebuffed and we in South Australia were on the right side of history long before it became fashionable.

CHAPTER SIX
# The Dunstan Government

Following the 1975 state election, an election held in the dying days of the increasingly unpopular Whitlam Government, Labor clung to power with the support of the Member for Port Pirie, Ted Connolly. Recognising the parlous political outcome of the election, Premier Dunstan rushed to Port Pirie late on election night to secure Ted Connelly's support for the government in exchange for Connelly's appointment of Speaker. The key benefit for Connelly in this arrangement was having a government car and driver for his use between Port Pirie and Adelaide. His support for the government was as reliable as any Caucus member, enabling the government to continue as before. In addition, the Labor Government's position in the Legislative Council had improved to the point where, on almost all issues with support of Liberal Movement members, the government could get a majority for its legislation.

I was personally delighted with the election result in Elizabeth. I was the only Labor member of the House of Assembly to achieve a swing to Labor at the election. Not bad for a member described by the Opposition as glib, politically immature and with deep radical connections. Whatever the *Advertiser*, the Opposition or the business community thought, the people of Elizabeth had made their judgement and they liked what they saw.

When the parliament met, Don asked me to visit him in his parliamentary office, where he informed me that he intended to increase the size of the Cabinet to 13 ministers. He explained that this required a constitutional change and if it were approved, he intended to support me in the Caucus ballot for the vacant Cabinet position. If I was elected by Caucus, he intended to make me the Attorney-General and Minister for Prices and Consumer Affairs. I was just 30 years old. I was delighted and thanked him for his support and confidence. Don noted that he didn't expect my Caucus election to be a foregone conclusion, as Terry McRae would also nominate and have some support, particularly among the Catholics. He asked me to be particularly careful to stay away from controversy over the next couple of months.

The constitutional amendment to increase the size of the ministry passed with only a small amount of dissent, with Robin Millhouse, at that stage the Liberal Movement Member for Mitcham, opposing it. Although the passage of the Bill was serious business for me personally, I found Millhouse's critique to be rather amusing. First, he claimed that if Don got rid of the dead wood in the Cabinet, he would only need about half the number of ministers, offering his suggestions for those who should go. Then, unaware of what was happening behind the scenes, he dubbed the Constitution Bill, the 'get Terry McRae into the Cabinet Bill'. Of course, it was neither and I was subsequently elected with Don's support by a comfortable majority over McRae. Sometime later, in 1978, during a Constitutional Convention meeting in Perth, Don and I were having dinner and discussing the various personalities in Cabinet, when he commented that although Len King, the previous Attorney-General was 'exceedingly good, as good as South Australia has had. However, occasionally I had trouble with him over social questions. Imagine how much worse things might have been with Terry?'

I think that, when I was sworn in as Attorney-General and Minister for Prices and Consumer Affairs, Don was very pleased to have someone who was young, enthusiastic and somewhat radical as his Attorney-General, perhaps considering me as a reflection of himself in 1965. I moved into the Attorney-General's office at 33 Franklin Street, met the ministerial staff and went straight into action. An avalanche of social legislation followed, which Don strongly supported but which had not seen the light of day under my predecessor, although it could be argued in his defence that the numbers in the Legislative Council had been the problem prior to 1975. However, a contributing factor was Len King's social conservatism.

The swearing-in by the governor was followed by a ceremonial sitting of the full Supreme Court, where I was welcomed by the Chief Justice, John Jefferson Bray, who congratulated me on my appointment to the 'exalted position'. The president of the Law Society also spoke, offering congratulations and the cooperation of the Law Society in my important work. The Law Society representatives may have been disappointed a few days later when they realised that I was no longer a member of the society. The Law Society constitution provided a full voting membership for the Attorney-General on the Law Society Council. I had considered this matter carefully and had decided that if I was to embark on a comprehensive law reform program, I didn't wish to feel a conflict of interest every time I met with the Law Society, which inevitably proved to be very often.

For this formal Supreme Court welcome, tradition required me to dress in full regalia, which included a long-bottomed wig, the only time I have ever had occasion to do so. As Attorney-General, I chose not to involve myself in what would have been the personal hypocrisy of attending the procession and church service for the opening of the legal year. That would have been the only other time I would have been required by tradition to wear this wig. I was then, and am still, opposed to the wearing of regalia in the court system. Later in my term as Attorney-General, I started a conversation with the Law Society and the District Court about abolishing the wearing of wigs and gowns, at least in the day-to-day operation of the courts. In retrospect I have to concede that this was not a high-priority issue.

Following the Supreme Court ceremony of welcome, we retired to the Chief Justice's chambers for coffee, and I suppose biscuits or sandwiches, during which time I was approached by Mr Justice Howard Zelling, who introduced himself as the Chair of the Attorney-General's Law Reform Committee. I assured him that I was keen for the committee to continue its good work and that it had my full support. He then shocked me by inviting me to join most of the members of the court for dinner at the Adelaide Club that evening, an invitation I politely declined. I discovered a short time later that Justice Roma Mitchell would not have been in attendance. Either she had a ban on the Adelaide club or was not welcome because the only women allowed into the Adelaide Club in 1975 were the wives of members. This rule changed soon after, maybe because of Dame Roma's ban.

During the coffee and biscuits get-together following the ceremony, the Chief Justice, John Bray, asked me whether 'I'd be taking silk as Don did?' The practice was that the Chief Justice nominated a list of prospective Queen's Counsel to the Attorney-General, for submission to the governor in Executive Council each year. The list was usually collaboratively compiled by the Chief Justice, the Law Society, the Bar and the Attorney-General. John Bray asked his question, assuming that I would add my name to the list. At the time, as Attorney-General, I was the leader of the Bar. However, in terms of the profession, I was a very junior solicitor. Having myself nominated as a QC would have been ludicrous in the extreme and would have rendered me a laughingstock. I advised Bray accordingly.

Ron Payne, who had been acting Attorney-General since the 1975 election, was also Minister for Community Welfare, meaning that when I took over there was serious backlog of administrative and policy work in the office. Greg Crafter had been Len King's senior private secretary and I intended to keep him on, a proposition which he happily accepted. With his help, I soon moved the backlog of administrative files. At the time the role of Attorney-General involved a huge amount of administrative and quasi-administrative work. Over many years, the burden of work had built up and much of it could not be delegated either for legal or prestige reasons, such as signing Justice of the Peace Certificates. To be appointed as a Justice of the Peace is seen as important and prestigious by the successful candidate, and a certificate signed personally by the Attorney-General is part of the ceremonial process.

When my appointment as Attorney-General was announced, I received a congratulatory telephone call from Lionel Murphy, by then on the High Court. As usual, Murphy had numerous pieces of advice for me, the most important being to ensure that my desk was not loaded with so much routine administration that I didn't have time for the policy work that would improve the lives of our supporters – and everyone else. I took that advice on board, establishing structures that relied heavily on the good judgement of the staff. Reading files was both laborious and time-consuming, and mostly a waste of my limited time. The senior staff generally knew what my attitude would be on particular matters and took that into account when making recommendations. All administrative files were read by one of my staff and then a recommendation was made, which I usually adopted without reading the background material, although I was always aware that authority can be delegated but not the responsibility. I found this approach worked well and, with only rare exceptions, moved the paperwork mountain, without getting into too much trouble.

I haven't researched the departmental structures recently, but I recall that when I became Attorney-General 12 separate departments came under my ministerial control: Land Titles Office, Supreme Court, Local and District Court, Magistrates Court, Coroner's Court and the City Morgue, Crown Solicitor's Department, Solicitor-General, Statute Consolidation section, the Law Reform Committee, the Licensing Court, Superintendent of Licensed Premises, the Public Trustee, the Superintendent of Cooperative Societies (Credit Unions and Building Societies). The Legal Services Commission, the Residential Tenancies Tribunal, the Crime Statistics Unit and the Government Investigation Section were added later. In addition, I was the minister with responsibility for the Prices and Consumer Affairs Department, later the Public and Consumer Affairs Department. The departmental structure that I inherited was an administrative nightmare, and work had been underway for some time to consolidate the disparate elements of the portfolio. This was not an easy administrative task, as many of the departments and divisions had their own Act of Parliament and statutory powers. Other issues included the courts, which were strongly protective of their independence. Eventually, consolidation was achieved, and we ended up with three departments, with some divisions and sections subsumed as divisions of the main departments.

When I first became a minister, I could easily have been overwhelmed by the amount of work. Apart from my administrative responsibilities, I had parliamentary duties, legislation to prepare, weekly Cabinet documents to read and the Elizabeth Electoral office to service. I soon adopted the approach of 'one day at a time', which has stood me in good stead since. The Attorney-General's office was staffed by some terrific, old-style public servants, Gus Mudge, Olive Harvey, Brenda Young and the Secretary Bill Landcake, among them. They were later joined by Doug Claessen, who held criminology credentials. The Crown Solicitor was Toby Gordon, another excellent officer, who later, after the administrative consolidation, was appointed as head of the Attorney-General's Department. The priority was to get a press secretary, with Carol Treloar subsequently appointed, along with my old friend and university colleague Peter O'Brien as senior private secretary.

The O'Brien appointment presented a bit of a challenge since each minister was only allowed one senior private secretary. I had inherited Greg Crafter and was happy with that arrangement but I wanted O'Brien as well, so I decided to see Don to argue my case. I explained that I had an extraordinarily large workload and needed two senior private secretaries, and that if I had to choose, I would reluctantly let Crafter go. Fortunately, a compromise was reached, with Crafter appointed as senior private secretary to the Attorney-General and O'Brien as senior private secretary to the Minister for Prices and Consumer Affairs. The only other staff member to join the team, some time later, was Jack Richards, a long-term Dunstan loyalist from Norwood. Don asked me to take on Jack and I was happy to have him as a kind of in-house ombudsman. With my office adequately staffed, the action began in earnest. One of my first tasks was, with support from the staff and the department, to compile a list of the legislative and administrative reforms I deemed important and to allocate a priority to each item.

In the first sitting week of parliament and during Question Time, my first crisis as Attorney-General arose. A week or so earlier in the Woomera Justices court, a group of accused, all Indigenous, had been due to appear. The law at the time governing Justices courts in SA required two Justices of the Peace on the bench to constitute a valid court. On the day in question, one of the rostered JPs (a local pastoralist, which is not surprising) had failed to arrive at court, presenting the police with a major problem. They had a lockup full of accused persons, who would have to be housed for a month, until the next scheduled court hearing. The local police sergeant had been in a remote post during a previous drought and had been sworn in as a justice to enable him to witness drought relief applications. This day he was at the Woomera Court intending to act as the prosecutor. The issue was 'solved' when he moved to the bench with the other justice, while the junior policeman became the prosecutor. Problem solved. The defendants were dealt with and all were convicted. This was an appalling breach of the principle that justice should not only be done but should be seen to be done.

In my reply to the parliament, I indicated that I would review the matter and would take appropriate action, which proved to be more problematic than I had anticipated. The Aboriginal legal rights team wanted all the convictions overturned or those convicted pardoned by the governor. Technically, the court had been properly constituted, meaning that it would be very difficult to justify intervention by the governor. Eventually, Legal Aid was funded to appeal to the Supreme Court, and the court set aside all the convictions from that day. This matter, however, was on my desk for months. It serves to illustrate how one issue can become a major political crisis.

After three years of parliamentary struggle, on 17 September 1975, the Homosexual Reform Bill was finally signed into law by the governor. It was a great outcome, and SA had led the way as it was doing in so many other fields at the time. Although I have always considered the abolition of capital punishment as my most notable achievement, getting the criminal law out of the bedrooms of the state came a close second.

Early in November 1975, I attended my first Attorneys-General conference, held in the period leading up to the dismissal of the Whitlam Government. Kep Enderby, Attorney-General in the Whitlam Government at the time, Brian Miller, the Attorney-General in the Tasmanian Labor

Government, and I represented Labor governments, with Enderby as chair. At the morning tea break, he and I drafted a very innocuous resolution, simply saying that this meeting of the Attorneys–General supported the conventions of the Australian Constitution. In any other circumstances, this would have been inconsequential and would have been carried unanimously. In the political climate of the Senate blocking supply, it was a bit more politically focused.

I approached Miller and asked him to second my motion, as Enderby as the chair could not do so. Unbelievably, Miller refused on the grounds that it was introducing politics into the Attorneys-General meeting. I then asked him if he would vote for the resolution. He indicated that he would not support the motion. I then talked to Enderby, and we decided not to move the resolution. While forcing the Liberal Attorneys to vote against upholding the Constitutional Conventions was good politics, having a Labor government Attorney-General voting with the Liberals was a decidedly bad look. What Enderby and I had not realised at the time was that Brian Miller was not a member of the Labor Party. He was an Independent member of the Tasmanian Legislative Council and was only part of the Labor Government insofar as the government had a member in the Upper House representing it in order to introduce Bills and so on.

I had advised Premier Dunstan that I would not practise law while I was a minister, although I hadn't really done any legal work since becoming a member of parliament. Don hadn't sought the undertaking, but I thought that it was the proper course of action. A diligent member of parliament was a full-time occupation. As a minister and a Lower House member, I had about 80 hours of work per week, which was more than enough. In any case, Don had warned me of a situation that had arisen when he was Attorney-General in 1966. The Crown Solicitor had begun to send briefs to the legal firm in which Dunstan was a partner. Whether with the intention of entrapping him under the constitutional provision proscribing MPs from holding offices of profit under the crown or not, that would have been the effect. When I became Attorney-General, I had the departmental secretary send an instruction to the various departmental divisions, specifically advising them not to brief my law firm, for the obvious reason.

It had been my practice to keep in touch with my partners at Duncan Barrett and Hannon by joining them for drinks at the firm's offices, on most Friday afternoons. I was at one of these informal events, when one of the junior staff commented that my status as an MP was 'good for the firm. We are now getting briefs from the police prosecutors.' I was shocked and immediately asked when this practice had begun and how many the firm had received. I learned that only one had been received to date and I quickly instructed the staff to send it back, explaining that it was an attempt by the police to have me removed from parliament under the office of profit provisions of the constitution.

Early in 1976, I was invited to attend a Labor Party fundraiser in NSW with the then Leader of the Opposition, Neville Wran. Lionel Murphy had made the arrangements and I was met at Sydney Airport by Neville Wran's driver. We collected Neville from his office on our way to the fundraiser at a Chinese restaurant somewhere in China Town. I suppose about 80 people were present and I gave a warmup speech focusing on homosexual law reform, which was the topic agreed earlier with Neville. My speech was followed by Neville giving a political, tub-thumping election speech. All went well and after the formalities we proceeded to 'work the room', visiting each table of paying guests. This was before the days of mobile phones, with their cameras. Nevertheless, some guests did have cameras. Neville took my arm and whispered to me, 'Don't be photographed with that man'; 'Avoid being seen with that woman she is so and so's girlfriend'; 'This is the table of cops who run the state'.

I recognised Abe Saffron from photographs I had seen, but happily avoided a meeting. Later in the car, Neville was laughing about the guests. As the story emerged of the details of those who'd been in the restaurant, I was horrified. Sydney's finest from gambling, crime at large and prostitution, to say nothing of people on the fringe of so-called legitimate business, were in attendance. Apparently, the night was extremely successful and more than $60,000 was raised. That event was a real education for a young naive Attorney-General from South Australia. However, I was learning fast. We didn't want the human detritus of NSW filtering into South Australia, which had been relatively clean of corruption, particularly at the political level.

In May 1976, I had an appointment as Attorney-General with one of Adelaide's property tycoons of Greek origin. This was Con Polites who, by 1976, was a larger-than-life character in Adelaide. He had started his working life as a market gardener in Port Pirie, where he was born. He was a flamboyant man, as well as being a fairly crude operator. All the buildings he owned, and there were many, were marked with a large blue-and-white (Greek colours) sign, with his name 'Polites' visible for all to see. Before this meeting, I had met him maybe once before. Initially, Polites had made his money by buying residential properties and, later, commercial properties, for rental purposes. People used to joke that he had more tenants than the Housing Trust. At the time, he was the closest thing Adelaide had to a slum landlord. He was known amongst lawyers for renting his dilapidated residential properties to tenants at a cheap rent on condition that the tenant would undertake repairs and upgrading. Thinking that they would live in the house at a cheap rent for some years, the tenants often did a good job, using quality materials. When the upgrades were complete, Con would raise the rent for the repaired property to the market, or a higher, rate, which was an extremely unscrupulous practice. He was also known for retaining properties for long periods of time, waiting for them to appreciate in value with the market.

According to the note from the staff member who had made my appointment, Con was interested in what we were planning with residential tenancies and, as he owned several licensed premises, whether any changes to the *Licensing Act 1967* were foreshadowed. The following is my recollection of our encounter, the conversation beginning with some well-aimed flattery:

> Gee, you're doing well Peter. At your age having all this power. It's incredible really and when you think, you already have that law firm. Gee you're doing well. I really admire you. Actually, I'm unhappy with the lawyers we've been using and I'm thinking of changing. Do you think your firm could handle my work?

I replied that I'd had little to do with the firm since I'd been in parliament and that he would need to see one of the working partners. He then came to the point of the meeting and asked me if I would do him a small favour. He wanted to be appointed a Justice of the Peace.

Unbelievable, I thought: a slum landlord with licensed premises, including night clubs, wants to be a JP! I immediately played a straight bat and pointed out that there was a process for applying through the department. He responded by explaining that it was not his intention to exercise any JP powers, he just wanted to have the letters 'JP' after his name. I then said something to the effect that didn't he think that having his name over all the commercial buildings he owned in Adelaide was recognition and status enough? Not surprisingly, he didn't agree, commenting that some people actually criticised him for this but he wasn't sure why. I admitted that I was one of them. After that, Con and I never hit it off, which was no loss since he was a supporter of the Liberal Party, although the Liberals were not prepared to reward Con with a JP appointment. Unsurprisingly, Polites never contacted my legal partners.

The built environment was an important issue at the time but sadly the Dunstan Government had made a serious error by allowing the iconic South Australian Hotel to be demolished to allow an undistinguished high-rise hotel to be constructed on the site. Although it was the case that the preliminaries and approvals had occurred under the Steel Hall Liberal Government, once in government and with political will, Labor could have saved the 'South'. At that time the government did not want to appear anti-business and so refrained from taking any action. This was just before the period when protecting heritage buildings became popular and important. From that day forth, I think Don regretted the decision.

In 1972, when the future of what is now known as Edmund Wright House was being discussed, the government saved the building and had it renovated for use as a reception facility and offices for the Registrar of Births, Deaths and Marriages. Over the years Edmund Wright House saw the celebration of thousands of civil marriages and was immensely popular in this role. Later in the 1980s, as a minister in the Australian Government, I appointed many civil marriage celebrants. An unfortunate side effect of that decision was that the ready availability of civil marriage celebrants and the general decline in the popularity of marriage meant that the demand for celebrations in Edmund Wright House declined; the department moved out and the building was left derelict.

After Don's experience with the South Australian Hotel, it was relatively straightforward to convince him to support the saving and reuse of historical buildings. With the passage of the Bill to establish the Legal Services Commission (described in detail in the next chapter), we were searching for a suitable building in which to accommodate the new commission. It needed to be on the ground floor in the city and near public transport and, in line with my desire to have the commission's services decentralised in regional areas, a relatively small office. The beautiful colonial building at 26 Flinders Street was being upgraded by the public buildings department and Cabinet agreed to house the Legal Services Commission headquarters there.

In Port Augusta, the previous colonial police barracks were now derelict. The legendary Port Augusta Mayor, Joy Baluch, approached me about refurbishing and using the building. I readily agreed and the building was renovated for use as a court. When completed, it was a beautiful re-creation, becoming both a tourist attraction and a working court building.

The decentralisation of the Consumer Affairs Department and the resultant creation of one-stop shops throughout the state, along with regional offices for the Legal Services Commission, meant there was a need for additional government office accommodation in some locations. In Port Augusta, for example, I was enthusiastic about establishing a solar-powered, modern, efficient and unique building. A block of government-owned land on the side of a hill in a suitable location was identified. The concept was that the building would be four-storeyed, run up the hill, with street access from the road at the side of the building, at each level. I discussed this idea with Premier Dunstan and with his enthusiastic support, a young Public Buildings department architect was assigned to prepare concept designs for the building. Unfortunately, for whatever reason, the building was not pursued after I had left the portfolio. It may be that the head of the Consumer Affairs department at the time, who was not enthusiastic about decentralisation, let the project quietly disappear under the successor minister.

CHAPTER SEVEN
# Dunstan's Attorney-General

I was determined to not simply be an administrator but an innovator on behalf of the people the Labor Party sought to represent – the working class, the poor and the dispossessed – and so I set to work. Across four years, from 1975 until early 1979, as Premier Don Dunstan's Attorney-General, I embarked upon a major reform program, introducing significant legislation into the South Australian Parliament.

As I indicated earlier, top of the list was the abolition of the death penalty, which had no place in a modern civilised criminal code. Although the Liberals were largely opposed to this reform, the Bill passed and brought South Australia into the modern world. Labor Party members for their part were bound by a longstanding policy. Although I rate this as the most significant achievement of my life in politics, some people will see it as symbolic. To my mind, however, the success of the legislation abolishing the death penalty symbolises that a society is abandoning its barbaric past, when death, torture and corporal punishment were seen as suitable responses to offending.

The next on my list was the crime of public drunkenness, reform of the law in this area being long overdue. My general philosophy was and remains that laws should be relaxed where they impinge on individuals and the way they live their lives. The previous law relating to public drunkenness had been seriously misused by the police, with the police and the Police Association making it very clear that they believed that law and order would break down if this measure was passed. In retrospect, the Labor Government was again on the right side of history.

The following is an anecdote that amply demonstrates why the reform was so necessary at the time. Keep in mind that the core of this anecdote is true, although some of the detail may have been embellished by history. John Bray, QC, was a brilliant and wonderfully eccentric barrister and acknowledged poet, and Don Dunstan's appointment as Chief Justice. It was Bray's custom to drink at the Sturt Arcade Hotel in Grenfell Street with Adelaide literary identities Max Harris, Geoffrey Dutton and others, a practice he maintained during his time as Chief Justice. He never held a driver's licence and always walked around the city.

One evening, about 9 pm, the Chief Justice was walking along Carrington Street towards his home in Hurtle Square. He was a shambling, untidy figure at the best of times, and, meandering along at that hour, he may have looked a bit ragged with his loping gait. Two young policemen in a patrol car pulled up and, caps on, approached Bray.

> 'Hello sir, where are you going?' asked one.
> 'Home', replied CJ Bray.
> 'You're drunk sir, and this is a public place. Please get in the car', directed the young cop.
> 'I'm not drunk, but you are right. This is a public place and I'm the Chief Justice', responded CJ Bray
> 'In the car', barked the young cop. Bray got into the police car and one of the cops called the Watch House Sergeant at Angus Street police headquarters.
> 'Hi, Sarg', we are just bringing in a drunk who thinks he is the Chief Justice', laughed the young cop.
> 'Oh god what next? What does he look like? Where did you find this one?', queried the sergeant.
> 'He is old and scruffy and was walking down Carrington Street', responded the young cop.
> 'Where?', enquired the Sargeant.
> 'Carrington St', replied the young cop.
> 'Let him go', the Sargent responded nervously. 'He *is* the Chief Justice. On second thoughts, drive him home.'

This account is not only apposite but serves to simultaneously justify the abolition of the offence of public drunkenness and explain the misuse of the offence by the police. Only recently was the veracity of this point underscored when an Aboriginal mother was arrested for being drunk in a public place in Melbourne, later dying in the police lockup. Forty-five years later, the law in Victoria still hasn't been brought into line with modern practice.

The next reform was criminalising rape in marriage. From this distance it is hard to believe that such legislation was necessary, but in the 1970s married women were legally appendages of their husbands. The Christian marriage vows required women to love, honour and *obey* their husbands. The traditional marriage ceremony had fathers 'giving away their daughters', that is, their property. Banks required the approval of the husband before allowing a married woman to open an account. Unbelievably, the criminal law allowed a husband to 'have his way' with his wife. Let us call it what it was and is – rape in marriage, then lawful in South Australia.

A report had been received from the Criminal Law and Penal Methods Reform Committee, chaired by Dame Roma Mitchell (Mitchell Committee), on this matter, but it did not go far enough, in my view. With encouragement from my then press secretary, Carol Treloar, a strong feminist, a Bill was drafted and taken to Cabinet. The aim of the Bill was to simply abolish the protection afforded by the criminal law to husbands who raped their wives. I was amazed to find it encountered some resistance in Cabinet before being adopted, some members believing that the measure would meet with opposition from established church groups. That view proved to be correct. The churches were very concerned about this reform, notably the Catholic Church, which believed that the law breached the sanctity of marriage, which, in their view, should not be subject to temporal law. According to opinion polls, there was some disquiet in the community about the proposed law since rape in marriage was not considered to be a problem in society. People couldn't see that this issue was emblematic of the position of women in society and this aspect was important in itself. True to form, the Adelaide *Advertiser* railed against the reform through its political editor, Stewart Cockburn.

A small hiccup in the progress of the legislation occurred in the Legislative Council, when the three Liberal Movement members were threatened and pressured by the churches to oppose the Bill. In the end, a fairly innocuous amendment was eventually agreed, and the reform was finally passed. Similar legislation has now been adopted Australia-wide. Significantly, the SA legislation marked the first occasion in the English-speaking world where rape in marriage was outlawed. Prior to this, the common law provided a husband with 'conjugal rights', the right to sexually force himself on his wife and use reasonable force to 'have his way' with the victim wife. The justification for this appalling situation was the marriage contract, the church's blessing and biblical teachings. Since this international first, women's position in Australian society has vastly improved and this Bill was an important step in that progress.

The next step, following on from this world-first reform, was to alter the procedures for rape and other sexual offences trials. The Mitchell

Committee had recommended reforms in this area, including pre-trial procedures, to ensure that the victims were treated as humanely as possible. Previously, the thought of having to confront the perpetrator again, in person at trial, was a terrifying prospect for the victim, deterring some from reporting rapes and other sexual offences. These recommendations were adopted and passed into law and the stress of the criminal trial for a victim was greatly ameliorated. Furthermore, as a consequence of enacting these recommendations, women were finally treated exactly the same as men for purposes of jury duty.

Despite there being many more issues to address, these reforms accelerated efforts towards women's equality. Prior to the 1970s, Australian women, once married, could not keep their jobs in the public service or in a bank and in many other industries. They could not sit on a jury until the mid-1960s. Often pharmacists would not sell contraceptives to women and initially the pill was only available on a doctor's prescription to married women. Large areas of hotels were legally 'no go' zones for women. Government child support was paid to fathers. Women were unable to get restraining orders against their husbands. Apart from being unable to open bank accounts without their husband's approval, mortgages to married women were virtually unknown. Equal pay for equal work was still a dream and a married woman's official place of residence was that of her husband's. Most of these appalling restrictions on women, and particularly married women, now have been removed in what is the most dramatic and positive social change in my lifetime.

The birth of my second son, Jock, occurred on 9 June 1975. He was a big, robust and healthy baby, physical qualities he has had throughout his life. Of my three children, he is, in my view, the most like me. Whether he would agree with that judgement, I don't know.

In 1976, I established the administrative structure to allow enforcement action under the Sex Discrimination Act, with Mary Beasley appointed as the first Commissioner for Equal Opportunity. These reforms were some of the first such steps in Australia and helped to lead to the groundbreaking change in the status of women in Australian society over the ensuing 40 years.

I was invited by the North Adelaide Football Club in October 1976 to be guest speaker at the club's monthly luncheon. I arrived, accompanied by my press secretary, Carol Treloar, to discover that the lunch was for men only. The president of the club began to explain the policy behind the ban on women, with the intention of excluding Carol from the lunch.

I quickly told him that I had heard enough. Either Carol was welcomed, or I was off. The club president capitulated and agreed to Carol's presence without further argument. The policy behind the ban was related to women having sensitive ears and the club's desire not to expose those delicate ears to the offensive, sexist, abusive language that was apparently acceptable at the lunch amongst the male members. I began my speech by putting on the record my opposition to the president's attempt to impose the club's ban on Carol. I pointed out that under the *Sex Discrimination Act 1975*, clubs would need to have non-sexist membership rules unless they applied for an exemption and that I expected that there would be few exemptions. I have no doubt that I won few friends at that lunch, although I recognised at the time that such minor confrontations are important in changing society's attitudes and lifting the position of women.

Another first in Australia was the recognition of de facto couples. I could see absolutely no reason in the modern world why de facto couples should be treated by the law any differently from married couples. Although the Cabinet agreed with my proposed legislation, this issue provoked considerable opposition from the churches, which again saw the government as entering an area where previously they had almost exclusive domain – the area of marriage. The Bill was ultimately passed (*Family Relationships Act 1976*) and subsequently copied nationwide. In a similar vein, another reform introduced by me was the abolition of the legal consequences of illegitimacy. Part of the cruel history of so-called Christian civilisation has been the way illegitimate children, through no fault of their own, have suffered discrimination, both by society and the law. Changing society's attitudes required education. The legal consequences of illegitimacy required an Act of parliament. A Bill was drafted and passed with little opposition, enshrining into law that all children in South Australia have equal status before the law.

Having witnessed innocent people, particularly working-class people and minorities, being defrauded by unscrupulous businesses, I ensured that a Bill was prepared to allow courts to review the terms of small or consumer contracts and to disallow unfair terms. This met with a great deal of opposition from the Law Society, judges and the business community. A fundamental principle of the common law governing commercial or business activity is the inviolability of contracts. Although I was removed as Attorney-General before the legislation passed the parliament, I had a minor success to the extent that my friend, Frank Walker, then NSW Attorney-General, took up my draft Bill and had it passed into law by the

NSW Parliament. Subsequently, when the law had operated for some time in NSW, it was passed into law in South Australia.

As an ABSCOL volunteer tutor while at university, I had seen many examples of overt and covert racism against Aboriginal people and others. In this context, another important reform, introduced around this time, was the *Race Discrimination Act 1976*, which outlawed acts of racial discrimination and had an important impact on changing racist attitudes and behaviour over the ensuing years. The Act particularised what was meant by 'race' and the grounds of discrimination based on race. That said, much education is still needed in this area.

Laws can only be applied effectively and fairly if people have access to the law, irrespective of their means, prompting me to introduce legislation, which was passed, establishing the Legal Services Commission. The purpose of the commission was to ensure that legal aid was available to all in need. Under its first chair, David Wilson, either private or in-house legal services were to be made available to needy clients. Such services do not come cheaply and, as Treasurer, Don was unhappy about the potential for this recurrent expenditure to blow out in future years.

To remove this expenditure from the Budget, I proposed that the money to fund these services should come from the interest on the large funds in solicitors' trust accounts. The banks and the Law Society were understandably appalled. The banks had the use of these substantial funds, interest-free, and were reluctant to see this advantaged situation changed. Likewise, lawyers with large trust accounts were seen as preferred customers by the banks and were given large overdrafts and generous mortgage terms. Of course, suggestions of such preferential treatment were emphatically denied by the Law Society. Eventually, the government won the day, and now trust account interest funds legal aid, representing yet another reform adopted across the nation. The Legal Service Commission's first CEO, Susan Armstrong, established the administration, practices and policies of the commission under the general policy prescription set out in the legislation, with offices throughout the state.

My next initiative was the establishment of the Office of Crime Statistics. After a review by the consultant Dr Greg Woods, an Office of Crime Statistics was set up, headed by the American criminologist, Peter Grabosky. Prior to this, the only crime data available in South Australia was provided to the media by the police. The police statistics had frequently been viewed as self-serving. The Office of Crime Statistics figures were gathered from the courts, at all levels, and from the Community

Welfare department, in the case of juveniles. According to the Cabinet minute establishing the office, the police department was also supposed to provide the appropriate statistical information; however, this did not occur until Commissioner Salisbury was sacked and replaced by Acting Commissioner Laurie Draper. The Crime Statistics Office numbers were seen as credible and accurate, with the quarterly reports issued from the Attorney-General's office providing an opportunity for more balanced discussion in the media and elsewhere. In addition, they limited the capacity of the police to run political campaigns based on 'shock horror' crime wave information.

One of the magistrates, Peter Liddy, vigorously opposed the requirement to report court statistics to 'this bureaucracy' and directed his clerk not to cooperate. He was later charged, and convicted, as a notorious paedophile. I have always wondered if Liddy was being blackmailed or protected by the police at the time, although of course this is mere speculation. Likewise, 'Bad' Barry Moyse, the then President of the Police Association, was a vigorous opponent of the Office of Crime Statistics. Later, when head of the Drug Squad, he was convicted of drug trafficking and sentenced to 20 years.

A further reform involved the Lands Titles Office. The Torrens Title registration system, introduced in South Australia in 1858, was a world-first and is now the standard system for land title registration across the world. When I became Attorney-General, the process of converting land titles from the old General Registry system to the Torrens Title system had not been completed – more than 100 years after its introduction. I asked the Register-General whether legislation was required to expedite this process, particularly since land titles generated in the old system are much more susceptible to fraud and other consumer scams. He indicated that all that was required was a modest increase in resources, which were then provided.

It was always my view, and that of the government, that the government should cheaply and conveniently make as much information available to the public as possible. Of course, there are exceptions to that general statement, such as ministerial papers and Cabinet documents. I think it is an individual's right to go to court to seek information held by the government but which is being withheld. Government should be for the people not against the people. Freedom of information laws were drafted but not enacted before I was appointed to a different portfolio and was no longer Attorney-General.

My attitude on freedom of information is not limited to government information. I think people have a right to much more information, for example, about private businesses, than they currently receive. Most people involved in legitimate businesses would probably agree with that statement. My general view is that vastly more information about major public companies should available, not only in the interests of the few shareholders but also in the interests of the community at large. Large corporates such as BHP make investment decisions every day that dramatically affect the lives of people in Australia and elsewhere, and I believe information relating to those decisions should be made public to ensure some public accountability. Citizens need the capacity to access whatever information the government (or private organisations for that matter) holds on them to enable them to verify its validity and accuracy. I have also always been opposed to cross-referencing between government departments; for example, if information is provided to the tax department, it should not necessarily be made available to the social security department.

Prior to introducing legislation to establish a Corporate Affairs Commission, the administration of various corporate bodies was spread across several government departments, a highly inefficient set-up. During the 1970s the registration and administration of all corporate bodies in South Australia was brought under one administration. Prior to this reform, it had been possible for 'corporate crooks' to arrange their affairs so that various components were covered by various departments, thereby effectively eluding control of their activities. A similar initiative to ensure comprehensive administrative oversight relates to the investigation of companies. A special office had been established by Dunstan to focus on scrutinising suspect companies and individuals in the corporate field and, where necessary, to launch prosecutions. The office consisted of lawyers, accountants and police officers who were specialists in dealing with matters involving company and commercial fraud and malpractice. The police department had opposed police officers being co-opted to this section and attempted to discourage police placements, a problem resolved with the appointment of Acting Police Commissioner Laurie Draper to oversee the police force.

In 1977 I set up the Regulations Review Unit, whose role was to methodically review all the regulations in South Australia to ensure that they were consistent and up to date, in terms of technology, and that they did not conflict with other regulations, rules and Acts etc. By way of example, a regulation passed in 1900 required a motor vehicle travelling at night at more than four mph to have a person carrying a light at the front of the vehicle; obviously, by the 1970s this regulation required upgrading. That was the role of the unit, with the reform process leading to a consolidation of the regulations under each Act and their ready availability to the public. This was before access to information via the internet and it was outrageous that a citizen or interested corporation could not easily identify the laws with which they were required to comply.

My predecessor, Len King, had contracted the former Parliamentary Counsel, Edward Ludovici, to consolidate the South Australian Statutes, a task first undertaken in the 1930s but which by the 1970s needed updating. I set out to complete this process by arranging the printing and publication of the consolidation by the Government Printer. A small problem emerged, in that Ludovici was a perfectionist and was working towards the consolidation being complete at the date of publication. Considering the amount of legislation being generated by the Dunstan Government, he was finding this task impossible. I simply picked a date as a cut-off point and the volumes were published, inevitably a little behind the legislation on the publication date.

In the 1970s, around a half a century ago, I set up a departmental committee to report on law reform to ensure 'sunlight rights', or solar rights for property owners who had or wished to install solar panels. In English law, there has been a right to ensure that the light of existing windows is maintained. This seemed to provide little, or no, protection for the solar light required for a solar panel to produce electricity. I was very enthusiastic about solar power, and I was concerned that without a right to solar light, a property owner might install a solar system only to have a neighbour construct a building obstructing the direct sunlight required by the solar system. There was some prospect that the planning and building laws and even the tort of nuisance might play some role. What was clear was that the law was, at best, vague and needed clarity and preferably new legislation. I decided to set up an interdepartmental committee, involving the Planning Minister, Hugh Hudson, and the Local Government Minister, Geoff Virgo, who also had carriage of the Building Act. When I informally approached each to determine their attitude, both were very sceptical. Hudson thought it would be more red tape restricting planning and development. Virgo thought solar was a low priority. I backed off, and on the next opportunity, I spoke to Don about the matter. He considered that it was worth pursuing but warned me that I was getting a reputation for being an expansionist minister, too ready to interfere in other ministers' portfolios.

Over the past few years, I have often been asked why the Dunstan Government 'did nothing about drug reform'. The answer is as follows: Dunstan and I wanted to reform drug laws and Don was prepared to expend the necessary political capital to achieve the desired reform. There was, however, some opposition in the Cabinet and Don decided to proceed cautiously, by appointing Professor Ron Sackville as a Royal Commissioner to report and make recommendations on how to proceed. Sadly, by the time of his report, Don had resigned, and I was no longer Attorney-General. The report and its recommendations for action were shelved.

Certain sections of the police force, including the powerful Drug Squad, led by Sam Bass (later the Liberal Member for Florey), were vehemently opposed to decriminalising cannabis. My senior private secretary Peter O'Brien had been a drug user in the past, although not while working for me. Prompted by what evidence I don't know, the Drug Squad decided to raid his house in North Adelaide at 11 am on a day when O'Brien and I were at work in the Attorney-General's office in the city. On hearing news of the raid, we both raced to O'Brien's house, fearing an attempt to plant drugs. Fortunately, Peter's then partner had been reluctant to admit the Drug Squad, and we arrived only moments after they had been allowed access. The subsequent search uncovered nothing and the Drug Squad left empty-handed. I was furious at this cavalier behaviour, which I saw as an attempt to intimidate me. I demanded an apology from the police commissioner, on behalf of O'Brien, which was given. The fact that the apology was offered so readily is, in my view, an indication that whatever evidence the Drug Squad had before the raid was not sufficient to satisfy the commissioner, who by that stage was Laurie Draper.

As Attorney-General, I established the Committee into the Rights of Handicapped Persons, an enquiry chaired by Mr Justice Bright, who had recently retired. This initiative was the first attempt in Australia to tackle discrimination against people with disabilities. We didn't have the opportunity to implement the committee's findings, but its report pointed the way forward in dealing with such discrimination. When parliamentary secretary to the Attorney-General in the Keating Government, I was able to resurrect this issue, resulting in the passing of *Disability Discrimination Act 1992*. Why disability discrimination was not dealt with by subsequent governments in South Australia remains a mystery to me.

Privacy is a somewhat indefinable concept: it means something to everyone and may mean different things to each of us, including the absurd argument that we don't need to have our privacy protected because 'I have nothing to hide', although it is unlikely that any of us have nothing to hide. Bank records, financial history, immigration status, health records, employment history, religious beliefs, political beliefs and of course sexual matters are just some of the areas that most people would argue are justified in being protected from publication. I was enthusiastic about exploring the introduction of a tort of privacy to protect the privacy of individual South Australians.

Legislation to create a right to privacy had been introduced by Len King but had been so vigorously opposed in the community that it had been withdrawn. In its breadth and detail, it involved complex matters. Existing criminal penalties under Australian law for breaches of confidentiality in post and telegraph legislation represented about the limit of Australian laws in relation to privacy. I asked the Solicitor-General, Brian Cox, to form a small departmental committee to investigate privacy law and to report. Don was enthusiastic about a privacy tort, and, in due course, we intended to introduce legislation. The report was completed after Brian Cox was appointed to the Supreme Court in late 1978 and no action was taken before I was transferred to a different portfolio.

I have always been in favour of more community involvement and more community participation in government and the government had a policy of worker participation, of which I was an enthusiastic supporter. It was always my view that the electorate should feel part of the legislative process. I decided to seek to amend the Associations Incorporations Act to provide a framework for democracy in associations incorporated under the Act. If associations were obtaining the benefits under the Act, it was, in my view, not unreasonable that their constitutions should reflect proper democratic values. Apart from small associations such as local sporting clubs, large and powerful groups such as the Royal Automobile Association and the Red Cross were also covered by the Act. The Bill provided for the election of worker and community directors. Cabinet approved the Bill, but its introduction prompted an avalanche of opposition. It was my belief that, as we introduced reforms, we should keep the electorate informed about the reasons behind the proposed reforms. In this instance, there had been inadequate consultation and little community support gained for the Bill and it had to be withdrawn.

As all these reforms were occurring, the Sydney criminal Abe Saffron had been establishing a chain of licensed hotels and night clubs in Adelaide, seven altogether, including the Elephant and Castle and La Belle.

In the 1970s, the New South Wales and Queensland police forces were rife with corruption. I was worried that Saffron, a key player in that corruption, was moving into South Australia and would soon infiltrate the smaller South Australian police force. I wanted to take Saffron on but was not sure how to do it. Then, in March 1978, a Sydney mate of mine, an investigative journalist by the name of Tony Reeves, contacted me to ask whether I could read a dossier in the South Australian Parliament that included a record of an interview between a deceased Brisbane prostitute, Shirley Brifman, and senior NSW police. He was aware that, once it was recorded in Hansard, it was subject to parliamentary privilege conditions. I asked to see the documents before making a commitment.

A package of three documents arrived at my office. The first was Abe Saffron's police record and mug shot. The second was a record of a police interview with Tony Reeves and Barry Ward, another journalist, relating to the murder of Juanita Nielsen, who had been campaigning against a development in Victoria Street, Kings Cross. The third was the Brifman transcript. Having read the material, I decided to deposit all of it into Hansard late one night, when there would be little likelihood of opposition to my seeking to incorporate it into Hansard without its being read. I have relied heavily on Anne Summers's reports of these matters since I cannot recall the exact details, as the matters were being coordinated in my office by Peter O'Brien, now deceased. I am almost certain we obtained the documents from Reeves, through some coordination with my friend Anne Summers at the *National Times*.

Reeves, who was undertaking a brave investigation into the death of Neilson, had obtained the Brifman record of interview with senior NSW police, which exposed the corruption of various other cops. Ian Alcorn, a Commonwealth Police officer, had passed it to Reeves. The plan to incorporate it into Hansard worked and the local media, including the *Advertiser*, didn't even realise the bombshell that had been dropped in their backyard until the publication of the *National Times* the following weekend.

This incident confirmed the extent of Saffron's venal influence in New South Wales and I was worried about his capacity to exercise a similar influence in the much smaller police force and political pond in South Australia. In conjunction with the police, I developed a strategy to ensure that Saffron would be unable to gain a foothold in South Australia. At the time, we felt that we had enough evidence to claim that Saffron was not a fit and proper person to hold a liquor licence in SA. The 'fit and proper person test' was a requirement for a licence under the *Liquor Licensing Act 1977*. When one of his licences came up for annual renewal before the Licensing Court, I had the Superintendent of Licensed Premises oppose the renewal, using the fit and proper test. That was the beginning of the end of Saffron, whose interests were represented in South Australia by the accountant Peter Vardon Fairweather.

Fairweather asked to see me. A meeting, which included plenty of witnesses, was organised in my office. With both senior police and the Superintendent of Licensed Premises at the meeting, Fairweather was advised that Saffron, on the basis of his poor character, was not welcome in South Australia. I indicated to Fairweather that we intended opposing each licence renewal, meaning that all that Saffron would end up owning in the state would be seven unlicensed premises. Fairweather argued that this was unfair treatment since Saffron previously had been welcomed in South Australia. Eventually, it was agreed that Saffron would be given 12 months to arrange for an orderly disposal of his South Australian properties, but that if any inappropriate dealings involving sales to related entities were identified, then the deal was off. As a result, Saffron's corrupting influence was removed from South Australia. I have no doubt, in the light of the number of South Australian police who have been shown to be corrupt, that this move was critical to thwarting institutionalised police corruption in the state.

A short time after the meeting with Fairweather, I was enjoying dinner with friends at Neddy's Tu Restaurant, which was configured as a series of separate rooms. During the evening, a waiter came into our room with a bottle of champagne and six glasses, informing us that an admirer had bought it – or words to that effect. Without giving it much thought, we consumed the bottle. Later that night, Fairweather appeared at the door to our room, and with a smirk said: 'Evening Attorney, enjoy the wine?' The next morning, I phoned the Leader of the Opposition, David Tonkin, who had been supportive of expelling Saffron, to inform him of these events. I did not want to appear on the front page of the *Advertiser* as having enjoyed Saffron's hospitality.

I also had a large body of reform underway in my portfolio of Prices and Consumer Affairs. Accordingly, the number of prosecutions doubled in the first year I was minister.

In my ministerial role, I set about rationalising the credit union industry, establishing protection for depositors. New credit union legislation was introduced that enabled credit unions to compete with the banks more effectively. More effective supervision of credit unions was introduced and a system of guarantees for depositors was also implemented.

The activities of a small cross-section of land agents were always of concern to the Consumer Affairs Commissioner, prompting the introduction of major consumer protection amendments to the *Land and Business Agents Act Amendment Act 1974*, which included prohibiting agents from buying and selling on their own account. While I was Attorney-General, the president of the Real Estate Agents' Association, Cliff Hawkins – a very decent person – held the attitude that the only way to improve the standing of real estate agents was to get rid of the rogue element. Cliff was always very supportive of the measures I took to clean up the industry.

During the period I introduced the *Residential Tenancy Act 1978*, which involved the provision of an inexpensive, quick-resolution tribunal. All residential tenancy bonds were required to be paid into the tribunal, with the interest from the bond account paying for the tribunal's administrative costs. Landlords initially opposed the new system but became more favourably disposed when they saw it in action. Disreputable landlords were exposed, non-paying tenants were evicted quickly and damage to property was repaid from the bonds. The system developed in South Australia was soon adopted in other jurisdictions. In relation to the operation of the tribunal, the Law Society disliked what was known as the '21-day rule', which required the tribunal to determine complaints within 21 days of notification of a dispute, the society's unspoken objection to this provision being that if a dispute between a landlord and tenant could be resolved in 21 days, then why not other disputes? In addition, busy lawyers did not like having to make themselves available at short notice for hearings in what, in their terms, was a minor low-fee tribunal. However, I viewed the 21-day time limit as critical to the effective working of an informal tribunal, whose role was to dispense speedy justice. The Housing Trust avoided Residential Tenancies Act scrutiny. Alex Ramsay, the General Manager of the Housing Trust, had convinced his minister, Hugh Hudson, that the Housing Trust should be excluded from the ambit of the Act. While I could see no reason to exclude Housing Trust tenants from the benefits of the Act, Hudson opposed having the Trust covered by the legislation and the Bill was amended by Cabinet accordingly. The Law Society later lobbied the Tonkin Government and the Attorney-General of the day, John Burdett, and had the 21-day rule removed from the Act.

This extensive reform program, implemented during 1975–79, also encompassed attempts at legislative reform in other areas of my consumer affairs portfolio, which early in my term as minister included addressing the high level of consumer complaints about insurance contracts. I arranged for the parliamentary counsel to draft a Bill to, in effect, introduce a code of good conduct for the industry and for consumers. Sadly, the government-owned State Government Insurance Commission (SGIC) was opposed to the legislation, which was somewhat ironic, given that SGIC's success was largely due to consumers being annoyed with private insurance companies. Ultimately, the legislation was not enacted. One consumer protection that I successfully introduced was a trust account arrangement to protect individuals from defaulting builders and sub-contractors regulated under the *Builders Licensing Act 1967*.

A further success involved the status of the Public Trustee. Prior to my time as a minister, the two private executor companies in South Australia – Elders Trustee and the Executor Trustee and Agency company – were protected from the competition posed by the Public Trustee. I removed this protection and allowed the Public Trustee to compete without restriction. I encouraged the Public Trustee to establish and extend a free will-making service for the public, an innovation again upsetting the Law Society.

I still tried to represent the Elizabeth electorate as best I could, despite a huge workload. In 1976, a proposal came to Cabinet to establish elite music programs in three metropolitan high schools, at Brighton, Woodville and Marryatville. I was outraged that the working-class areas of Elizabeth, Port Adelaide and Christies Beach were neglected. The submission was withdrawn for further consultations and when it returned to Cabinet, Fremont High school in Elizabeth had been added. The Fremont music suite was opened in 1978 and continues to provide high-quality music education and a music pathway for students in the Elizabeth area.

At this time, Adele Koh, Don's future wife, was depicted by some of the less kind conservatives in South Australia as 'Dunstan's handbag', a convenient cover to disguise his true sexuality. Nothing could have been further from the truth. Adele, when she was working for Don before they married, quite often visited my office in Franklin Street for coffee and a chat, and we of course encouraged her visits because they represented a bridge to the premier's office. Peter O'Brien was particularly matey with Adele, but so also was Carol Treloar. Unfortunately, Don got the idea that Peter O'Brien was having an affair with Adele and was enraged, phoning me one morning and instructing me to sack O'Brien. My response was to tell him that I was on my way over to discuss the issue with him. When I got to his office, I explained that it was utterly without basis and that I had no idea where the rumour had originated. After a short discussion he had calmed down and the matter was never raised again. Don offered no evidence, no smoking gun, nor did he indicate the source of the idea of an affair. As an aside, the incident demonstrates how absolutely in love he was.

CHAPTER EIGHT
# Tragedy and change

At the end of the 1976–77 summer cricket season, the SA Cricket Association (SACA) indicated that it would not permit the SA Women's Cricket competition to play its final match on the Adelaide Oval, the argument used by SACA being the need to protect the pitches from overuse. The women were claiming that the decision was sexist and demonstrated the low regard in which women's cricket was held by SACA.

When I was Attorney-General, it was the custom to have an Attorney-General's XI play the Governor's XI in a social match in March each year. In 1977, SACA management was approached about using the Adelaide Oval for this match. SACA agreed, but a week later we swapped our match with the Governor's XI to the Adelaide University oval. In the meantime, we arranged for a scratch match that involved the Women's Cricket Association playing the Attorney-General's XI on the day we had booked Adelaide Oval. The game was well under way before SACA officials realised. After this event, the women's cricket team never again had a problem booking Adelaide oval for their final!

During my time as a minister in the Dunstan Government, the Cabinet worked in a remarkably democratic fashion. If an issue was vitally important to Don, his view prevailed but he generally didn't intervene and exercise his power, except on rare occasions. Sometime in 1977 things seemed to operate less smoothly for me: Hugh Hudson, and to a lesser extent, Geoff Virgo, both began to put my Cabinet submissions under the microscope, which was somewhat annoying. As a result, Don often needed to intervene to support my submissions. There was very little pre-Cabinet lobbying of other ministers and if Don heard of any such activity, he would have been less than happy.

It was my practice on Mondays before the Cabinet meeting to have lunch with some of my staff and to go through the Cabinet papers. On one occasion, Carol Treloar and I went to the very small La Terrace restaurant on Northcote Terrace. When we arrived, we were surprised to find Don and Stephen Wright, with Cabinet papers set out before them. After pleasantries, Don said we must not combine our lunch, otherwise other Cabinet members would assume that we were colluding over the agenda items. So, we sat at another table. As we were settling in, Hugh Hudson and Ionie Brown, his senior private secretary, arrived. Again, Don made the point about no collusion and in a restaurant with only about ten tables, the three Cabinet members and staff sat at separate tables. As I recall, there were no other customers. There was some chatter between us, but, if anyone had asked, Don would have been able to say that the three ministers being at the same restaurant was pure coincidence; and that we sat at separate tables and did not discuss Cabinet matters. Weird, but true.

Cabinet members inevitably have sensitive egos and are very protective of their administrative patch, and the Dunstan Cabinet ministers were no different. Initially, I was probably insufficiently sensitive to these issues and, as a result, gained a reputation for interfering in other ministers' portfolios. Furthermore, I was not infrequently clashing with the police over legislation and other issues. For example, the Mitchell Committee had a broad remit, covering the criminal law, prisons etc. and reported to the Attorney-General. In addition, the Attorney-General was the minister in charge of the parliamentary counsel. Inevitably, the Mitchell Committee recommendations, with a draft Bill attached, went to Cabinet from my office, thus often usurping the Chief Secretary as the minister for police and prisons.

In the days before the ready availability of information over the internet, details of legislative initiatives in other parts of the world were hard to come by. My friend Peter Kellett, when undertaking university study in the US, had given me a copy of the Oregon Bottle Bill. I subsequently gave the Bill to the Minister for the Environment, Glen Broomhill, who, as I noted earlier, embraced it enthusiastically and it became the basis of the ground-breaking South Australian Container Deposit Legislation. Glen was rightly proud of that legislation, given the struggle he had to get it through the parliament, and saw it as the crowning glory of his political career.

During my time in the South Australian Parliament, the Caucus exercised significant power and influence. Cabinet would not make decisions that were against party policy, nor against the majority in Caucus. If the Cabinet or the premier believed that the Caucus could hold a different view on a particular topic, then the topic would be referred to the Caucus and there resolved. Don always won, as the Caucus numbers were confirmed beforehand.

In the Hawke Government, the Cabinet would make a controversial decision and then take it to the Caucus, with the Cabinet locked in behind its position and with Hawke effectively telling the Caucus, 'to put up or shut up'. In South Australia, the Cabinet operated as an absolute democracy of the 13 ministers, involving very serious debates around the table. I'm not denying that meetings in the premier's office between the ministers involved in a particular issue may have occurred – I was at many of them – but if agreement couldn't be reached, then the issue would be taken to Cabinet to be resolved. Don insisted on transparency and no lobbying prior to Cabinet. In politics, this was a unique approach for dealing with contentious issues. Don, of course, was a strong debater and could carry meetings most of the time. My point is that many debates were resolved in Cabinet, which rarely happened in the federal government, where key ministers would agree in advance and then impose their views on the rest of the Cabinet.

In 1977, the Minister for Transport, Geoff Virgo, had a proposal before the South Australian Cabinet to build a new Motor Registration building on government-owned land on the corner of Wakefield Street and Victoria Square. Already under the control of the Transport Department, the land was deemed the only suitable government land available. Preliminary design work had already been undertaken on the proposed building, a typical 1970s 10-storey building. It would have dominated that section of Victoria Square and accorded with the desire at the time for important government departments to be situated on or near Victoria Square and close to the State Government Administrative Centre, which housed the Premier's Department. The construction of the building, however, would have completely overshadowed St Frances Xavier Cathedral, which would have abutted the proposed building site to the east.

It transpired that the cathedral community had long wanted the cathedral to be visible from Victoria Square. However, for this objective to be achieved, the community would face several obstacles. First, the church didn't own the land, and even if the government agreed to sell, the church lacked the money to purchase the land, thus effectively resulting in a dead asset, as open space. Second, many in the church community considered that, even if the Catholic Church could raise the money, it would be better spent on completing the cathedral (argued by the conservative wing of the church) or on much-needed school buildings in the developing suburbs (argued by the small 'l' liberal wing).

As I walked into the Cabinet room, Premier Don Dunstan, whom I later realised was supporting the proposal for open space, welcomed me, asking me for my position on the proposal to build the new Motor Registry on Victoria Square next to the cathedral. 'Geoff', said Premier Dunstan, 'claims that we have no choice, as there is no suitable alternative site owned by the government. Des [Corcoran, Deputy Premier] believes the land should stay as open space. The Cabinet is split. What is your view?' I confirmed that I was in favour of the site remaining as open space, to which Don replied: 'Good, then we are decided. I will mark the file: "building approved for financing and all departments to cooperate in locating a suitable alternative site close to Victoria Square and the Administrative Centre".' A site in Gawler Place was subsequently identified and the building, with minor modifications to the previous design, was approved for construction and built. In light of this anecdote, it is germane to note that government departments side with their ministers, so that a Cabinet defeat is seen a personal humiliation for the minister.

In April 1977, I suffered an embarrassment, although one of no real consequence, despite the incident making the front page of the *Advertiser*. I had been late for a committee meeting in the parliament and had rushed out of the ministerial car, leaving my driver to bring my briefcase to the office. He noticed a ticking in the case and alerted Greg Crafter, my senior private secretary, to the problem. Exercising caution, Greg called the police bomb squad, who were quickly on the scene, detonating the briefcase and revealing my dictaphone as the source of the ticking.

Another incident concerning me that amused the *Advertiser* related to Bryant & May, the British match company. A citizen had written to me advising that he had suspected for some time that the company was defrauding consumers. Each matchbox bore the words 'average contents 60'. He claimed that his research indicated that the average was 54 matches per box. He then invited me, as the Minister for Consumer Affairs, to calculate how many billions of matches Australian consumers were being denied each year. In that context, this was potentially a serious example of product misrepresentation. I asked the Commissioner for Consumer Affairs to investigate. He did so and reported that the consumer was correct. At this point, the matter was leaked to the *Advertiser*, which through a cartoon and its reporting, along with an editorial, ridiculed the whole exercise. I was really annoyed by this and tried to respond by calculating how much the consumers were being short-changed each year, but the *Advertiser* wasn't interested. Under the law now, there would be capacity to seek a class action; in the 1970s all that was required was that the company change its packaging to read 'Average contents 50'.

By 1977, I had been the Member for Elizabeth for about five years and Attorney-General for two. The federal seat of Bonython covered Elizabeth and Salisbury. When the former Member for Bonython, Martin Nicholls, announced his intention to retire, I was immediately under pressure to seek preselection for the vacant seat. This pressure came from local Left unions and from some of the unsuccessful candidates in the Elizabeth preselection, which I had won in 1972. Ray Roe was particularly eager to support me for Bonython and, of course, to free up the seat of Elizabeth. In addition, Lionel Murphy (by then on the High Court) and members of the NSW Left, Arthur Gietzelt and Tom Uren, were pressuring me to run to keep Bonython voting with the Left in the federal ALP Caucus.

Don Dunstan was supporting Neal Blewett and was putting maximum pressure on me to stay put. He had some pretty strong arguments for me to remain there; he and I were working very closely together on other issues and he wanted to continue with the reform program that I was undertaking. He also said that he didn't 'want a bloody by-election even in a safe seat'. I suspect he was also concerned that, if I resigned, it might have been difficult to keep Terry McRae out of the ministry; McRae was unlikely to adopt the same social reform agenda that I had been running. In addition, I had a dedicated staff, who were working at a furious pace, and I felt I owed them some loyalty – they would have lost their jobs if I resigned. I decided finally not to run, and Neal Blewett became the Member for Bonython and a great Minister of Health in the Hawke Government. Who would have won the preselection if I had run? Who knows, but I lived in Elizabeth and was probably at the height of my popularity in the Labor Party at large.

Throughout this period, my personal life was in turmoil and by 1978 my first marriage had ended in divorce. In 1978, I bought what was to be my home for the next 25 years, in Gibbon Lane, North Adelaide.

By any measure, 1978 was a tumultuous year in South Australian politics. In February, the Governor Sir Keith Seaman was engulfed in a scandal following the revelation that he had been involved in a 'grave impropriety' prior to his appointment. Keith Seaman had been a Uniting Church Minister and the Superintendent of the Adelaide Central Mission

(Methodist), located around the corner from my office in Franklin Street. I often saw him in the street. He was a good guy who cared about the dispossessed.

In March of the previous year, his predecessor, Pastor Sir Douglas Nicholls, had resigned as governor following a stroke and the government was casting around for a successor. After the experience of an earlier governor, Sir Mark Oliphant, who attempted to interfere in the governance of the state, Dunstan was understandably very cautious about an appointment. I suggested to Don that Seaman might be a worthy candidate to replace Nicholls and that we should appoint him. He agreed, and proper due diligence was carried out. He seemed well qualified and appeared to have no skeletons in his closet. After an interrogation by me and Don, he was recommended to the Cabinet and the appointment met with universal approval, although Hugh Hudson did say in jest, 'Jesus Don, we've just had one bible basher [referring to Pastor Doug Nicholls] do we have to have another?'

In February 1978, the *Advertiser* incorrectly reported that Seaman was about to be sacked and referred to his 'grave impropriety', which turned out to be merely adultery. This may be a serious offence in the church but in a secular world it was hardly a sacking matter. The issue had been dealt with prior to his swearing-in as governor: the Uniting Church had investigated the matter, found him to be guilty of the alleged behaviour but had not applied a penalty. Don was initially furious, not about the crime, but because Seaman had chosen to deliberately conceal the matter when he was specifically asked by Don in my presence whether there was anything in his past which likely to bring him, or the office, into ill repute or scandal. Seaman answered in the negative, which was a deliberate lie. As I said, Don was furious at this perfidy but decided to ride out the storm and Seaman survived. I suspect that the *Advertiser* story about Seaman getting sacked was a leak from the premier's staff, who had seen how angry Don had been, although he eventually calmed down.

Lionel Murphy had advised me to be courageous in all things, but particularly in appointments. I took that advice to heart. I decided to appoint people to positions based on my judgement as to whom was the best candidate, and not according to lists of queued candidates from the Law Society, the Bar Association or the Justices Association. These appointments, under the various pieces of legislation, are the unimpeded responsibility of the Attorney-General.

Up to that time, it had been the role of the executive of the Justices

Association (Royal Association of Justices of South Australia Inc.) to nominate a list of prospective Justices of the Peace to the Attorney-General to be rostered for sitting on the Justices courts, for which they receive sitting fees. In the past these nominees had overwhelmingly been retired military, police officers and similar individuals. Justices were appointed according to state electorate size, with large waitlists for each electorate, particularly the middle-class electorates. I had appointed most of the people – rather than a select few – on these lists of recommendations if they were suitable candidates. My action, according to the Justices Association, overwhelmed the state with Justices of the Peace, as well as greatly upset the Law Society. The increased number meant that JPs were readily available to witness documents free of charge across the state. Lawyers as Commissioners for Declaration (Comm. Decs), who must be legal practitioners and who could perform the same service of signing documents as a JP, were allowed to charge for this service. Justices were not permitted to charge for providing the same service and, understandably, lawyers were not happy about this 'unfair' competition. I appointed many new Justices to the court, resulting in a much larger group of JPs from whom to recruit for the Justices courts, these appointees coming from a diverse range of backgrounds and without preconceived ideas of what a criminal looked like.

When I attended a Justices Association cocktail party in October of that year, I announced a proposal whereby Justices over the age of 70 would no longer be listed for court work. The establishment JPs who ran the association were mostly over 70 and were vehemently opposed to the idea. As a result of these changes, the Justices courts began to display a degree of independence from the police. Even though these courts were administratively separate from the police, a 'club', comprising the police prosecutor and the JPs, had often operated against the interests of justice.

Similar reforms to the personnel of the Magistrates and Local and District courts were initiated. In the 1960s and early 1970s the court system at the lower levels was relatively unsophisticated. Magistrates, some of whom had been on the bench for decades, were often frustrated, angry and contemptuous of the public, and often influenced by the police. Younger, more enthusiastic, magistrates were appointed, along with a resident magistrate in Port Augusta to serve that city and Whyalla, Port Pirie, Port Lincoln and the West Coast. I made residence a condition of employment for the Port Augusta magistrate. Sadly, after I ceased being the Attorney-General, the system of magistrates visiting from Adelaide to the courts in the state's regional cities was reinstated.

In 1978 I made a number of appointments to the District Court, including the academic lawyers Brian Grieves and Arthur Rogerson, both of whom brought a different perspective to the court, as well as Iris Stevens, the first woman to be a judge of the District Court. In June 1978, five more Queen's Counsel were appointed – Ken McCarthy, Graham Prior, Ted Mulligan, John Von Doussa and Kevin Duggan – from a list supplied to me by Len King, by then Chief Justice, after discussion with the Law Society and the Bar Association. Since no women were proposed, I flagged the need to appoint women with Chief Justice King and we agreed that the next list would include some women.

Appointments to the Supreme Court were generally restricted to a list of Queen's Counsel and were based on their seniority of appointment as a QC, despite there being many excellent candidates, including lower-ranking QCs and other members of the legal profession. This latter group included judges of the District Court, as well as magistrates, who, by convention, were excluded from what was seen as promotion. The reasoning underpinning this convention was that, if a candidate for higher judicial office desired promotion, he or she might constrain their judicial activities in order to ingratiate himself or herself to the government. I thought that this was nonsense, and it didn't seem to apply to Masters of the Supreme Court, who had in the past been promoted to the position of Supreme Court Justice. I upset the legal establishment, including several Supreme Court Justices, by promoting District Court Judge Michael White to the Supreme Court.

Soon after, there was a need to appoint three further Supreme Court Justices. I was keen to appoint Elliott Johnson and I mentioned the matter to Don. By that stage, late in 1978, we were dealing with the fallout from the Salisbury sacking and decided that, politically, we didn't need another controversy by appointing a member of the Communist Party to the Supreme Court. I don't regret the decision in that context but was pleased that he was appointed subsequently. He proved to be an excellent judge. Instead, I appointed Chris Legoe, QC, to the Supreme Court, an appointment that also upset the profession, given that Legoe was junior in QC rankings to several others.

All in all, as far as judicial appointments are concerned, I believe that my revitalisation of the appointment system has subsequently served South Australia well and, although it was seen as radical at the time, a structure was established that ensured that the best person was appointed rather than simply the next person in the queue.

On three occasions, I had dinner with Don Dunstan at his Norwood home. Don, of course, was a great host and a magnificent chef. This was in the period prior to my meeting Julie. I was starting to feel guilty about not returning Don's hospitality. Late one night, in October 1978, when we were in the parliamentary bar and not long after Adele had died, I foolishly invited Don to my semi-renovated house for a meal some time during the following week. The next morning, the full horror of the implications of the invitation struck home. Not only was my house only partly renovated, but my kitchen, as described by my now-deceased friend Peter Kellett, was little more than 'a room with a pie warmer'.

I discussed my dilemma with my friend, Andy Thorpe (also deceased), who suggested that I organise Phill Cremey from Ayers House restaurant to home-deliver, advising that I instruct him to 'Down market his food a bit, brief you on the ingredients, cooking methods and time of cooking etcetera'. Andy, also friend of Don's, offered to come as one of the guests and to entertain/distract Don and the other guests while the food was delivered, and then served by me. The other guests were Peter Kellett (who was in on the secret), Peter Crayford and his partner, and the artist Cressida Campbell. The night came. The wine flowed. As arranged, the food arrived on time, at 9 pm. I recall that the main course was Chicken Cacciatore; the details of the dessert are lost in the mists of time. The whole charade was carried off to perfection and never at any stage was I forced to blatantly lie about the cooking of the food. As far as I am aware, no one let on and Don continued under the delusion that I was an able enough cook. Forty years on, I blush when I recall the deception. Fortunately, thereafter, with Julie by my side, such embarrassing events were never repeated. With Julie in residence, dinner parties and long lunches became a regular feature of life. Oh, how we entertained. The house was perfect for the lifestyle: a pool to entertain our and other friends' kids for hours as we drank, ate and enjoyed ourselves.

In July 1977, Carol Treloar left for overseas travel and was replaced as press secretary by Trevor Watson, who proved to be equally expert at handling my relations with the media, which were often fraught. By November, pressure was building on the government over allegations that the police special branch had large numbers of files on law-abiding citizens. Most of this public commentary was coming from Peter Ward, Dunstan's former staff member and close adviser. Don and Ward had fallen out and Ward had gone to work for the *Australian*, owned by then by the much-reviled Rupert Murdoch. Underpinning Ward's disquiet was his belief that Don had not done enough to bring the police under control in relation to the so-called 'pink files', held on homosexual people. Prior to Michael White's report, detailed below, it may be that Ward did not realise that files were also kept on people holding Left political views.

Don and I agreed on an investigation by a judicial officer. We had just appointed District Court Judge Michael White as an Acting Justice of the Supreme Court and maybe he was on my mind for that reason. He was not a friend of mine or of Don's, although we knew him through the legal profession. He had no Labor Party or other Left associations and was a practising Catholic and an honourable person. We agreed that he was suitable for what was inevitably a very sensitive task. Michael, when approached, agreed to undertake what was considered to be a simple and straightforward task. His report to the premier, however, delivered early in 1978, was a bombshell and revealed that files were kept on thousands of South Australians. Pretty much anyone who held anything other than conservative views was likely to be under suspicion and the subject of a file.

The SA Government directed the Police Commissioner Harold Salisbury to destroy the files. Salisbury refused point blank, after which a Cabinet meeting was held, where it was agreed that Salisbury should be offered the options of destroying the files or resigning. He refused both, and in accordance with the Cabinet decision, he was sacked. Salisbury immediately cried foul, on the specious and ludicrous grounds that he was employed, in effect, at the pleasure of the Crown – the Queen – not the elected Government of South Australia. Stewart Cockburn at the *Advertiser* was a friend of Salisbury's and campaigned through its pages for his reinstatement. A group of conservatives formed a Salisbury Support Group and organised a protest, which was large and no doubt from their perspective, very successful.

Premier Dunstan and I decided to respond and organised a meeting in support of the government's action and the sacking of Salisbury. The meeting was held on the Festival Centre Plaza. Don and I addressed the assembled citizenry from the Juliette balcony at the rear of the parliament building. The plaza was full, and the meeting was extremely successful and greatly lifted Dunstan's spirits. That day and that image indelibly remain with me. Following this event, he and I had tea in his Parliament House office, and he indicated that, with the *Advertiser*, the Opposition and the establishment driving the issue, it was not likely to go away, particularly with the Legislative Council threatening a select committee. Don explained that he believed a Royal Commission could be the solution and he indicated that he had the Supreme Court Justice Roma Mitchell in mind for commissioner. The Royal Commission was established, with the ensuing report exonerating the government's action in sacking Salisbury. It also found that Dunstan had no knowledge of special branch's work and files prior to Mr Justice White's report. The government was completely cleared of any wrongdoing.

Many people have argued in retrospect that Don was a poor judge of character, his appointment of Salisbury being ample demonstration of this. Salisbury may have been an adequate police officer in England, but he was British to the bootstraps and a monarchist, and not by any stretch of the imagination, a democrat. I supported the sacking of Salisbury and the way it had been done. Under Salisbury's leadership, the police were essentially out of control and inviolable: that nobody had been charged with Dr George Ian Ogilvie Duncan's murder and that the perpetrator police officers were merely allowed to resign from the force was evidence of that. We were the elected government, even if we were the wrong party for Salisbury and his supporters, including Oliphant, Cockburn, and his wife Jennifer Adamson, the Health Minister in the Tonkin Liberal Government. The Salisbury saga publicly exposed that special branch political files were in existence in all states and that special branches were doing the legwork for ASIO.

At Easter 1978, Don's wife, Adele Koh, was tragically diagnosed with terminal cancer. She expressed the wish that this terrible news be kept from the public, a request to which the media mostly complied, with the exception of Derryn Hinch in Victoria. Don was attempting to nurse her at home, while continuing with his normal workload, a nearly impossible task. Andy Thorpe was also doing a terrific job helping to nurse Adele and was keeping me informed about the real situation in relation to Adele's health. Her reports were bleak compared with the optimistic information emerging from the premier's staff. Adele's death was a savage blow to Don and one from which he did not recover until long after his resignation. In retrospect, Adele's death, given its impact on Don's health, was one from which the government itself didn't recover. From this distance I can see that, as everything continued on a business-as-usual basis, we were inevitably heading to an irretrievable situation.

The Labor Party in South Australia had long been run by a group known as 'the machine', a group consisting of Geoff Virgo, Senator Jim Toohey, Clyde Cameron, Don Dunstan and Mick Young and whose ideological position encompassed what loosely could be described as Centre

Left, although every ideological perspective was represented in the makeup of the various positions chosen by the party. For example, Senator Arnold Drury was from the Right, senators Jim Cavanagh and Don Cameron (Clyde's brother) and Martin Nicholls were from the Left in the Australian Parliament. Until the mid-1970s, the State Parliamentary Caucus was basically ideology-free. Don would have been the one Left member, in that he was a radical, but no one else even looked like a socialist.

The modern faction system in South Australia developed slowly from about 1974. The unions wanted seats in the parliament. Jim Dunford, Jack Phelan, Keith Plunkett, from the AWU; Frank Blevins from the Seamen's Union; George Apap from the Storemen and Packers'; Terry Hemmings and John Scott from the Metal Workers'; Ray Roe from the Postal Workers' etc. obtained preselection for safe seats. There had been some unhappiness amongst the unions about Anne Levy getting a safe berth on the Legislative Council ticket, while Don had made it clear that he opposed the preselection of Jim Dunford. From that time on, the Left unions from the Trades and Labor Council started considering ALP matters more formally.

The involvement of the Left unions slowly developed, and I began attending meetings regularly in 1979. The group was more anti-Right than Left at this stage, although the Right was only a small group. It wasn't really until Don left the parliament that processes became more formalised, in part because of the disagreements over uranium mining and the entry of factional disputes from New South Wales, which were transferred to the National Executive when Arthur Gietzelt and Tom Uren and others became very enthusiastic about building support from like-minded people from other states who would support the line, particularly on uranium mining and the nuclear fuel cycle.

Uranium mining, a divisive issue in the party, became a lightning rod, galvanising the Left and generating strong feelings at the time. Civil libertarians and those on the Left thought it was economically wiser not to develop nuclear energy, at least until the problems with disposal of waste and other associated issues had been resolved – still unresolved today despite massive investment in research and development. The issue of uranium also fed into the disputes that developed in the AWU, given that uranium mining was within the remit of the AWU and the union was generally in favour of any sort of mining because it created jobs and potential union members. Roxby Downs had been discovered in 1975, and over the ensuing years the size and richness of the ore body was revealed. The Labor Party was waiting for the release of the report from the Ranger Uranium Environmental Enquiry (the Fox report) before adopting a position and was committed to taking advice on the safety of mining, enrichment and processing.

Initially, pre-Roxby Downs, Dunstan was opposed to uranium mining, although he kept an open mind and wanted to investigate further, travelling overseas to study the latest developments. I think intellectually he was in opposition to uranium mining and the nuclear fuel cycle but was cognisant of the political reality of the proposed Roxby Downs mega mine. My recollection is that Don had been reasonably comfortable with a cautious policy on uranium mining and the nuclear fuel cycle. Early in the term of the Dunstan Government, Hugh Hudson and Don had discussed uranium enrichment and processing. Don, however, was unconvinced and the discussions went no further. Later, when Roxby was discovered, the politics of the nuclear issue in South Australia changed. It was generally considered that it would be impossible to oppose the development of a world-class mine. One option being suggested was that the mine should go ahead without mining the uranium. In other words, mine the copper, the silver and the gold deposits; process on site; and return the uranium to the mine. Labor ministers, including myself, agreed that this was an unworkable solution, in that the uranium would be left conveniently in the ground, and at the next election, a Liberal Government would be elected and mining would begin. That argument was very difficult to deny.

In early July 1978, I made a speech at the Anti-Uranium National activists conference, in which I analysed the Fraser Government's legislation to facilitate uranium mining: the *Environment Protection (Nuclear Codes) Act 1978* (the Nuclear Codes Act). It was a carefully crafted speech, which pinned my anti-uranium colours to the masthead by attacking the federal Liberal Government. In my speech, I noted that the South Australian Government opposed the Fraser Government's legislation because it was contrary to ALP policy and furthermore that Fraser had failed to consult adequately with the states. I pointed out that the legislation went against the recommendations of the Fox report; that the legislation contemplated the establishment of uranium-enrichment facilities; and that it did not provide proper compensation for damage to health and property caused by nuclear accidents. I explained that the law did not adequately protect the environment and permitted destruction of Aboriginal cultural sites and the exploitation of Aboriginal people. I also pointed out that the curtailment of civil liberties was one of the more sinister aspects of the legislation. Citizens could be arbitrarily detained on the order of the Commonwealth minister, without recourse to the due process of the courts and the legal system. Police were empowered to enter premises and search and seize people's papers and property without judicial warrant. In addition, peaceful demonstrators could be imprisoned without court order and the minister had the power to suppress information relating to an accident; to halt any demonstration or pamphleteering activity; and to have the activists involved jailed without trial. I concluded by asking the question: if nuclear technology is so safe and foolproof, why should it be necessary for the government to pass such vicious anti-civil liberties laws, so sweeping in their application and hence potentially oppressive?

In early December 1978, I attended an Attorney-Generals' conference in Hobart. Kym Boyer, the Women's Advisor to the Tasmanian Premier Doug Lowe, whom I had met previously, had arranged a lunch for me with a few of her female friends, one of whom was Julie Badcock, to whom I was immediately attracted. Unfortunately, she had to return to work before I managed to get her contact details. All I knew about her was that her name was Julie and that she worked in the Tasmanian Education Department Public Relations section. Eventually, we established a relationship and she agreed to visit Adelaide for 10 days in early February 1979, right in the middle of the disaster of the Dunstan resignation. By the time she returned to Hobart, I was the Minister of Health and no longer the Attorney-General.

In January 1979, prior to his resignation, Don had travelled overseas on a rushed trip to study the latest developments in the nuclear fuel cycle. During his absence, I attended a meeting of the Left and, although other Caucus members were present, I was the only Cabinet minister. At the meeting, we discussed the issue of uranium and the nuclear fuel cycle and decided to wait for Dunstan to clarify his position on his return and then, if necessary, coordinate opposition to uranium mining at the party level. Unfortunately, Don received a very biased report of the meeting and my role in it, interpreting my attendance as an act of disloyalty. A meeting of the Caucus was held. Although I'm unable to recall the exact details, I was left in no doubt that Don was extremely displeased with me. At the 1977 national conference, a policy of a moratorium on uranium mining had been adopted and at the 1978 state party conference, a ban on uranium mining was agreed. Dunstan had been attempting to manage the issue and had persuaded the Cabinet to support him in delaying the decision on the state government's position until he returned from overseas.

With my attendance at that Left meeting, he saw me as having gone against the Cabinet position. My argument, if I'd had the opportunity to present it, would have been that I hadn't made any public comment in breach of the Cabinet position and had attended a private meeting of Left party members and that details of that meeting had not been publicly leaked.

Don obviously had heard the version fed to him on his return to Australia. Steven Wright, his senior private secretary, had accompanied Don on the January 1979 overseas visit and was frequently on the phone to Peter O'Brien, my senior private secretary, seeking information about the rumoured book that subsequently became Des Ryan and Mike McEwin's biography of Don Dunstan, *It's Grossly Improper*. During these phone calls, Steven intimated that Don was strengthening his opposition to uranium mining. Don returned from overseas on 5 February 1979 in poor health. The parliament met three days later, and soon after, Don collapsed and was hospitalised. On 15 February 1979, Don resigned as premier and from the parliament.

Although I was distraught when Dunstan's resignation was announced, I have since wondered if the person who poisoned me to Dunstan was equally upset. I suspect that my reaction to Don's resignation was somewhat different from that of those waiting in the wings for promotion or who were feeling a sense of relief that the days of pink shorts, Monarto and a frenetic pace of government were over.

The 1977 ALP National Conference decision to oppose uranium mining meant that Don's position of leaving the issue open was clearly the only policy option available to those in the Cabinet who were in favour of mining uranium. The Left lost the argument over uranium mining at the National Conference in 1981, which was probably inevitable. A small state like South Australia was faced with a significant economic benefit implicit in the potential of a mega mine, and also its small size meant that it would not have had the numbers to alter the outcome. The Left can however take credit for keeping the nuclear fuel cycle out of Australia. Clean alternative energy sources have supplanted nuclear in terms of cost, safety and reliability.

I think it's important to emphasise that I don't believe that Dunstan ever truly thought that he would be forced to resign until maybe just the last few days or even hours before he announced his decision. There was no plan for succession. Earlier there had been talk about Don moving into the federal parliament, the first occasion being between 1968 and 1970 when opponents of Whitlam were casting around for an alternative. The second occasion was at the end of the Whitlam Government in 1975, when Clyde Cameron, who had been sidelined by Whitlam, offered to resign and support Dunstan for the electorate of Hindmarsh. I'm unaware of the details, but I suspect that Don, who was just about at the height of his power, would have given the proposal short shrift.

Given David Tonkin's lacklustre leadership of the Liberal Party, his loss to Dunstan in 1977 and Don's reasonably commanding support in the community, Don probably could have expected to remain as premier until he tired of the position, perhaps sometime in the late 1980s. Some of the plans being developed or in train had very long-term horizons, including Monarto and industrial democracy. Other long-term plans or ideas were being contemplated. One was the idea that Adelaide – the City of Adelaide – should have sectors that, through government assistance and influence, would become focused as mini ethnic communities: the East End as the Italian area; the West End as the Greek; and the Gouger/Grote Street area as Chinatown. That dream has been partially realised but not to the extent he envisaged.

Don was very interested in carefully managed decentralised town planning. He believed that the idea of building Elizabeth on the northern Adelaide plain had been flawed and should never have occurred. The Elizabeth concept was based on building an industrial area on the semi-desert plain and importing mainly British working-class people to live in the town and work for GMH. That was not the way Don thought things should be done. I remember having dinner with him and we discussed this issue. After all, I was the Member for Elizabeth. Monarto, the Dunstan Government's proposed new town, was significantly further away from Adelaide than Elizabeth and had the Adelaide Hills in between as a barrier. Monarto, he considered, had a much greater prospect of developing a separate city entity as opposed to being a dormitory suburb of Adelaide.

It was clear to me that Dunstan believed, or hoped, that he was going to be premier for quite a while to come; it is not unreasonable to suggest that Don anticipated he had a Playford-length premiership ahead of him. Of course, as the details of Ryan and McEwin's book began to emerge, combined with the stress of the job and the impact of Adele's death on his health, his resignation, in retrospect, was probably inevitable.

I'm of the opinion that during the 1970s the people of South Australia recognised that something exciting was occurring in their state, that history was being made. In a speech in 1976, I made the point that, very often when you live through periods of historical change, you do not appreciate what is going on. Looking back, however, as far as the Dunstan Government was concerned, I believe that the people of South Australia did have a sense of optimism and anticipation. That the Dunstan Labor Government in South Australia was able to achieve all that it did, despite all the powerful forces aligned against it (and that raged against it), gave me real hope in the possibility of changing the system from within. In addition, history was to prove that substantial reforms, once implemented, are hard to roll back or reverse. Virtually all of the reforms of the Dunstan Government, including those law reforms I implemented, are still on the statute books and continue to benefit South Australians to this day.

That was the sad end of the Dunstan Government and an extraordinary period of enlightened administration in South Australia. I owe Don Dunstan an enormous debt of gratitude for the opportunity he gave me to be his Attorney-General. None of the great reforms outlined in this memoir would have occurred without his support, something I am the first to acknowledge.

CHAPTER NINE

## The Corcoran Government and marriage to Julie

After his resignation Don decided that Hugh Hudson was the person who should replace him as premier. Des Corcoran, who had been a very loyal deputy and competent in his way, had good support in the Caucus and decided to run. Hudson could not have won unless Don had been around to manage the process, which his health crisis prevented. Corcoran became the Leader and Premier. I had supported Corcoran and was surprised when he moved me to Health, although I didn't dispute the move. In retrospect, I concede it was understandable. I had allowed myself to become 'the dangerous Left wing whipping boy', which was acceptable while I had had the protection of Dunstan, but with Don no longer on the scene, Corcoran needed to make it clear that he was his own man, and moving me to the Health portfolio was part of that message.

Because I had believed that Don would be premier for another 10 years, I had given the future leadership little thought. I recognised that if I were to consider a leadership role, I would be required to change my persona and make compromises, which at that time, I was not prepared to do. I thought that I would be able to continue running a vigorous reform agenda under cover of Dunstan's popularity. I had little concern for my standing in the community at large, as long as I was well regarded by him and by my constituents in Elizabeth. With the benefit of hindsight, it was hardly surprising that Des Corcoran wanted to signal to the *Advertiser* that he had effectively clipped my wings and that he had dispensed with the frenetic pace of reform associated with the Dunstan Government. It is often said that fortune favours the brave. I was brave for my time as Attorney-General, but when Dunstan's health collapsed and he resigned, my luck, to some extent, ran out.

At the first Cabinet meeting following the swearing-in of the Corcoran Government and after my move to Health, Des discussed my changed responsibilities. He had agreed to leave Corporate Affairs with me, as the critical negotiation over the national corporate affairs scheme was ongoing. I became the Minister for Health and Corporate Affairs. A couple of days later, in the context of the health-related matters on which I had been working as Attorney-General, I suggested to Des that the Drug Royal Commission administration, the Rights of Handicapped Persons Committee, and Food Standards remain my responsibility. His response to the first was that no more time would be 'wasted on drugs'.

At the state ALP conference that year, Andrew Dunstan (Don's son) moved a resolution in favour of legalising marijuana and Des vigorously opposed the motion, ensuring its defeat. In relation to Handicapped Rights and Food Standards, Corcoran took responsibility for these, although nothing ever came of my approach. It was obvious that Corcoran's desire was to shut me down.

During that first Cabinet meeting, when it came to the Industrial Democracy Unit, Jack Wright, the Minister for Labour, was given responsibility. Ron Payne, who was a Hugh Hudson supporter, asked Des in Cabinet:

'Is this the end of this stuff?'
'No. It's not dead', replied Des. 'Jack [Wright] will control [Phil] Bentley and his crew [working in the Industrial Democracy Unit]. It's on life support until the election.'
'You can't just dump this stuff, what about the party policy?', I asked.
'What about it?', Hugh Hudson replied.

That was effectively the end of a brave experiment.

Once I had recovered from the shock of moving to Health, I realised that it was not necessarily a massive demotion. It was an important portfolio in terms of the expenditure of funds and the services it delivered, and previous ministers had not shown much policy initiative. The department head, Dr Brian Shea, had been the minister in all but name and had determined the issues, which the various ministers followed. I quickly reached a good working relationship with Shea, who, I believe, rather liked the idea of an activist minister for a change. The health sector hadn't had a shake-up in decades, and I saw many areas where I could make a significant policy difference and I got straight into it.

The one bonus of the move to Health was that an International Health Ministers' conference was to be held in Athens and the South Australian Health Minister was scheduled to represent Australia. The relationship between Julie and me had become very important to us, so we decided to marry to enable her to travel the conference in Greece as my partner. A wedding was quickly organised in Hobart for Sunday 8 April 1979, between a sitting of the parliament and the start of the Athens conference on 17 April. Happily, Easter fell in between, and we organised to have a short honeymoon on the wonderful Mediterranean island of Santorini.

The wedding was held in the garden of Julie's parents' home. Kath and Sam Badcock lived in the Hobart suburb of Taroona. It was a lunchtime event and, in my eyes, just perfect. Little formality, a civil registrant and lots of fun with family and friends. I arrived in Hobart on Saturday wearing the cream suit I intended to wear for the wedding. I was not keen on wearing a ring but Julie wanted to wear one, so we reached a compromise, whereby she wore a ring and we exchanged stylish watches. She had a Swiss Army brand and I a Raymond Weil, which I wear to this day. We had bought the ring in Adelaide. When we went to collect it, I realised I had left my wallet in the car, meaning that she had to pay for it, for which she forever after teased me.

The next day as we were dressing for the wedding, Julie pointed out that my cream coat had 'pancake makeup on the lapel' and that I couldn't wear it. The suit had just been dry-cleaned. I explained that a woman admirer at Adelaide Airport had given me, a public figure, a hug – and there was no 'other woman' for her to contend with. The problem was solved when I bought a bottle of dry-cleaning fluid on the way to collect some friends for the wedding.

The best man, Peter O'Brien, and his partner Karen, along with my friend and legal partner Gordon Barrett, flew in on Sunday morning. O'Brien was carrying $5000 cash, part of the funding for the trip to Greece. In the taxi from the airport, they drove past the Wrest Point Casino and Peter directed the taxi to stop for a 'quick look'. This episode led to an hour-long roulette play, the loss of $3000 cash and the arrival at the wedding ten minutes before the scheduled start. This incident begs the question of why I didn't sack O'Brien – both as best man and senior private secretary – on the spot. The answer is firstly that I didn't know about the loss of the money until after the wedding; the second reason is more complex: O'Brien, apart from being a very good officer, was very entertaining and, in a very stressful job, light relief is very welcome. I had calmed down about the missing $3000 after Peter had arranged to pay it back and the books were balanced in terms of the departmental budget office, so no harm was done.

Fortunately, I was in possession of the wedding ring, so Julie was not particularly stressed when the best man arrived only just in time and somewhat drunk. The wedding went off smoothly and was a fabulous social success. Lionel and Ingrid Murphy gave us two exquisite Lalique glasses, which we used for the toast at the wedding and for other big-occasion toasts during our married life. Before Julie died, she brought them to Lombok and instructed me to smash one of them on her death, with Georgia, our daughter, to do the same on my death. Lovely symbolism from Julie: she wanted the glasses used only to celebrate our love.

The following day we headed from Hobart to Melbourne for an Olympic Air flight to Athens. Olympic Air had upgraded us from economy to first-class. Although I always travelled economy class when travelling overseas at government expense, I didn't object to the upgrade. Knowing we had no official business on arrival in Athens, we settled in to enjoy the flight. Once in Athens, we caught a taxi to the Grande Bretagne Hotel for a long recovery. On Thursday, Julie and I took a ferry to Santorini and had a great four-day honeymoon, staying in a pension and riding mopeds all over the beautiful island. We returned to Athens on Sunday evening to find O'Brien in a high mood, having discovered that a Greek Apotek (pharmacy) was a drug store. This was the only time, so far as I know, that he broke the 'no drugs' rule on which I had insisted when employing him, his defence on that occasion being that whatever he was using was not an illegal substance, at least not in Greece. The conference passed uneventfully, from our point of view. The exception was that I participated in the (inevitable) pro/anti-abortion debate, in favour of a woman's right to choose, much to the unhappiness of the then Australian Ambassador to Greece.

When appointed as Health Minister, I was acutely aware of my lack of knowledge of the health area, having previously had no need to investigate the system since I was reasonably fit and healthy. At least when appointed Attorney-General, I had the benefit of a legal studies background and some limited practice and consequently could 'talk the talk'. Not so in health, and I decided to play it cautiously until I found my feet. I soon recognised that my approach of seeking areas of the Health portfolio in need of law reform, while desirable, would be entirely inadequate in dealing with the deficiencies of the Health portfolio at large.

The administration was in dire straits and would need more comprehensive action than merely developing a few Bills for Cabinet and having them passed by the parliament. The conference in Athens was an opportunity to speak to experts in many fields and I wasted no time in drawing on the expertise of those I met. I soon had a feel for the issues and international trends in health policy in similar Western societies and developed a list of priorities and some thoughts on approaches.

With all their complexity, Aboriginal health was an obvious area of need and of particular interest to me. Women's health had never received adequate attention and now that feminists had seen some progress in women rights, people had begun to address the inadequate service delivery in women's health, social services etc. The one limited involvement I had with the health area was a result of hearing the horrendous stories told by my friend Dale Hassam, a psychiatric nurse who had worked at Glenside Psychiatric Hospital. I decided to attempt to undertake some administrative reform in mental health. My interactions with the other World Health Organization (WHO) conference delegates indicated a groundswell of concern amongst health professionals over the impact of smoking on health. I was already a strong opponent of the pernicious tobacco industry and I took on board several ideas that seemed likely to be politically possible in South Australia. Finally, I spoke to the WHO administrators and invited them to hold their next conference in Adelaide. Long after my demise as Minister for Health, this invitation was realised, with the World Health Organization Conference on Healthy Public Policy held in Adelaide in 1988.

A few days after the end of the conference, Julie and I flew to the Greek island of Leros to represent Australia at the Anzac Day commemoration. Leros had been a staging point for Australian and other Allied troops during the First World War's Gallipoli campaign and somewhat incongruously is heavily wooded with Australian eucalyptus trees. On our return to Australia, Julie managed to secure a position as cadet counsellor at the Adelaide *Advertiser* (despite her husband's high political profile) and we settled into a hectic married life.

Equipped with the information gathered at the Athens conference and the departmental briefings, I began to embark on serious work in the Health portfolio. To the list of priorities I had already determined, I added a focus on preventative health. I soon realised that, in the expansive Health portfolio, a large amount of the minister's work involved administration, encompassing vast numbers of boards and committees, the personnel for which were nominated in whole or in part, by the Health Minister. Many of these positions required medical personnel to be nominated. I personally knew about three doctors, and only two of them well enough to ask advice about appointments. My initial appointments were not particularly controversial and, as I discovered later, any appointments out of the ordinary would have been denied by Cabinet. As I started to get an understanding of the portfolio and to take initiatives to Cabinet, I realised just how exposed I was without Dunstan's protection. Anything involving new money was automatically opposed by Hugh Hudson, the Treasurer, a situation not necessarily the case with other ministers, but other initiatives of mine were also put under the microscope. In fact, the Health portfolio was a mess and needed comprehensive administrative reform. That was nothing new. The so-called maladministration had existed from the Playford era and in my short tenure as Health Minister I was unable to make an impact; real reform was not addressed until John Cornwall became minister in the 1980s.

The existing problems weren't characterised by corruption in the narrow sense: corruption here involved a system that appeared to operate in the style of a series of fiefdoms, an approach that had been allowed to exist and proliferate for decades. Most of the units in, or funded by, the department were a law unto themselves. The Queen Victoria Hospital, for example, which was run as a charity, with its operating costs covered by government funds, had costs-per-bed-occupied far exceeding those of the Royal Adelaide Hospital (RAH) on a comparable basis. As a major teaching hospital, the RAH should have had higher costs than those of a maternity hospital. By way of further example, policies more in tune with the 1920s were being applied by the Alcohol and Drug Treatment Board, prompting me to focus initially on the policy priorities that I had identified rather than tackle the administration. I also arranged for a good lawyer and legal draughtsperson from the Attorney-General's Department to be seconded as a legal consultant to the Health ministry to assist in resolving legal matters when and if they arose. This was done at an administrative level as a favour to me by the public service head of Attorney-General's.

While I understood the position of Aboriginal people in relation to the legal system and the law addressing racism against Aboriginal people more broadly, I knew little about Aboriginal health issues. To better understand Aboriginal health and to develop a strategy to deal with what I saw as a continuing crisis, I decided to check on the health services being provided on the Anangu Pitjantjatjara Yankunytjatjara Lands (APY Lands), in the towns of Indulkana and Ernabella. We drove from Adelaide in the ministerial limousine. When I arrived in Indulkana, I discovered that the new government school had been built without adult toilets. The architects had provided small-sized toilets for the children but no adult toilets for the staff. Although the school wasn't my responsibility, I undertook to help resolve the problem.

I visited the health clinics at each town and spoke to the community nurses who, at the time, were all non-Indigenous. As far as I could tell from my brief visit, each of these women was very dedicated and doing a good job in extremely difficult circumstances. They were 'Jills of all trades' – health workers who covered a multitude of areas: they undertook preventative health and they were dietitians, midwives, community health workers and, when the doctors visited, surgical assistants.

Following Whitlam Government initiatives, the salaries of the community nurses were paid by the Commonwealth Government, with the more complex medical services provided by fly-in, fly-out medicos from Alice Springs, Port Augusta and Adelaide. Emergency medical services requiring hospitalisations were provided by the Flying Doctor or Aerial Ambulance service. One of the nurses explained just how complex the provision of these services for Indigenous people was. From my brief time there I could see that the whole system needed reform and I was determined to establish an interdepartmental committee of enquiry to advise. Unfortunately, such a step needed the involvement of the Department of Aboriginal Affairs and, hopefully, the Commonwealth department. Unfortunately, the Minister for Aboriginal Affairs claimed that it was his responsibility, and nothing was done before the 1979 election was called.

While in the APY Lands, I became aware of widespread petrol-sniffing. It was a major health issue and I determined that, when I returned to Adelaide, I would do all that I could to ban petrol vehicles in the APY Lands and to have them replaced with diesel vehicles, thus removing the source of, and need for, petrol for sniffing. Unfortunately, the white owner of the petrol station on the Stuart Highway near Indulkana campaigned to get the local Elders to oppose the ban on petrol-powered vehicles. Why would the owner of the service station care? If he wasn't selling petrol, he would have been selling diesel? Well not quite. The owner had a side business bringing old cars from Adelaide and selling them to local Aboriginal people on credit. There weren't many cheap diesel-powered vehicles available in the 1970s, so banning petrol vehicles from the APY Lands was going to drastically affect his used car business. Most vehicles on the APY Lands were government-owned or -supplied vehicles and many were already diesel. It would have been relatively easy to insist that all these vehicles be diesel. However, for the policy to be effective, there would need to be a ban on private petrol-fuelled cars. Unfortunately, my Cabinet submission on this issue indicated that the Elders did not support the ban, with Cabinet then using that as the excuse to defeat the proposal. How many lives would have been saved and how much brain damage avoided had it been adopted.

In 1945, following the Second World War, 72 per cent of Australian males, of a population of seven million, smoked. By 2018, with a population of over 20 million, the percentage was down to 13 per cent and since then has declined further. Lung cancer death rates – just one of the many ill effects of smoking – are in long-term steep decline. This dramatic social change in my lifetime has been achieved by a wide range of policy initiatives, including packaging reforms and taxation. By the late 1970s, the medical profession itself had begun to consider supporting restrictions on tobacco availability. I saw this area as an important health policy reform. If we were to do something about decreasing the incidence of lung cancer and other tobacco-related diseases, it was obvious that we had to reduce cigarette smoking and tobacco consumption. Possible approaches included increasing the cost, restricting tobacco advertising, reducing the level of tobacco sponsorship of sport and the arts, restricting smoking in public places, such as hotels and, finally, imposing health warnings on packaging, as had been introduced in other jurisdictions. The Deputy Premier and Treasurer, Hugh Hudson, was a dedicated smoker, so when I raised the matter for an informal discussion in Cabinet, it was summarily dismissed. It became clear that reduction of tobacco consumption was not going to be a priority in the Corcoran Government. Overall, this has been a fight with overwhelming benefits for society at large. I am saddened, however, that the Corcoran Government was not brave enough to take up the fight. Restricting tobacco sales to minors was the timid extent of the steps taken in South Australia during the 1970s.

During a discussion with one of the delegates at the WHO conference in Athens, he had pointed out the contradiction implicit in spending money from the Health budget on hospitals to treat the sick rather than spending money on ensuring the people stayed healthy and therefore less likely to need hospitalisation. He commented that, even though the medical profession paid lip service to the need for public health education and a healthy society, the reality was that they preferred expenditure on hospitals and the treatment of sick patients, since it was their *raison d'être*. The facilities designed to keep the public healthy on the other hand were starved of resources. Of course, it was much better to spend money on encouraging people to exercise, to stay fit, to eat healthy foods and to avoid obesity, rather than on hospitals and surgery to repair bodies after the damage had been done.

It should have been possible from within the Health budget, and without additional cost to the government, to reduce hospital budgets and establish community health facilities for women and for those with mental health issues, and educate people towards healthy lifestyles. It soon became clear to me that hospital administrators fiercely defended their turf, and their budgets. Notably, health reform and hospital restructuring were to be the political death of the Health Minister John Cornwall later, in the 1980s.

I discussed this issue with the departmental head, Brian Shea, and, while he agreed with my proposition, he indicated that achieving a reallocation of resources would be an extremely difficult task, explaining that any proposals to restrict or limit hospital budgets would automatically prompt the specialists and administrators at a particular hospital to increase waiting lists for elective surgery, a situation always very unpopular with the public. Nonetheless, Shea and I agreed to a strategy that was likely to free up some resources. Hospitals were to be given the opportunity to make savings and those that did were to be given an efficiency dividend, resulting in the availability of modest amounts of money for the establishment of community health centres and specialist community-based mental health facilities. These remained in place until John Cornwall introduced wholesale restructuring of the department's systems. We also envisaged a network of women's health centres and I arranged to have this initiative inserted into the ALP health policy for the early election called by Corcoran late in 1979.

A women's community health centre had been established at Mary Street, Hindmarsh, in the mid-1970s, as an initiative of the Women's Liberation Movement, with funding from the state government through Premier Dunstan's Women's Advisor, Deborah McCulloch. The collective that ran the centre later established a separate rape crisis centre, initially at Mary Street and later at the Queen Elizabeth Hospital at Woodville. In earlier times, there had been some specialist facilities for women, but they had focused on mother and baby issues rather than on more confronting issues, such as rape, assault and domestic violence. Unfortunately, the relations between the department and the centre were poor, and I attempted to improve the situation. Later in the 1980s, however, the government withdrew funding and the centre, set up as a collective, was forced to close.

Both then and now, my attitude to drug reform is that drug addiction and abuse needs to be treated as a health issue, with rehabilitation rather than lengthy prison sentences. Not only do we need to legalise marijuana, but we must also expunge the records of marijuana offences and eliminate mandatory minimum sentences in general for such non-violent offences. It is unacceptable that poor people are imprisoned for selling marijuana. Australia needs real drug reform and wider criminal justice reform. If I had survived longer as Attorney-General, I would also have abolished fines for minor traffic infringements and replaced them with loss of points on their driver's licence.

Since my teenage years, I've had little personal interest in drugs, with the exception of alcohol. I have rarely been a user of other drugs. While at university I used ephedrine to stay awake as I studied for exams. I found it fitted the purpose but since then have never felt the need for its use to stay awake. If my body was tired, a quick nap seemed a more sensible response for me. Julie occasionally liked to smoke dope. Given my position in the parliament, she was, of course, very careful. One day in the mid-1980s, we visited wineries in the Barossa Valley with friends. Julie, being designated driver, drank very little wine, enabling me to enjoy a good quantity of wine. On the way home, somewhere near Roseworthy, she decided that she would stop and have a joint. On the rare occasions that she was having a joint, she was always very careful not to smoke in the car, which would have left a lingering smell. She parked the car next to a wheat paddock that was close to being harvested. Since it was a lovely afternoon, we decided to jump the fence and spread the rug we had brought from the car on the ground about 25 metres from the fence. She lit the joint and we were thinking of doing what might come next, but before we could proceed, a car containing SA's finest opponents of pleasure pulled up behind our car, intending, I assume, to determine why an empty car was parked in the 'middle of nowhere'. In panic, Julie threw away the joint and we emerged from our wheat retreat and approached the cops. Seeing the rug, they soon understood what was going on and decided that nothing more illegal than trespassing on private property was occurring and thus they departed. Just as we were about to get back into the car, Julie noticed smoke rising from the wheat field. We rushed back to discover that the joint had started a very small fire. We quickly opened one of the bottles of wine we'd bought that day and poured it onto the fire. A shocking waste of good wine.

Coffin Bay is a delightful small town on South Australia's Eyre Peninsula, where the economy of the local region relies on the oyster industry and tourism. The bay itself is an almost-enclosed waterway, rather like a lagoon, in which the oyster beds are located. More than a hundred small holiday homes – 'shacks' – had been built on the sand hills surrounding the lagoon on land leased from the Department of Lands, with a licence that could be suspended at any time. When undertaking routine tests on the water, the Health Department discovered that the *E. coli* count in the lagoon exceeded World Health Organization recommendations for water in which oysters were being grown. The department's view was that the excess count was being caused by sewage from the shacks. It became clear that some of the shacks had septic tanks, while others had sewage disposal, which consisted of leaching completely untreated sewage into the sand. Neither system was suitable. The problem was flagged for my attention and I was presented with two alternative solutions, based on what was considered the correct health policy response.

The first option was to announce the presence of a high *E. coli* count in the lagoon water close the oyster industry and then provide or build a sewerage system for the shacks. This would eventually reduce the count to safe levels and allow for the re-establishment of the oyster industry. However, such a course of action was expected to take two years and would have devastated the oyster industry to the extent that it might not have survived. In addition, the Coffin Bay oyster brand would be substantially damaged. The second option was to cancel the shack licences until the sewerage system was operational, which would have meant that the shack owners were denied their use for about two years. While this option lay within the government's power, it would have virtually guaranteed a riot.

The Health Department had not collected a representative sample of oysters to test for *E. coli* and I requested that this be done: none of the oysters contained *E. coli* above the World Health Organization recommendation, offering a glimmer of hope. I had already briefed Premier Corcoran, who was also the Minister for Works, and he was agreeable to a scheme to establish a small sewerage treatment works and a sewerage reticulation system for the shacks. However, he wanted the shack owners to pay the cost. I agreed and the two departments started to coordinate the government's response. This included a meeting of shack owners, which I attended. We had agreed not to mention the water sample problem and to attempt to sell the sewerage scheme based on good government.

Even without providing information about the water tests, I couldn't deny that the need for the sewerage system was to protect the future of the oyster industry, which prompted most of the shack owners at the meeting to demand a contribution from the oyster growers. So, I then organised a meeting of commercial oyster growers – some of whom were also shack owners – and they very reluctantly agreed to make a contribution to the cost. Eventually, the government paid half, the shack owners one-third and the oyster growers, the remainder. I considered that the oyster growers got off lightly. The upshot was that the sewerage system was installed and opened some time after my term as minister was over. No one suffered poisoning from Coffin Bay oysters; the Coffin Bay oyster brand was unaffected; and the shack owners obtained an inexpensive sewerage system. The water *E. coli* count was reduced to below the WHO-recommended maximum level and the original *E. coli* count test was not released and never became public knowledge (until now).

Late in 1979, Premier Corcoran, without consulting the Cabinet or the Labor Party Executive, announced a snap election to obtain a mandate in his own right. This decision was made even though the government had nearly two years of its term left. It is now history that the Labor Government was defeated in what amounted to a thrashing.

On the Thursday prior to the 1979 election and recognising that the defeat of the government was inevitable, I decided to accept the invitation of the Libyan Ambassador to attend a cocktail party in Canberra to celebrate an important day in the Libyan calendar. This was not as obscure as might at first appear. SAGRIG, the South Australian Government Agricultural Extension Service, had extensive contracts in Libya. I had even toured one of the SAGRIG projects on a visit to Libya in 1973 as a guest of the League of Arab States. Our delegation drove from Benghazi for about two hours to a wadi in the desert. Here we were given a sumptuous evening meal, after which, around 10 pm, a small fleet of Volkswagen beetles emerged from the desert and out of one of the cars stepped Gaddafi … without sunglasses. He was polite, spoke reasonable English and spent about two hours with the delegation. After that we returned to our hotel in Benghazi.

While in Libya, I had been taken to see one of the SAGRIG forestry projects: a freshwater table about four or five metres below the surface had been identified on a 100-hectare piece of desert, on which SAGRIG was successfully establishing a blue gum eucalyptus forest. As the trees were planted, a piece of two-inch water pipe, three metres long, was inserted into the sand alongside each tree, with two metres protruding above the ground. A donkey cart with a water tank went up and down the rows of trees watering them through the pipes and the trees sent their roots down to get to the water. After a few months, the pipes were driven further into the sand and the process repeated. Eventually, the tree roots would reach the water table and the forest would develop without any further need for intervention. The plan was to repeat the process on another block. Projects such as this one are indicative of how innovative and extensive the South Australian Government's commercial activities were during the Dunstan years.

As a result of this interest and contact, I had become a favourite of the Libyan Ambassador. So, O'Brien, Julie and I flew to Canberra for the night. Imagine our disappointment to find that the function was dry. Of course, we should have known – Libya is a Muslim country. We stayed the minimum time required for politeness, around 20 minutes, and left. I located Lionel Murphy, and we went to his and Ingrid's house, and over some very fine wines the always optimistic Lionel lobbied me about moving to Canberra and a career in federal politics.

At the 1979 election, I retained the seat of Elizabeth but with a reduced majority. In February 1979 Greg Crafter had won preselection for Norwood after Dunstan's resignation and won the by-election. Unfortunately, he lost the seat narrowly at the 1979 state election. After a Court of Disputed Returns enquiry, a further Norwood election was ordered and Greg won the seat and held it until defeated years later. My press secretary, Trevor Watson, went on to become a well-known and distinguished ABC international correspondent before resigning to work as a Sydney-based PR adviser. Peter O'Brien, my senior private secretary, also lost his job but soon obtained a position as Secretary of the Independent Schools Teachers Union in Queensland. On moving to Queensland, he sold his house at 24 Gibbon Lane to my lifetime friend Peter Kellett and another chapter in the Gibbon Lane saga began.

CHAPTER TEN

# The Bannon Opposition

I had no desire to be the Leader of the SA Labor Party and had said so many times. After Corcoran resigned, Dunstan, Corcoran, Clyde Cameron, Mick Young and I all supported John Bannon to become the Labor Party State Leader and Opposition Leader. Bannon announced that he proposed to maintain only a parliamentary executive until halfway through the term, after which Caucus would elect a Shadow Cabinet, to be marketed to the public as the team that would become the government after the next election.

After discussing the matter with Julie, I decided to spend some time on the backbench, until the election of the Shadow Cabinet. I was rundown and exhausted after five years as an extremely busy minister and unbelievably frustrated after my experience in the Corcoran Government. I did not stand for the executive. However, I made the mistake of not advising Bannon of my decision in advance. Consequently, Bannon decided I was simply sitting it out on the backbench until he slipped up or lost an election, believing that I considered I would have been in a good position to take over as leader.

Bannon had portrayed himself as a younger Dunstan. Sadly, he was anything but. He was a good debater and there is no doubt that was his great strength. He turned out to have a timid nature, unable to stand up to stronger personalities, but such judgements were for the future. Sometime in the early 1990s, Dunstan and I were having dinner. We agreed, in retrospect, that the best replacement for Don would have been Lynn Arnold. But of course, Don's forced resignation was far too soon for Lynn to be in the running to replace him. Don was very disappointed with Bannon, as were we all. Apart from the collapse of the State Bank and being focused simply on winning government rather than on policies to assist the electorate, the Bannon Government achieved little of note. Rather than a reformer, he was a manager, and considering the State Bank disaster, not a very good one. The common thread throughout the Bannon years was extreme caution.

I did seek two positions at the Caucus meeting after the 1979 election loss. I successfully stood for election as one of the two parliamentary representatives on the University of Adelaide Council. This position was not heavily contested within the Caucus; hence, my success. The other position was as the Caucus representative on the ALP Council and Convention. This position held only one vote on each body, but the majority of the Caucus determined that I would not hold the position. I enjoyed my term on the University Council and played an active role. The other University Council members were polite but nervous that I might, as a result of my experience on the council, develop some ideas for reform and seek to change the *University of Adelaide Act 1971*. Over generations, the university, purportedly to protect the independence of the institution, developed a convention that the University of Adelaide Act should only be amended with support of the council. I saw that convention as self-serving nonsense and was astounded to find that one of the university subcommittees – the Finance Committee – did not report in any detail to the council. It was the key university body, not the council.

On two occasions at University Council, I moved to force the Finance Committee to open its books to the scrutiny of the council and unsuccessfully ran for a position on it. Essentially, the committee was dominated by Adelaide Club businessmen, who pontificated on the university's shareholdings and how the shareholder votes were cast, all of which was closely guarded secret. Likewise, these matters were apparently no business of the University Council. On one occasion, I took these matters up privately with the vice-chancellor, who explained that the existing arrangements benefited the university because it was often able to buy shares in special issues. 'You mean through insider trading?' I observed. 'That won't look too flash on the front page of the *Advertiser*'.

With the departure of Peter O'Brien to Queensland and the Labor Party no longer in government, life for me and Julie started to resemble something that might have passed for normal. We lived at 30 Gibbon Lane, North Adelaide, for 24 happy years. It was our daughter Georgia's first home and the weekend and holidays home for my boys, Mac and Jock, during a period of shared parenting. Later Mac lived with us during his university studies, from 1992 until 1996. Julie, ever the inspiration, undertook numerous renovations in a never-ending process. This saw the purchase of the backyards of two adjoining properties to the north, which were added to ours, leading to the installation of a swimming pool, a glass gazebo and later, a studio above a double garage.

After my frustrating experience in and with the Corcoran Cabinet, I thought, while on the backbench, that it was important to strengthen the position of the Left or progressives in the State Caucus. In the main, this involved consolidating the Left leadership of the unions. Winning votes from sub-branches (winning the delegates' votes) to the ALP Convention and Council was also important. In early 1980, I visited each of the Left union secretaries and some of the secretaries whose unions were notionally Left. In the main, they were good people committed to advancing their members' interests. That didn't mean that they weren't personally ambitious, but the two aims are not necessarily mutually exclusive. In a briefing to each union secretary, I explained the huge difference between the Dunstan and Corcoran governments and emphasised that if we wanted to deliver for the working class, we needed good, strong Left people in the Caucus. Most union leaders at the time were smart people, and when the internal workings of the government had been explained were ready to do what was necessary.

Some unions agreed to increase their union affiliation to the Labor Party. It was often the case, particularly with small unions, that they would under-affiliate to the ALP, as a savings measure; that is, they would affiliate for a lesser number of total members than was actually the case in order to make a saving in their membership fee. Others agreed to appoint as delegates non-union members who were reliable for the Left and who were guaranteed to attend State Council and Conventions, and on time. Don Dunstan was successful in winning preselection for Norwood in 1952 because the Printers Union delegation, all travelling in one car, had a flat tyre and arrived late. They were planning to vote against Dunstan and their absence was the difference between winning and losing. I also sought to understand which unionists had personal political ambitions to ensure that these ambitions could be met, if reasonable. Frank Blevins and I and a few others worked out which Right wing unions had weak leadership and could potentially be subject to successful union election challenges. In particular, the Electrical Trades Union looked like a good prospect. Bob Geraghty successfully challenged the secretary and, over time took over the leadership of the union. Another strategy considered was to encourage unaffiliated unions to join the ALP, although on reflection we agreed that this approach could be counterproductive since some unions, for example, teachers, independent schools' teachers, clerks, police officers, nurses and the Public Service Association, did not necessarily have progressive leadership.

We won several sub-branches through a simple strategy. The Left was generally seen as in the ascendancy and people interested in parliamentary careers were tending to float towards the Left. Many of them, including Susan Lenehan, Kim Mayes, Nick Bolkus, Phyl Tyler, John Scott, Derek Robertson, Gay Thompson and Vicky Agirov, were advised that if they wanted to garner support, they needed to win their branches for the Left. Sometimes these sub-branch contests were extremely animated. Although I can't recall making the following comment, George Apap, Secretary of the Storemen and Packers' Union, claimed that he had asked me for advice about how to handle the forthcoming Semaphore sub-branch annual general meeting. My alleged reply was: 'Get a strong man to guard the light switch and another to protect the minute book'.

South Australia was unlike NSW or Victoria in terms of inter-factional or political violence, although some very unpleasant incidents occurred, indicating that the potential lay just below the surface. The secretary of the small Ships' Painters and Dockers Union, with only about 250 members, a client of my law firm, was approached in Adelaide by a couple of 'heavies' from the union's national office in Melbourne. Ships' painters and dockers at the time were casual workers, employed to do basically unskilled maintenance work for a short time while a ship was in port. Either the union allocated the work to members, or the boss ran a bull ring and selected the required number of workers from those who showed up at the worksite at the advertised time. The heavies from Melbourne advised the South Australian secretary that a new arrangement was to be established, whereby each worker was to pay a $10 levy for each day worked. The SA secretary indicated that the members would never agree to such a scheme, to which the Melbourne official responded that they would because the secretary would make it his business to convince them and if he didn't they would break his legs to encourage him to change his mind. And they did. At the meeting at the Osborne Hotel that evening, the secretary was thrown across the gutter in the side street and someone jumped on his knee and smashed it. He refused to report the matter to the police; and, as I understand it, the outcome was that the new levy was implemented.

By the time of the ALP Convention of 1980, the Left had a reasonably reliable vote of 55 per cent. It didn't mean that we could control, or win, every vote, but the opposing forces had to fight hard and promise favours to win. At the 1981 June Convention, Susan Lenehan defeated the

Right's Les Drury for the state seat of Mawson, which was seen as a very big victory, given that Drury had been the sitting member from 1977 until he lost the seat in the 1979 bloodbath. In addition, Kym Mayes and three others won support for winnable seats on a Left ticket. Left candidate John Scott was selected to replace Clyde Cameron in Hindmarsh and Nick Bolkus was successfully preselected for the Senate. Nick had been a friend and comrade for some years, and I was thrilled at his preselection, seen as a significant victory for the Left. How wrong was I to be celebrating! The saying 'No good work goes unpunished', comes to mind. But again, I am getting ahead of myself.

In total, these preselections resulted in the Left vote in the State Caucus being around 12 members after the 1982 election, not a majority, but enough to have a voice. Bannon was happy with these preselections, because in terms of winning the next election, they provided quality candidates in marginal seats, where it mattered.

In the late 1970s, several preselected candidates caused grief to the party, including the bungling, incompetent Keith Plunkett, who had been foisted onto the electors of Peake. Keith Plunkett had been an Australian Workers Union organiser and Jack Wright had been the Secretary of the South Australian branch of the same union, and the pair were mates. Jack entered the House of Assembly as the Member for Adelaide in 1971 and Keith might have been described as a devoted, almost slavish, supporter of Wright. Keith had what used to be described as a 'short fuse'. Jack Wright rewarded the loyal, but under-talented, Plunkett with the seat of Peake in the House of Assembly. In this position, Keith, of course, was able to continue to provide loyal support and a Caucus vote for Jack Wright. At the 1979 election, Plunkett was the new candidate for Peake, with the retiring Member for Peake, Don Simmons, the ALP campaign director for the seat. On one occasion, as Keith was door-knocking, some conflict occurred between Keith and a voter. The next day, Don Simmons sent Keith door-knocking in the adjacent electorate. Keith didn't know the difference. Don Simmons told me his job was to win the election and the best way to do so was to keep Plunkett away from the voters.

After the 1979 election, the Opposition backbenchers had to share offices in Parliament House, and, for my sins, I was forced to share an office with Plunkett. Initially it was okay. I had nothing in common with Keith, but I soon realised that he was eavesdropping on my phone conversations and reporting back to Jack Wright. This was confirmed after the contents of a 'bullshit' conversation were fed back to me by an angry Jack the following day. After his eavesdropping had been exposed, Keith entered our office in my absence and smashed a paper mâché artwork. It was a representation of a relief map of Australia looking like one big mine, with Tasmania as one big dam. That piece of artwork had been given to me by Julie as a present and was a favourite of mine. I never forgave Keith and never will. Of course, Plunkett was that particular type of AWU member who loved mines, regardless of what was being extracted. The piece of art must have irritated him from the moment we began to share the office.

At the 1981 Caucus ballot, Jack Wright had been elected as Deputy Leader of the Parliamentary Labor Party, a position which automatically made him a member of the Shadow Cabinet. A ballot of Caucus members was subsequently held to fill the remaining Shadow Cabinet positions. In the State Caucus elections, the names of all the Caucus members were printed on the ballot paper and voting was undertaken by crossing out the name of the person for whom each caucus member voted. Exhaustive ballots were held and counted, until the required number of Shadow Ministers had been elected. After the first ballot, the returning officer announced, 'Hopgood elected and one informal vote'. After the next ballot, 'Arnold elected with one informal vote' and so on. The informal vote reoccurred in each subsequent ballot until the election was completed. Later, I asked returning officer Frank Blevins what was going on. He explained that 'someone was trying to elect Jack Wright to a position on the Shadow Cabinet, which he already held'. Keith was showing his only talent – loyalty to Jack Wright. Towards the conclusion of the exhaustive ballot, Keith must have been becoming seriously stressed as, in his mind, Jack Wright kept missing out on being elected.

In the House of Assembly on one occasion, Keith was reading a speech that somebody else had obviously written for him. In the middle of his speech, the House adjourned for the dinner break. Keith left the pages of his typed speech on his desk. During Keith's absence somebody (allegedly Robin Millhouse) had shuffled the pages of the speech. After the dinner break, Plunkett returned and without realising what had happened continued to read the now unintelligible speech – which of course was recorded in Hansard – amongst guffaws from those who were in on the joke. Pity help the poor Hansard staff.

Along with other workers, the AWU covers shearers, who begin their season in Western Australia, then travel to South Australia and finally move through the Riverland and Victoria and north through NSW into Queensland. This across-state movement by workers means that a degree of coordination is required between AWU organisers from adjoining states for membership drives, with friendships developing between the organisers and shed delegates of the various states. In addition, the shed delegates get to know which state has competent and caring organisers. While the South Australian organisers were generally highly regarded by the shearing shed members, the AWU administration in Victoria was seen as moribund and alienated from the members, with many of its organisers viewed as incompetent. Bob Smith, one of the few Victorian organisers who was competent, decided to oppose the Victorian state secretary in the upcoming union elections and sought help from the South Australian organisers. The South Australian AWU leadership asked the SA Left for assistance, and we readily agreed. Pamphlets were prepared and advice given about strategy and tactics. Bob and part of his team had a victory, such that control was delivered to the Left in the large AWU component in the Victorian ALP, which had previously been dominated by the Right. This was a seismic shift, and it quickly became clear that some outside help – from South Australia – had been involved. Gerry Hand, who was part of the Left faction in Victoria and later went on to be a minister in both the Hawke and Keating governments, asked me if we had been involved and I happily advised that we had. Gerry was terribly upset, although others in the Victorian Left were more sanguine. Ray Hogan, of the Miscellaneous Workers Union, was delighted with the outcome. However, my involvement was leaked to the Victorian Right's numbers man, Senator Robert Ray, who apparently swore revenge, although not to my face. These events were to have a significant negative impact on my future career in the Australian Parliament. In the eyes of the hard men of the Victorian Right, I was a marked man.

In 1982, the Left held a national conference in Canberra, with delegations from every state and territory. The meeting appointed Gerry Hand, Bruce Childs – until 1980 Assistant General Secretary of the NSW Labor Party, at which time he was elected to the Senate representing New South Wales – and me as convenors of the national Left, with power to make decisions between national Left meetings. Not long after this, we called a meeting to discuss the looming contest between Bob Hawke and Bill Hayden. The Left in the federal parliamentary party at that point was locked into ongoing support for Hayden. I attended the meeting, expecting that it would vote to maintain the status quo. Such was my shock when Tom Uren, Arthur Gietzelt and Gerry Hand – all from the Left faction – spoke in favour of Hawke. Tom, becoming quite emotional, told us all how much he loved Billy Hayden, 'like a brother'. I was astounded at this result since I wasn't aware of the background, which was not explained at the meeting; however, it became apparent later. The argument put to the national Left was that only Hawke, with his stratospheric popularity, could guarantee an election victory. Tom and Arthur were both aged around 63 in 1983; and if Labor didn't win the next election, both would have been too old to be ministers after the subsequent election. No doubt that factor played a role in their thinking. In Gerry's case, I discovered later that he was one in a betting ring consisting of Bob Hawke, Mick Young, Jack Wright, Eric Walsh, Jim Deane – the South Adelaide footballer and publican and a mate of Mick's – and others, now forgotten.

A slight digression: each member of the betting ring built up a friendship with a horse trainer; Hawke with Tommy Smith, Jack Wright with Grahame Heagney, Mick Young with Bart Cummings, Jim Deane with Colin Hayes etc. Each would contact his trainer mate on Thursday seeking information on what was good for a weekend bet. They would then share the information and decide on the best bets. Gerry, being part of this syndicate, was close to Hawke.

The Right's master tactician, Robert Ray, had organised a plan to get Hawke elected Leader and to dump Hayden. The key players were all Victorians – John Button, Gerry Hand, Hawke and Robert Ray. Hawke had the support of the Victorian and Queensland Right and some of the NSW Right. This clearly wasn't a majority. Hayden had the Centre Left and the Left, a majority in the Caucus. Without the Left moving its support to Hawke, it would have been impossible for Hawke to win. As things stood, there was little chance of the parliamentary Left doing a *volte face*. Robert Ray and Gerry Hand devised a strategy involving a meeting of the national Left, where, in a small meeting, Tom, Arthur and Gerry might be able to carry the day, which they did. The support at the national Left meeting for Hayden came from Western Australia, South Australia and Queensland. Ray Devlin, later a senator, from Tasmania told me subsequently that he had been asked to attend the meeting by the secretary of the Miscellaneous Workers Union in Tasmania and to follow Tom and Arthur. The Northern Territory delegate was from the North Australian Workers Union, a branch of the Miscellaneous Workers Union.

Victoria, New South Wales, Tasmania and the Northern Territory prevailed in favour of Hawke. Ray Gietzelt, Arthur's brother and the legendary national secretary of the Miscellaneous Workers Union, was a mate of Hawke's from the Australian Council of Trade Unions (ACTU) and his influence was palpable. I was pretty devastated the following day when the eastern states papers carried a leaked version of the meeting, stating that the Left had changed sides. At the time I didn't realise the role the meeting would play. The meeting had been quite civil, the pro-Hayden forces believing that the discussion was nothing more than an expression of opinion. The Left Parliamentary Caucus made the decisions about whom to support as Leader, not the national Left. Based on headlines, it was portrayed that the Left was moving.

Ultimately John Button visited his friend Bill Hayden and convinced him that Hawke had the Caucus numbers and that Bill should resign the leadership, which he did.

Stories of Hawke's various exploits are legion. Rupert Murdoch moved to the United States in the mid-1970s after purchasing the San Antonio *Union Tribune* newspaper and he was in the process of establishing a national tabloid: the *Star*. In the US, most papers are distributed through news stands and there are few newsagents, unlike in Australia. Distribution was a major problem when establishing a national newspaper. Murdoch sought assistance from Hawke, at the time in charge of the ACTU, who was able to introduce Murdoch to Jimmy Hoffa, one-time leader of the Teamsters Union, which is the US equivalent of the Transport Workers' Union in Australia. In 1974, Hawke arranged a meeting between Hoffa and Murdoch. By this time, Hoffa was no longer leader of the union but was still influential. The outcome of the meeting was an agreement in which Murdoch was able to transport his papers cheaply across the US, a great competitive advantage. What grease was used to achieve this deal and what benefit Hawke obtained, I have no idea. What is clear is that the leader of the ACTU at the time facilitated a deal that cut US workers' income and conditions.

In February 1981, a state Labor Shadow Cabinet was elected, and I was allocated the Transport portfolio. Bannon's close confidant, Chris Sumner, was inevitably the pick for Shadow Attorney-General. I had asked to be appointed Shadow Chief Secretary, with responsibility for police and corrections. Apparently, the activities encompassed by the police and corrections portfolio would have been too close a fit to the Attorney-General portfolio for Bannon's liking, given that Bannon was threatened by his ill-founded assumption regarding my leadership ambitions. Transport was an area in which, at the time, I had little knowledge. Despite what was an obvious slight, I embraced the area enthusiastically. However, I had only been in the shadow Transport portfolio for a few months when Bannon's betrayal occurred.

At the 1981 State Labor Party Convention, I stood for one of the two South Australian delegate positions to the ALP National Executive. Being a National Executive member would automatically mean that I would become a National Conference delegate. At the time, the election system used by the South Australian party was a type of winner takes all. The Centre Left expected to win both positions. I nominated, as did state secretary Chris Schacht and Mick Young, the Member for Port Adelaide. Mick, who was popular across the party, topped the poll and normally his preferences would have elected Schacht. However, this did not occur. Some of Mick's votes leaked to me and I was elected number two by 1,100 votes, from a possible 130,000, which represented a small margin. The returning officer reported to the Convention that Young and I had been elected. His report was accepted by the Convention and the ballot was declared. Legally, that should have been the end of the matter. To use the legal term, the returning officer's role in that ballot was *functus officio*.

It was discovered subsequently that the Builders Laborers Federation had been issued with three credential coupons, each marked with a value of 750. In fact, each of the three credential coupons should have been marked with a value of 250. As a result, the Builders Labourers had cast 1500 votes to which they were not entitled. People made a not unreasonable assumption that the Builders Labourers had voted for me, although there was no direct evidence to support that assumption. If the votes had been allocated correctly and the BLF had voted for me, I would have lost by 400. The situation became public because the Builders Labourers delegates boasted in the Trades Hall bar about the mistake in the credentialling. Incidentally, the credentials committee and the returning officer were Centre Left functionaries, so there was no suggestion that the ballot had been rigged by the Left. I could have argued that the ballot had been declared and that was the end of the matter and refused to resign or agree to any other action. In the circumstances, that course of action would have made me look churlish and left me as a somewhat illegitimate delegate.

Initially, I offered to resign so that a ballot between Schacht and me could be held. Mick Young had been legitimately elected and his position was not under question. The Centre Left rejected that offer. Schacht, although he was the state secretary, was not particularly popular and I was very confident that I would win in a head-to-head contest with him. However, the Centre Left did not agree and, after some discussions with Bannon, I agreed to a new ballot on the night of the next State Council monthly meeting. The voting system used at the State Convention was known as a 'card vote', reflecting the affiliated number of members of the sub-branch or union.

According to the rules of the State Council voting system, one vote was allocated to each delegate, with the disputed National Executive election held by the State Convention using these rules. A further vote should have adopted the same process. There was another issue, that of whether the State Council, clearly an inferior body to the State Convention in legal terms, could overrule a decision of the Convention. Clearly it could not. When I spoke to Bannon, he agreed with me on that point. I then telephoned my supporters on the State Executive and asked them to support a new convention ballot, as had been agreed with Bannon. Bannon then went to State Executive with the proposal, which I expected would be carried.

The Centre Left, however, holding a significant majority on the State Executive, decided that ballot would be held by State Council and would include Mick Young, Schacht and me. The meeting of the State Executive was held on a Thursday evening, prior to the regular State Council meeting, and finished as the latter was beginning. Since I was not on the State Executive, I was unaware of what had gone on. As Bannon moved from the State Executive meeting to the State Council, I spoke to him very briefly. He indicated that the matter had been resolved as agreed earlier between us. That was the nub of the betrayal.

As a result of this conversation, I assumed that a ballot was to be held at a special State Convention in a month's time. The resolution from the State Executive had not been printed and distributed because of time constraints between the conclusion of the meeting of State Executive and the commencement of State Council. The resolution from the State Executive presented at the State Council Meeting had been formally moved by Bob Gregory, Secretary of the Trades and Labor Council, and again formally seconded by Frank Blevins. The upshot was that the report of the State Executive was adopted without dissent. After the meeting, in the milling-around as delegates left the hall, John Scott, Secretary of the Metal Workers and a strong supporter of the card vote, asked why I had accepted the proposal for a ballot to be held by State Council.

That was the first time that I realised what had happened. When I raised the issue with my comrade Frank Blevins, who had been at the State Executive meeting, he indicated that Bannon had told the executive that I had agreed to the resolution proposed earlier. Another deception and betrayal.

I decided to stay calm and consider my position for a few days. That was 9 July 1982. I reflected on what had happened and spoke to several local and interstate colleagues. By August, I had decided that I could no longer work for, or with, John Bannon. The National Executive position, which I would have won in a Convention ballot against Schacht, had been stolen. Bannon had played a critical part in the exercise, and I was having none of it. I declined to nominate for the National Executive ballot to be decided by State Council on 6 August and the next day resigned from the Bannon Shadow Cabinet.

Julie and I then took a few days holiday in NSW. Contrary to press reports, we didn't go skiing. When I returned, I held a press conference and revealed all – much to the horror of the party apparatchiks, Bannon and most of the Labor Caucus. My move was interpreted wrongly by the media as either the end of my career or the beginning of the undermining and removal of Bannon. As history demonstrates, neither was correct. I had simply decided to withdraw from the field of battle and to live to fight another day.

John Bannon's flawed character, including disloyalty, was demonstrated emphatically in the way he treated John Cornwall, his Health Minister, later in the decade. Although damaged in the short term, my standing in the party in fact recovered quickly and improved over time, as party members hankered for the days of the reformist Dunstan Government. Through my record as Attorney-General, I had huge political capital with party members, if not at that stage with the public.

In 1984, I was elected to the National Executive by the Convention. Mick Young, by then a minister on and off (due to various slip-ups and misdemeanours) in the Hawke Government, did not nominate and with only two nominees, Schacht and me, there was no ballot. However, it was clear from other ballots at that Convention that, under the winner-takes-all system then applying, if two Left delegates had nominated, they would both have been elected. Not long after this, the Centre Left pushed for a proportional representation system for party ballots, where multiple candidates were to be elected, a proposal which the Left supported.

In 1981, Bob Brown, later a Senator for Tasmania, toured mainland Australia, campaigning to save the Franklin River – under threat by both Labor and Liberal Tasmanian governments – from being dammed. Julie knew Bob Brown from her time as a journalist in Hobart and we, along with Peter Kellett (PK), who had a walking/trekking business called Eco Trek, went to hear Bob speak. Afterwards, we had a conversation with him over a drink and he offered to facilitate a Franklin rafting trip for me, Julie and a small group. We accepted his offer and made the plans and arrangements. This trip couldn't have happened without PK's outdoor skills and we met in his kitchen to plan the trip for January 1982. Our party met Bob at the Collingwood River bridge, where he presented us with a copy of the Franklin River rafters' notes, essential for a safe trip. We undertook our epic adventure in individual blow-up rafts. It turned out to be one of the highlights of Julie's and my life together.

Clyde Cameron, a former Whitlam Government Minister, and his wife Doris, were touring Tasmania and they had arranged to meet us at the end of the trip. Clyde took the last few photos of our trip from the cruise boat that picked us up on the Gordon River after we exited the Franklin. Clyde presented us with cold beers, which were most welcome after paddling alcohol-free for 10 days. As a result of this experience, I drafted a resolution to save the Franklin, which was submitted to the Elizabeth ALP sub-branch, where it was passed. It was then submitted to the 1982 South Australian ALP Annual Convention, where it was again passed, but not without some opposition.

When I moved the resolution, it was by no means certain that it would pass, as some Left unions were worried about losing construction jobs in Tasmania. The Right wing was also opposed and so were parts of the Centre Left, who were frightened of losing votes in Tasmania. Eventually a couple of Centre Left delegates were persuaded to move an amendment that watered down the whole thrust of the motion. Andrew Dunstan got up to speak. Perhaps unfairly, I had expected him to support the amendment. However, he wholeheartedly supported the resolution, saying he had been horrified when, a few years earlier, the Tasmanian Government ignored national opinion and flooded Lake Pedder. The amendment was lost overwhelmingly on the voices and the resolution was adopted.

It was subsequently submitted to the ALP National Conference as a resolution at State Conference. As a delegate, I intended to move the resolution; however, the move to save the Franklin was heavily opposed by the Tasmanian Right and had split the national Right faction. I was concerned that the motion might have been defeated, unless supported by the small independent faction. Bruce Childs and I, as convenors of the national Left faction, spoke to John Button, one of the independents. He said they would support the resolution but only if he could move the motion. I reluctantly agreed and he moved, and I seconded the resolution. It was debated, opposed by sections of the Right, and finally passed.

The resolution became the basis for the Hawke Labor Government's successful move to use the foreign affairs and corporations' powers of the Australian Constitution to prohibit the building of the proposed Franklin River Dam. The Australian Labor Government's legislation to achieve this outcome was challenged but upheld by the High Court, which included my mentor, Mr Justice Lionel Murphy. I want to emphasise that the driving force that saved the Franklin emerged from a discussion in the kitchen of 24 Gibbon Lane and to stress the role played by my now-deceased friend Peter Kellett. This victory represents an example of how individuals, with sufficient perseverance and influence, can affect important national decisions (remembering also Peter Kellett's important role in the South Australian Container Deposit legislation).

Lionel Keith Murphy was a unique human being, a first-rate lawyer, an excellent politician, a scientist of some note and a man of considerable natural charm and of great principle, tempered by pragmatism. He had a genuine interest and curiosity in every person with whom he came into contact. To claim that he was a breath of fresh air on the High Court is an understatement.

On one occasion early in 1984, I was at Lionel and Ingrid's house in Canberra for dinner, after which we had retired to the lounge room and were drinking and talking generally about all things political. The conversation not surprisingly turned to the Franklin River episode. By that time the issues had been resolved in parliament. I explained my initial involvement and Lionel then proceeded to explain his: how he had negotiated the four-vote majority on the High Court to uphold the constitutionality of the Commonwealth legislation. While the High Court held that the Commonwealth had legitimately prevented the construction of the dam, it was a close-run thing. Justices Murphy, Mason, Brennan and Deane were in the majority and Sir Harry Gibbs, Justice Dawson and Justice Wilson were in the minority. Thus, it was decided by a majority of one. In this context, Lionel's account is incredibly significant. Apparently, at the outset, only Justices Anthony Mason and Murphy were for upholding the Commonwealth exercise of powers. Gerard Brennan was undecided, and William Deane wanted to save the Franklin from being dammed but had grave doubts about the Commonwealth's legal power to intervene. Murphy set out to convince Brennan and Deane to support the Commonwealth exercise of power.

Lionel arranged a series of dinners, to which each of the justices was separately invited. He soon discovered that Brennan, on social justice grounds, thought that the Franklin should not be dammed but he didn't believe that the Commonwealth powers extended to a ban on the damming. He was certainly not going to vote to extend the Commonwealth powers in the manner required, just to be part of a minority, *obiter dicta* – a judge's expression of an opinion not essential to the decision. He believed that there was a clear majority against the Commonwealth: Chief Justice Harry Gibbs and Justices Ronald Wilson, Daryl Dawson and William Deane. Lionel then asked Brennan if he would reconsider if he could be part of a majority. Apparently, Brennan agreed that he would.

Deane needed an entirely different approach. He was against the extended Commonwealth powers initially but he had ambitions to be appointed Chief Justice after Gibbs's retirement. At the dinner with Deane, Lionel raised the issue of the Chief Justice position. Deane expressed the view that, as Lionel was a Labor man, he was the most likely candidate. Lionel told Deane that he had told Hawke – who was expected to be the PM for at least a decade – that he, Lionel, was too old and that the Labor Government should appoint a younger person, who would obviously occupy the office for a longer time. Lionel was a decade older than Deane, and this was before Lionel had been diagnosed with terminal cancer. He encouraged Deane to contemplate this opportunity, but indicated that he, Lionel, would lobby for Deane. According to Lionel, he never actually had to lobby Deane directly on the Franklin case. Once Deane had grasped the idea that Lionel was not seeking the Chief Justice position and would back him, Deane became more supportive of Lionel on the court.

As things turned out, a majority was emerging and when Deane indicated at a judges' conference that he was likely to uphold the Commonwealth legislation, Brennan fell into line and a majority was achieved. Sadly, Lionel died in 1986 and William Deane never became Chief Justice. He did, however, become Governor-General, appointed by the Keating Government. Both Deane and Brennan had been Fraser Liberal Government appointments to the High Court.

In the early days of the Hawke Government, the highly regarded former national secretary of the ALP, my deceased friend David Combe, a lobbyist, was accused by ASIO of compromising Australia's national security through his dealings with a Soviet diplomat, Valery Ivanov. On 22 April 1983, Ivanov was expelled from Australia by Prime Minister Bob Hawke and ministers were directed not to use Combe's lobbying services. Rumours of Combe's involvement with Ivanov and the black ban soon began to circulate and before long the Left had begun to accuse

ASIO of conspiring to bring down the government. Mick Young, the Special Minister of State and Vice-President of the Executive Council (and himself a former ALP national secretary 1969–72), was forced to stand down from the ministry on 14 July 1983, when it was revealed that he had breached Cabinet security by talking to a mate, the journalist Eric Walsh, immediately after the 21 April 1983 Cabinet decision to expel Ivanov. Mick Young was reinstated in January 1984.

Hawke appointed Justice Robert Hope as a commissioner to enquire into the affair and his enquiry exonerated Combe. By then, however, Combe was nearly bankrupt, his business was in ruins and his marriage in tatters. This was Hawke's response to a great and loyal servant of the Labor Party. I was furious and led the charge from within the Left to get the government to pay Combe's legal costs and to assist in finding him a job. I was not in the Australian Parliament at this stage but I was receiving my information from David Combe himself and Senator Arthur Gietzelt. No doubt all conversations with Combe were recorded and heard by ASIO, so discretion was necessary. Similarly, during that period, it was almost impossible to have a phone conversation with Arthur because, apart from his deafness, he was even more telephone-paranoid than normal:

> 'Good day Arthur, it's Peter'.
> 'Careful no names.'
> 'Oh sorry, how are you?'
> 'Ok.'
> 'What's the latest?'
> 'Oh, nothing much.'
> 'Fair enough. Oh well, we will catch up some other time.'
> 'Okay'. End of conversation.

I would then telephone Bruce Childs, who had been talking in person to Arthur and was able to pass on the latest information. Our purpose was to get a government position for Combe, and we were successful, in that he was appointed as Australia's Trade Commissioner to Canada and Hong Kong. All reports were that he was an excellent officer, serving Australia's interests well. The idea that David Combe, a loyal Australian, would breach Australia's security or other interests was completely ludicrous, as proved by Justice Hope. David was a loyal servant of the Labor Party, and it is a deep stain on the Hawke Government and particularly Bob Hawke himself, that Combe's reputation was traduced in the way it was over this affair.

Soon after the Hawke Government's election in 1983, the government started planning a redistribution and an increase in the size of the House of Representatives as part of a package of electoral reforms. The outcome of the subsequent redistribution was a new seat for South Australia on the northeastern fringe of Adelaide. It was named Makin, after Norman Makin, a South Australian Labor MHR, who had been the first President of the United Nations General Assembly. The pundits considered it to be a marginal Labor seat. Although not covering or adjoining my seat of Elizabeth, I had enough knowledge of the area to consider it part of my political territory. I decided to seek preselection and transfer my political activities to the Australian Parliament. For years, several of my interstate friends had been encouraging me to enter the federal arena, and after the Bannon betrayal and my self-imposed exile to the backbench, the timing was perfect.

Unfortunately, the ALP state secretary, Chris Schacht, also had ambitions of being the Member for Makin. Eventually, with the support of the Left, I was successful in securing the party's endorsement. A few of the Centre Left Bannon supporters at the time, including John Cornwall, subsequently claimed that the Centre Left faction had cleared the way for me to get out of state politics and out of Bannon's way. I don't know whether this is correct, but, if so, it puts a very different gloss on the outcome of my dispute with Bannon and the picture painted by the mainstream media. In fact, it could be argued that the dispute led directly to my endorsement for Makin, and the new opportunities it offered.

I have criticised the Bannon Government and his successors Rann and Weatherill on many occasions since then as being focused only on winning government, thus wasting their time and opportunities. Some commentators have made the point that had I not had the falling-out with Bannon and had stayed in his Cabinet rather than going to Canberra, then those governments might have achieved more, their argument being that with Duncan, Arnold, Blevins, Cornwall, Levy and others, the progressive voices in those governments would have been more robust in achieving reform. I disagree. Both politically and personally, Bannon was essentially a very conservative person, as I have noted elsewhere. Although I appreciate the compliment to my political skills implicit in this commentary, the idea that I could have made much, or any, difference to the policy outcomes of the Bannon Government is laughable and should be dismissed accordingly.

In an email I wrote to John Cornwall, now deceased, following the publication of his book *After Work, After Play, After All*, I said:

I take your point about just how hard it was for you to achieve much reform in the Bannon Government and how much easier it had been under Dunstan. I would only comment that you let Bannon off pretty lightly in your memoir. I tell anybody who will listen that the problem with Bannon was that he was ever allowed to leave St Mark's College. I am not going into the entrails of him doing me over, but as you know, his gloss that he was a good and decent man was exposed when he decided to do you over and me likewise. Maybe you prefer not to speak ill of the dead. Fair enough. I prefer journalist Dennis Atkins's analysis that 'Bannon was a naive fool over the State Bank. If its growth story appeared too good to be true, it probably was'.

. . .

People like you and me have the crazy brave gene that is essential to achieve real reform. I don't know how most of our former colleagues can sleep at night knowing how they wasted their time as Ministers. Most in the Bannon Government were asleep for a decade and nothing improved under Rann and little under Weatherill.

Homelessness still exists or is worse, the educational achievements of the kids of the poor are still lamentable, and the position of Indigenous people! I could go on, but these three policy issues could easily have been addressed with dramatically improved outcomes. It would have required political will, some extra funding and the expenditure of almost no political capital. Oh, how others wasted their time.

John Cornwall vigorously replied, generally supporting my comments.

Some people may not be aware of the phrase 'went to water': its origin lies literally in what happens to ice when it melts from a robust solid state to a malleable and wet state. My comrade, Bob Mac, wittily observed that it must have been extremely hot in those Labor Cabinets under Bannon, Rann and Weatherill, because when good people entered those Cabinets, they 'went to water'. Sentiments I endorse entirely.

After Don Dunstan had recovered his health he was treated as a political pariah by his chosen successor John Bannon. As observed by John Cornwall in his memoir:

> He [Bannon] had been placed on the fast track by Dunstan following his election as the Member for Ross Smith in 1977. He entered state Cabinet in 1978 and at the same time, he had been virtually anointed by Dunstan as a future leader.
>
> It is interesting to contrast this with Premier Bannon's treatment

of the former premier almost a decade later, when Dunstan returned to South Australia from a controversial appointment as Director of Tourism in Victoria. Dunstan had only accepted the appointment when it had been made clear that his services were not wanted in SA.

Premier Bannon, however fleetingly, was not about to allow his quest for 'perpetual popularity', to be interrupted by giving Dunstan a job and in Cabinet he frequently expressed his misgivings about doing so. It was more than 12 months before we were able to take advantage of Dunstan's enormous experience in government administration. In the second half of 1988, he was eventually given a modest, but very difficult, consultancy to develop options for Aboriginal local government in consultation with Aboriginal communities.

Dunstan's appalling treatment during his post-parliamentary life has never been explored fully. Although Angela Woollacott in her recent biography of Dunstan alluded to the issue, she fails to give the full picture and appears to have been influenced by Bannon supporters. Once his health had improved, the obvious role for Dunstan would have been as the South Australian Agent-General in London, but this was never offered to him. In the biography Woollacott refers to the position of Australian Ambassador to Italy. It is true that attempts were made to have that position offered to Dunstan.

Neal Blewett and I travelled together on a flight to Adelaide shortly after the 1987 election. I had just been appointed a federal minister and around that time speculation was rife about the termination of Don's contract as Victorian Tourist Commissioner. Neal and I were discussing Dunstan's future, with Neal commenting that an ambassadorial position would suit Dunstan's talents well and that Italy would be an appropriate posting. He offered to speak to his Centre Left colleague, Foreign Minister Bill Hayden, but pointed out that since the 1983 leadership issue, he and Hayden had not been as close. I was one of the last in the Left who had stuck with Hayden against Hawke and Bill knew that. I indicated that I would also speak to Hayden. We both did and Bill was sympathetic to the idea and agreed to recommend Don's appointment to Hawke. Blewett told me early in 1988 that Hawke had indicated that he would offer the position if Bannon agreed.

Bannon was Premier of South Australia at the time and about to become National President of the Labor Party. It was also the time when Hayden was about to be elevated to Governor-General, departing from Foreign Affairs without any movement on a Dunstan appointment. Later, when Gareth Evans was Foreign Minister, I took the matter up again, although the position was never offered. A black ball from Bannon seems to be the most obvious reason.

As John Cornwall observed, it was Dunstan who had virtually created Bannon politically by arranging for his preselection for the safe seat of Ross Smith, fast-tracking him into the State Cabinet and anointing him as State Labor Party Leader. It is unlikely that Dunstan could have done much more to assist Bannon. Bannon, for his part, did not return the favour. Dunstan's treatment at the hands of Bannon is one of the more egregious incidents I witnessed in my political career. The last thing the ultra-cautious Bannon wanted was any focus on Dunstan, or for Dunstan to be appointed to any position in which he would have had a public profile. Dunstan had awoken South Australia. Sadly, Bannon sent it back to sleep.

CHAPTER ELEVEN
# The Hawke Government

After I had secured the preselection for Makin, I was given the hint that I should start vigorous campaigning in the expectation of Prime Minister Hawke calling an early election. There was no clear evidence at that stage that Makin was in fact anything other than a Labor-leaning marginal seat, at best. I was concerned about the possibility of not winning it, and we worked hard and ran a good, although traditional, campaign. After preferences, the Labor vote was better than 54 per cent, which was comfortable enough. I was elected as the Member for Makin on 1 December 1984.

The by-election for Elizabeth – the seat I had vacated – was held on the same day as the Australian election, thereby reducing the cost and avoiding elector inconvenience. The Mayor of Elizabeth, Martyn Evans, a member of the Labor Party, decided to run for preselection. Ray Roe, also a member of the Elizabeth Council and who had been preselected for the state seat of Briggs to the south of Elizabeth, decided to withdraw from Briggs and try for Elizabeth, where he lived, rather than wait two years for the next state election. Ray was supported by his union, the Postal Workers', and the Left of the ALP. He won the preselection and Martyn decided to run as an Independent Labor candidate. They were both friends of mine, making the situation extremely difficult for me. I tried unsuccessfully to dissuade Ray from running in Elizabeth.

Lionel Murphy was always proud of his Irish ancestry and he and Ingrid were great friends with the Irish Ambassador to Australia at the time, Joe Small, and his wife. Ambassador Small organised a testimonial party for Lionel in September 1986, at the ambassador's residence. Lionel was in physically poor shape and most people at the party were shocked by his appearance. Neville Wran made a speech and Lionel responded with a speech full of the old spark. Keep up the fight. Don't forget why we are a movement. Never tread on the underdog. How lucky he had been in life to have such a wonderful family, friends and comrades. The only person in the room not reduced to tears was Lionel. It was a great send-off to one of Australia's most distinguished sons and one of the Labor Party's greatest achievers.

About 10 days before Lionel's death in October, when he was bedridden at home and on morphine, Bob Hawke came to pay his last respects. After some emotional preliminaries from Hawke and praising Lionel as a great servant of the Labor movement, Lionel indicated that he had one last request, to which Hawke responded that if it were in his power he'd be happy to fulfil it. Lionel explained that he'd like to see Mary Gaudron replace him on the High Court, arguing that 'It's time for a woman and apart from that she is the best candidate available'. He explained that her appointment was unlikely to be controversial, emphasising that the government would be applauded for appointing a woman. He concluded by noting that she would continue the important work that he had been doing in the court. Hawke promised to do his best to have her appointed. Justice Mary Gaudron was a much better appointment than any that would have arisen through the normal appointment process. Two days later, Lionel asked me and Frank Walker to say our farewells at his bedside and told us that story. He asked us to keep Hawke to his promise. To Hawke's credit, we didn't need to do a thing.

On 13 November 1986, Julie and I joined a parliamentary delegation to Sri Lanka and India. It was a goodwill visit to two Commonwealth countries and was intended to shore up somewhat neglected relations. We first went to New Delhi for consultations. It was two years after Indira Gandhi had been assassinated, and the political turmoil following the assassination was only just settling down. We met Rajiv Gandhi, the Prime Minister, at a cocktail party reception, along with numerous politicians who had been roped in for the occasion. The conversations were mainly about cricket, a subject about which I had limited knowledge and Julie none. We stayed in the wonderful, colonial-era Imperial Hotel, which at the time was slightly shabby, and were chauffeured around New Delhi in a fleet of the Indian equivalent of Morris Oxford cars and visited Agra and the Taj Mahal. Overall, my recollection of the parliamentary visit was of formal goodwill but of little substance and a wasted opportunity on both sides.

After India we flew to Columbo for our visit to Sri Lanka, where a completely different set of circumstances prevailed. The civil war had been underway for three years in the north and the east, and the Tamil Tigers were putting up a good fight against the Singhalese-dominated Sri Lankan military. The Tamils were generating considerable support internationally, particularly, of course, from India, and the Sri Lankan Government was determined to use our visit to convince the delegation of the merits of its case. The Australian Government's position at the time was that a sensible resolution would be a federation with five regional governments – three dominated by the Singhalese, where they were in a majority, one in the north dominated by the Tamil majority, and one in the east, where numbers were about equal. I supported the Australian Government position. Some years later, the Sri Lanken Government offered the Tamils that structure and, foolishly, they refused to accept the offer and continued to fight. History judges the leadership of the Tamil Tigers very harshly. Instead of a state government in the north and the possibility of another Tamil-dominated state government in the east, the Tamil Tigers were crushed militarily, and many Tamils were subsequently killed, persecuted or emigrated to countries such as Australia. The highlight of the visit is my memory of Julie riding on an elephant owned by the Speaker of the parliament, the Hon. E.L. Senanayake (Mahanuwara) on his estate in Kandy.

During the trip we visited Kandy in the highlands, where the tea plantations dominate. Here we became aware of a group of people whose civil rights I subsequently attempted to champion. While on the Speaker's tea estate, we noticed some very skinny and bedraggled people living in what appeared to be large, concrete, open-fronted bins. When I asked about these people, our host responded dismissively. Later, the young foreign affairs officer accompanying the delegation explained the situation of the 'Plantation Tamils' to me. Around one million people had been brought from Tamil Nadu, the Indian state adjacent to Sri Lanka, by the British about 150 years earlier to work on the tea plantations. The current generation of plantation Tamils had been born, raised, worked and died on the plantation on which their parents lived. They were completely uneducated and were stateless persons, without citizenship or passports. They were provided with just enough food to keep them perpetually hungry. The provision of food to feed their children was the method by which the plantation owners kept control. These people were slaves in everything but name. They were seen as lower-class and -caste underlings by the Sri Lankan Tamils of the north, where those who owned plantations used a similar method to control their Plantation Tamils. In the 1990s, when Gareth Evans was Foreign Minister, I brought this situation to his attention and under his direction, Australia did good work internationally on the plight of these people, who are now Sri Lankan citizens.

On 11 July 1987, I was re-elected as the Member for Makin, with an increased majority, defeating the Liberals' perennial loser Neville Joyce. Thirteen days later, I was appointed Minister for Land Transport and Infrastructure Support in the Hawke Labor Government. The Cabinet or senior minister was Gareth Evans, Minister for Transport and Communications. Gareth and I generally maintained good relations. On my appointment, I became one of the very few who had served as a minister in both a state government and in the Australian Government. Immediately following the swearing-in, members of my staff were contacted by ASIO for the purposes of organising their security clearance, a process that required each staff member to sign documents permitting ASIO to make enquiries about them. In the light of what had happened to David Combe, I knew enough of ASIO to have no faith in its activities or level of skill. Jim Hyde, my senior private secretary, initially refused to sign, but eventually did so, because without a security clearance, there was no job.

ASIO also wanted to check the security of my house in North Adelaide, purportedly to ensure the house was safe from terrorists. I was more concerned about ASIO bugging my house. Eventually, their officials in Adelaide visited and decided that the house was secure enough, except for the glass panels surrounding the strong wooden front door. Although the panels were of thick carved glass, they were not bullet-proof. Julie didn't want any change that didn't replicate the original panels. No problem for ASIO, they arranged for bullet-proof glass to be engraved with birds of paradise — although it was six months before the panels were finally installed. When Julie signed the documentation confirming that we were happy with the work, she saw the receipt from the Melbourne-based sub-contractors who had undertaken the engraving work. The cost was more than $24,000. Imagine the front-page story if that figure had been published? It would undoubtedly have been a headline reflecting badly on me not ASIO. This did seem to me to be a rather pointless exercise since I also had a house in Canberra, which received no attention from ASIO whatsoever. We had purchased it after the 1984 election. As a minister, I probably spent a third of my time in the ACT, sleeping in that house. In addition, several of my staff, as well as Julie and the boys, and after his election to the Australian Parliament, my friend Frank Walker, stayed there.

Soon after my swearing-in, some of my mates decided that the election victory and my appointment as a minister necessitated a party in Sydney, to which I readily agreed. Coincidentally, it turned out that my friend Meredith Burgmann was getting married and was planning a party at the Water and Sewerage Workers Hall in George Street the same night. In the mists of time, it's debatable whether we crashed her party or vice versa, but what matter? At that time, my friends in Sydney were from a wide-ranging group of socialists, libertarians, Left Labor and even a few anarchists, and they included judges, lawyers and peace activists. Meredith Burgmann, Frank Walker, Stewart West and Greg Woods were part of this group of friends and I think Wendy Bacon (sister of a future Tasmanian Premier, Jim Bacon) and George Peterson were also part of the group. I like to claim that I am the last person still alive to have hosted all of those attendees at a social function in Sydney. The party was going splendidly until a faction-based fight broke out in the men's toilet between Glen Batchelor (Meredith's betrothed) and another male, prompting some of the guests to depart rapidly.

The Transport portfolio, for which I was minister, covered amongst other things the Australian National Railways (ANR) Commission for a short six months, and during this period the ANR was being dismantled and partially privatised – to which I was strongly opposed. I only achieved two worthwhile reforms in the railways area, the first being an agreement in November 1987 with the states to transfer ownership of the nation's mainline standard gauge tracks to the Australian Government. The second was to end the longstanding practice of naming a locomotive after railways' ministers. Instead, I arranged to have two locomotives painted with Indigenous imagery by Jumbana, a group established by my friend John Moriarty. This initiative later led to the group being contracted by Qantas to paint two 747s with Indigenous motifs.

I was very friendly with the Adelaide-based managing director of Australian National, Don Williams. At the time I was minister, AN was organising a Bicentennial project, *Opera in the Outback* and a bush race meeting at Beltana, to be held during September 1988. Although by then I had long ceased being Railways Minister, Don invited Julie and me to *Opera in the Outback* as VIP guests. Dame Kiri Te Kanawa was beyond peer, and the event was a highlight of Julie's and my life together, at least socially. We also attended the race meeting and I was amused to find that Richard Morton, the brother of my previous wife Sally, was the course vet at the meeting. Richard offered to 'mark my race book' – to indicate his picks – but he failed to mark any horse in race seven. When I asked for his reason, he replied that as the veterinarian of this meeting, he couldn't certify that 'any of those nags can make the distance'.

Shortly after I became minister, the department organised a familiarisation visit to departmental facilities in Tasmania. The Australian Maritime College in Launceston was an Australian Government facility but the section with responsibility for marine-navigation aids, lighthouses and so on was in Hobart. The Transport Department had two F28 jets, whose role was to carry equipment for testing nationwide air-navigation systems. Up to a point, the F28s could undertake the routine testing to coincide with the minister's travel requirements. So, an F28 flew to Adelaide, picked up Julie and me and headed for Hobart. It soon became clear that this visit had been organised to get the new minister on side. The monthly helicopter resupply to the staff of the lighthouse on Maatsuyker Island, off the coast of southern Tasmania, occurred concurrently with our visit to Hobart and we were asked if we would like to be passengers on the resupply mission. The next day we flew to Maatsuyker, and what a fantastic privilege that was for us. We enjoyed a great barbecue with the lighthouse keepers who, although they are often characterised as enjoying their own company, appeared to enjoy ours. Sadly, but inevitably, the Maatsuyker Light was due for conversion to automation in 1990, meaning that lighthouse keepers would no longer be required on the island. That day the lighthouse keepers urged me to reverse the decision to close the staffed facility. When I returned to Canberra, I enquired about doing so, but the financial benefits were impossible to argue. From memory, the cost of the staffed facility, including supply, was $1.5 million per annum, compared with $200,000 for the automated facility, including maintenance.

From Hobart, we travelled to Launceston by car to visit the Maritime College. This was the first time a minister had visited since its opening some years earlier and we were made very welcome. Shortly after I had been sworn in, I had become aware of a proposition to purchase a former high school in a Canberra suburb for use as an aviation college to train air traffic controllers and others. Given that I was a committed supporter of decentralisation, I asked why the facility needed to be in the ACT. I was told that the senior people in the department, those who would be the lecturers, trainers etc., were in Canberra. That appeared fair enough, until one departmental officer told my staff that information was incorrect and that most of the key Aviation College lecturers were in Melbourne. While in Launceston, I asked the principal of the Maritime College whether all of the classrooms etc. were fully utilised and was assured that they were 'absolutely'. I expressed regret and explained that I was considering establishing the Aviation College under the umbrella of the Maritime College if the new facility could be grafted on to the existing facilities at little additional cost. I was quickly assured that the college's facilities could be restructured 'to accommodate the Aviation College at little cost'.

Once back in Canberra, I began to ask awkward questions. The capital cost of the former high school was $3 million, plus upgrading costs and furnishing. The Launceston option was less than one million – a no-brainer for the Department of Finance. Despite the Department of Transport bureaucracy being bitterly opposed to the Launceston option, I took the matter to Cabinet, where the Launceston option was adopted. The Aviation College operated successfully in Launceston for some years, mainly, as I recall, with fly-in fly-out lecturers and trainers. However, the department finally won the battle some years later, when a completely new airways system for Australia was introduced. The new system provided overall control of the airways from bases in Melbourne and Brisbane, with continuing local air traffic control occurring from control towers at the local airports. The Transport Department took the opportunity of using this development to move the college from Launceston to Melbourne.

Perhaps the most significant (and disturbing) issue during my time as minister involved Amann Aviation. Although the decision regarding *Commonwealth v Amann Aviation* in the High Court is in the public domain, its background contains no reference to the political context. The airways system was part of my responsibilities in the Transport portfolio and included the private contract for northern Australia's aerial coastal surveillance for the Customs Department. The contract had been awarded to Sky West some years before and was up for tender in 1987. From memory, the department had called tenders some time before I became the responsible minister. The tender had been won by a small company, Amann Aviation. To my knowledge, this occurred without any involvement at ministerial level. In other words, at that stage it was an entirely routine undertaking. Apparently, the Sky West business largely relied upon the coastal surveillance contract for its viability. The transfer of responsibility to Amann had a long lead time and Sky West continued to undertake the work under its expiring contract. Given my large portfolio, I was initially unaware of Amann Aviation, Sky West, or the coastal surveillance contract. Suddenly that changed.

Two things happened that, in retrospect, appear to be strangely coincidental. First, the senior minister, Gareth Evans, informed me that the prime minister had advised him that the coastal surveillance contract was likely to become a hot political topic, which would need careful handling.

In light of that, I was to ensure that the department provided weekly updates on the contract implementation and Amann's progress towards compliance, with the report to be copied to the PM's office. Secondly, the Opposition Transport spokesman began to ask questions in the parliament about the contract's implementation. He appeared to be exceptionally well informed as to Amann's progress or lack thereof. Gareth also noted that coastal surveillance was vital and that any failure on Amann's part would be a fundamental breach of contract. The implication, of course, was that any failure in Amann's performance would result in the contract being voided.

As the September date on which Amann was to take over approached, it became clear that the company did not possess the capacity to fully comply in terms of the total number of planes required, or indeed with various other contractual matters, such as long-range fuel tanks on all their aircraft. They would need another two months to fully comply. In the interim, they would be able to fulfil their contractual obligations for surveillance, provided they didn't have any mechanical failures with their limited number of fully compliant aircraft. The department and I did not consider that these circumstances legally constituted a fundamental breach in the context of a three-year contract. Gareth, on the other hand, involved himself on an almost daily basis and believed that a fundamental breach was likely. In effect, that was the situation when the matter blew up one day in Question Time.

Departments prepare a Question Time briefing book for the ministers on all the likely contentious issues in the various departments. Gareth, in the Senate, and I, in the House of Representatives, had identical books. On this day, the Opposition, displaying a higher level of astuteness than usual and being well briefed, waited until about halfway through the House of Representatives Question Time to ask a number of questions on this issue at the exactly the same time similar questions were being asked in the Senate. Among other things, they related to whether Amann Aviation was in fundamental breach of the contract. I responded, 'by the book', that no they weren't, not at that stage, whereas Gareth, on the other hand, gave an answer that, while more nuanced, amounted to saying that Amann had committed fundamental breaches.

I received a summons to see Hawke in his office after Question Time. When I arrived, he was talking to Peter Abeles (a long-term friend and confidante of Hawke, an Australian transport magnate and Hawke's witness to the Kirribilli Agreement, discussed later) on a red desk phone. Gareth had also been summoned but was yet to arrive. After Hawke finished his call with Abeles, which concerned the two Question Time incidents, I, making conversation, told Bob that as one of his ministers I wouldn't mind having 'that red phone number', to which Hawke replied agitatedly, 'And when you've done as much for me as Peter Abeles, you'll be entitled to it'. At that point, Gareth arrived, and Hawke begin to interrogate me about my answers. I responded that I had answered, 'by the book'. 'But fuck it, didn't Gareth tell you that Amann are in fundamental breach?', enquired Hawke. 'Yes, but that's not my view nor the department's view, nor the department's legal advice', I replied. To which Hawke crudely responded that 'we are running this government, not the fucking department!' Gareth then asked Hawke if he'd spoken to Abeles about taking on the contract, to which Hawke replied that 'they are ready to go'. I was somewhat confused by this stage and interrupted by asking what Abeles had to do with all of this. 'He has taken over Sky West, to save us from the potential embarrassment of not having coastal surveillance', Hawke replied. I was absolutely furious and made clear in no uncertain terms that I wanted nothing further to do with the issue.

It is now obvious what happened. Abeles bought Sky West for a very low price and then lobbied Hawke to get the Amann contract rescinded, with Hawke colluding in this perfidy. Although I have no proof, I reasonably suspect that the departmental reports on the progress being made by Amann supplied to me and Gareth and copied to Hawke were forwarded to Abeles by Hawke. Abeles was likely the source of the highly informed questions asked by the Opposition in the parliament. Incidentally, I never did get the number for that red phone on the prime minister's desk. The Amann Aviation affair and the way it played out completely coloured my view of Hawke. I've not previously discussed the affair and to have mentioned it at the time would have resulted in a backlash against me for perceived disloyalty. Until the High Court decision, it was only my legal view (and that of the Transport Department's legal advisors) against Gareth's view. The High Court changed all that by deciding that there was no fundamental breach by Amann Aviation and, therefore, Gareth was wrong. Considering the High Court decision, the reality was exposed. After this experience, I became completely disillusioned with Hawke and supported Keating as he moved into challenge mode in 1991. If Hawke had looked to see where his leadership support began to unravel, he would have needed to look no further than the Amann Aviation fiasco.

Amann commenced legal action, seeking $23 million damages and was awarded $410,000 by the Full Court. This case considered the issue of the measure of damages, which included a claim for damages for wasted expenditure (reliance damages) and expectation damages. The Court ordered that the appeal be allowed in part, with the sum awarded by the Full Court to be reduced to $3,989,899, plus interest. The Commonwealth Government then appealed to the High Court, arguing that Amann should not be entitled to any damages because it could not show that the contract had any lost economic viability. However, the High Court upheld the earlier ruling that damages could be awarded on the basis of actual costs incurred. The facts of the case are that Commonwealth accepted Amann's tender in March 1987. In response, Amann began to acquire and fitted out 14 specially equipped aircraft. Surveillance commenced on 12 September 1987, before Amann had all aircraft ready. On the same day, the Commonwealth gave notice that it regarded the contract as terminated for the failure of Amann to comply with contractual obligations. By the time the matter reached the High Court, it was accepted that the Commonwealth's notice of termination was not valid, with the result that the only question before the court was an assessment of damages.

The Transport Department had maintained a watching brief on banning smoking on domestic aircraft for many years. International flights to and from Australia were more difficult to regulate, as they were governed by international agreements and, at that time, there was no agreement in relation to smoking. If Australia had banned smoking on Qantas flights to Indonesia, and Garuda didn't respond by doing likewise, it would be claimed that Garuda would have had a competitive advantage – although I don't know why. With the power of the tobacco lobby, this issue was a hot potato, and despite the department and the airlines being generally in favour of a ban on smoking on domestic flights, the power of the tobacco lobby was so strong that nothing was done.

Early in 1987, a Private Member's Bill had been introduced to the parliament by Ron Edwards (ALP) in the House of Representatives and Senator David Vigor (Democrats) in the Senate, I assume as joint sponsors. No doubt because of this Bill, the Department for Transport had reviewed the whole matter, and towards the end of 1987 a file with five recommendations came to my office. The file was about 30 cm thick and had been started during the time of the Menzies Government. Gareth Evans was overseas at the time, and I think the file came to me as acting Minister for Transport. From memory, the five recommendations were as follows. First, maintain the status quo – do nothing. Second announce an enquiry to be headed by a judge. Third, ban smoking on domestic flights with a long lead time of five years. Four, introduce regulations to give effect to the policy behind the Bill, which was to ban smoking in general on domestic airlines but have an area sealed off for the other passengers with its own air-conditioning system where passengers could continue to smoke. The commentary associated with this option indicated that it was, after the do-nothing option, the most favoured option by the tobacco lobby. Finally, ban smoking entirely on domestic airliners. This option was generally favoured by the airlines but vigorously opposed by the tobacco industry.

The department had been unable to reach an internal consensus on which option to recommend and so the options came to me without a recommendation but with arguments for and against each of the options. The necessary documentation to give effect to each, including draft regulations and press releases as appropriate, was also part of the package. I consulted with my staff, who discussed the situation with the departmental officer who had responsibility for the matter. I then decided to adopt option five and signed the document, 'Adopt Option 5 and implement forthwith. PD'. We issued the press release in my name on the same day and all hell broke loose.

The cigar-smoking Hawke was furious and carpeted me, to no effect. Hawke was arguing process. I was responding on the issues. I couldn't lose. According to the departmental brief, the airlines supported the ban, including Ansett (Abeles), so Hawke's anger must have been on behalf of the tobacco lobby. Of course, if he had ordered a backdown from what was a very popular initiative, it would have looked as if he was under the thumb of the tobacco lobby, which was the case, since they were significant donors to the ALP at that time. Hawke could have sacked me, but that would have caused serious ructions in the government. Sacked for what? If he had reversed the decision, he could not be sure that I would not have resigned and again that would have been a dreadful look for the government. As things turned out, the regulation was introduced and domestic airline travel over Australia became tobacco smoke-free, from 1 December 1987. It would have happened eventually, but it might have been 20 years later, given the power of the tobacco lobby. It is amazing that we as a community allowed smoking in confined spaces such as on airliners for so long. Even now, when I think of what it was like as a non-smoker on planes in the 1980s, I begin to feel ill.

Overall, this was a fight with overwhelming benefits for society at large.

I have often reflected on whether the department deliberately forwarded the file to my office in Gareth's absence and whether it was done in the hope that I would adopt option five and resolve the matter. It is worth noting that Gareth was in favour of the ban, as he told me later. Of course, he was close to Hawke and almost certainly would have consulted the PM, who would have insisted on a 'no action' outcome.

I was involved in two further initiatives during this period. One was the new Brisbane domestic airport and the other the consolidation of air navigation regulations. To support the *World Expo 88* in Brisbane, a new Brisbane domestic airport was under construction. However, development was behind schedule and was not likely to open in time for the *Expo* opening, early in 1988. That was a problem, but that is another story.

The Transport and Communications Department was a vast bureaucracy, with dozens of divisions, sections and corporations under its supervision. The New Projects Division, consisting of architects, planners and various others, had responsibility for building this huge new airport. Concurrently, and without adequate coordination, another division of the department was dealing with airport security issues and was planning to require all domestic passengers at major airports across the nation to pass through metal-detection machines. The problem was that the new Brisbane airport was being built with passenger comfort in mind, with plans for 80 or more gates, each of which would have direct access from the vehicle drop-off area outside each gate. Under the new security requirements, each of them would require security screening, which needing to be staffed – at vast additional cost.

This lack of coordination was potentially not only a disaster but also an ongoing financial catastrophe in terms of recurrent expenditure. A meeting of all the relevant public servants was organised in Gareth Evans's ministerial office, with about 20 people in the room, including me. Gareth and I were rightly furious with the department and wanted to hear options for dealing with the problem. At that point, the department didn't have a solution, although later they worked out an expensive compromise, which we adopted. However, in the meantime, when asked for answers, the bureaucrats were simply reverting to a debate on whom was to blame, a circuitous argument that went on for some time. Suddenly, I saw Gareth, who had the thick departmental file on his knees, lift the file and remove the long metal spike holding the file together. Then in a rage he exploded, saying, 'I'm sick of hearing bullshit from you bastards! Come back when you have a solution!' With that, he threw the file across the room, scattering hundreds of pieces of paper around the office, and stormed out, with me following. One of Gareth's more memorable moments.

A new terminal building was built in the shape of a boomerang and the inside or shorter side of the boomerang was landside (that is, where passengers enter and exit the terminal). The building was expanded to incorporate a walkway landside of security, and two security access points were established – one for Ansett and the other for Qantas.

Early in my tenure in this portfolio, I was taken on a meet-and-greet familiarisation tour of department facilities in the ACT. During the tour I was shown the room where the official copy of the Air Navigation Regulations and other department-supervised rules were kept. The room measured about three metres by four metres (about the size of a bedroom), with its walls lined with shelves containing loose-leaf ring binders of the sort used in those days to file subordinate legislation. I was stunned by the extent of the files. It was then explained to me that the main legislation governing aviation in Australia had originally been based on the British Merchant Shipping Act, with the aviation regulations developed in a similar manner. Later, this approach changed, with the Australian legislation becoming based on US regulations. In other words, the whole system was a mess.

I arranged a meeting with the appropriate departmental officers to discuss this situation. I believed that the starting point should be a new Act. The department's officers argued that the current Australian legislation basically mirrored legislation in other Commonwealth countries, in that they had also adopted US regulations for aviation and, like the Australian situation, these had been grafted onto the local equivalent of the British Merchant Shipping Act, and that if we rewrote it, we would be out of step with countries with which we had similarities. I decided not to fight that war over something that was basically one of efficient administration. Next, I turned to the subordinate legislation, and the department agreed that a consolidation was long overdue. However, they warned that pilots and those whose occupations were governed by the regulations basically knew the key regulations by reference to a particular number, letter or combination of both and would not take kindly to having to relearn new numbers. A consolidation would inevitably require this.

This was before the pilots' strike and deregulation, a time when the pilots' union was powerful and ran the system. Ignoring this, I contacted a friend in Adelaide, Ian Bidmeade, who had worked on consolidating the regulations in South Australia. The work didn't need to be undertaken in

Canberra and he agreed to do the work on contract – a good outcome all round. Unfortunately, after I had been moved to the Education Ministry, the department was able to convince the incoming minister that this was not essential work and, as a savings measure, Ian's contract was terminated after only some preliminary work had been undertaken.

Early in 1988, I was moved from Transport to the Education portfolio, with John Dawkins as senior minister. In a sense, the timing of my move wasn't too bad, as Gareth Evans, Minister for Communications and the senior minister in the Transport portfolio, had accepted the Telstra and departmental line that timed telephone calls were a great economic reform. I was in the House of Representatives and knew what my constituents thought of timed telephone calls. Gareth, at the time, was in the Senate (that 'great unrepresentative swill', as Keating described it) and had no sense of the extent of the community opposition to the timed telephone calls 'reform'. Gareth and I had argued about the matter internally but, of course, he and the Cabinet carried the day, which they did until the Adelaide by-election on 6 February 1988, caused by the resignation of the Labor member, Chris Hurford, who was to take up a diplomatic post. Labor was thrashed, losing the by-election in a landslide. The Liberals had turned the by-election into a plebiscite on timed telephone calls and following the loss, the Cabinet was forced to reverse the decision.

CHAPTER TWELVE
# Change continues

I was appointed to my new portfolio as Minister for Employment and Education Services on 19 January 1988 and held this portfolio until 4 April 1990. I was disappointed to have been moved from Transport, but after the run-in with Hawke over Amann Aviation and the smoking ban on domestic aircraft, it was hardly surprising. I think Hawke felt that Dawkins was more likely to curb my single-minded enthusiasm, and he may have been correct. The relationship between my office and Dawkins's office was always characterised by a degree of suspicion. That didn't mean that the two offices didn't have an adequate working relationship. The indefatigable Jim Hyde, my senior private secretary, saw to that, but we always had a feeling of being under supervision.

The launch of Australia's Bicentenary year celebrations occurred a few days after my new appointment. On Australia Day 1988, an extraordinary day-long party was held on Sydney Harbour, culminating in a massive fireworks display. It was the forerunner of the now-annual fireworks display on New Year's Eve on the harbour bridge. The celebration on 26 January 1988 was marked by the arrival and sail-past of a fleet of tall ships, some of which had been travelling towards Sydney Harbour for up to a year. The Australian Government had hired the NSW Maritime Services Board's large luxury launch, which was coincidentally a fabulous gin palace, for the dignitaries' pleasure. How this NSW Government department managed to justify its existence or use is an interesting question. On board were Australian Government ministers and their partners, along with various VIPs – former prime ministers, governors-general and their partners – for a day on the harbour with lunch and drinks. Margaret and Gough Whitlam, Malcom and Tammy Fraser, John and Lady Kerr and their various retainers were among those on board.

We sailed at about 11 am and disembarked at about 4 pm after a fabulous day. Julie later remarked that the day almost compensated for all the excrement I had been forced to endure during my political life – or she as a politician's wife. The harbour and its facilities were stretched to the limit that day, forcing our boat to berth at a wharf somewhere in Balmain, where a gangplank consisting of two wooden planks clamped together was the only means of disembarkation. As the guests were leaving, and were milling around on the wharf waiting for buses and cars, our attention was suddenly drawn to John Kerr about to navigate the gangplank. Lady Kerr and the 'faithful' retainer were attempting to support the detested, unstable and overweight Kerr as he veered from port to starboard. As these gyrations took place, some of the ministers on the wharf began to cheer or jeer in the hope that the loathed Kerr might fall into the harbour. The cheering and jeering were interrupted by Gough's booming voice, 'Don't get your hopes up comrades, the thing's so bloated it would have floated'. Ah, the wonderful Gough.

During the Bicentenary celebrations, Queen Elizabeth II, 'Queen of Australia and Head of the Commonwealth', visited Australia to open the new Parliament House, on 9 May 1988. I and many others had hoped to see Australia become a republic with an Australian head of state before, or at, the Bicentennial celebrations. Aboriginal and Torres Strait Islanders and their supporters mounted a noisy protest in view of the forecourt, attempting to provide a focus to their many justified demands.

At that time I was the only person to have served as a minister in a state parliament and in the federal parliament in both Australian Parliament buildings – the Old Parliament House and the new Parliament House. I was tremendously lucky with the staff I had in my parliamentary and ministerial careers. Of my staff during my time in the Australian Parliament, two were subsequently elected to the SA Parliament – Frances Bedford and Robyn Geraghty. Jim Hyde became the head of public health in Victoria; Vicky Agirov had a stellar career as a computer expert, assisting community groups, and Deirdre Tedmanson and Colette Snowden became academics. I first met Frances Bedford, who became the Member for Florey, at the Holden Hill kindergarten and she subsequently came to work in my office, initially as a volunteer. According to Frances, I barely remembered her from the Holden Hill kindy, but thought she was useful when she found a file for me. I can't attest to that, but I told Jim to hire her after her stint of volunteer work of reorganising and filing. She soon became an irreplaceable staff member and forever teased me about her skill as a filing clerk. Demonstrating her typical generosity and caring attitude, Frances acted as Don Dunstan's correspondence secretary from 1997 until his death.

On one occasion, Deirdre Tedmanson and I had flown to Whyalla by chartered light plane for some Commonwealth business, the details of which I have forgotten – although I certainly remember our dramatic flight back to Adelaide. As we flew over Gulf St Vincent following our departure from Whyalla, the aircraft's alternator died – this being the piece of equipment that produces the spark that ignites the fuel in the engine. Without the alternator and with the radio and lights turned off to conserve the battery, we were heading for Adelaide airport. The engine was relying on a rapidly depleting battery for the spark. It was a full-on emergency, and all other aircraft were told to vacate the area. With Deirdre the colour of cream and me considering my swimming skills, we donned life jackets. The pilot was heading straight for the runway lights, and we were all fearful that at any minute the engine would die – at which point I helpfully enquired how far the plane could glide. The pilot's terse reply was that he didn't know. With the fire trucks' blinking red lights ready to welcome us at the end of the runway, we made it, but with how much charge left in the battery I'll never know. The pilot did a great job, but sadly I can't recall his name to thank him once again, after all these years.

In an economic statement in 1988, Treasurer Paul Keating had promised a new program – Skillshare. It was to be a government-funded, community-based program designed to provide a bridge to work for unemployed people, particularly for the long-term unemployed, and for unemployed youth to become 'job ready'. Given that many people were alienated from the job market by a range of problems, one of the underpinning principles of the Skillshare program was the recognition that one size does not fit all. My office, in collaboration with the appropriate departmental officers, had developed the Cabinet submission on Skillshare and we were thrilled when the Cabinet adopted the idea and allocated substantial additional funding for the program. The aim was to establish Skillshare groups across the country – both generalist or more specialist, community-based and not for profit.

The program was designed for maximum flexibility, depending upon the needs of the unemployed in a particular area. The individual groups were, in some respects, mini-TAFEs and, as the program developed, many Skillshare groups were able to articulate their training programs into the TAFE system; that is, Skillshare training certificates of achievement were recognised by TAFE. My ministerial staff and I were incredibly enthusiastic about developing and implementing this program: it was a chance to provide a one-on-one support service for people who had multiple issues or disadvantages, such as lack of education; reluctance to undertake formal learning; a range of mental health issues, which could be supported in conjunction with health professionals; and physical issues. Skillshare groups were either established by charity groups; for example, in Cairns, the Skillshare group was set up by an organisation in the Catholic Church and managed by the dynamic Sister Nadia Del Popolo, and was the epitome of what was possible with Skillshare, or were community-based and often sponsored by local governments.

Disgracefully, the ideologically driven Howard Government defunded the program and replaced it with the for-profit provider system operating today, which essentially generates profits for the private owner, based upon the number of people placed in work. That, of course, has focused attention on work-ready people and has left behind those in need of more intensive support.

On Sunday 20 August 1989, I organised a fundraiser – a night of nostalgia with members of the former Dunstan Government in the Renaissance Tower function centre in Rundle Mall. The 400 available tickets at $50 each sold rapidly, raising $20,000. Never before, or since, had such a successful fundraiser of that magnitude been held by a political party in South Australia. My concept was to get all the ministers who had served under Dunstan and who were still alive together for one last time – for a celebratory event. All those who were reasonably available (Brian Chatterton was in Italy) and in adequate health attended. The atmosphere was warm and generous. The old (in most cases) ministers were delighted to be recognised publicly, one last time, and the true believers were delighted to be able to say 'thank you' for what had been achieved. I was the MC, and each minister made a short speech, with Don giving the main speech towards the end of the night. It was a spectacularly successful evening, with people coming from as far afield as Whyalla and Melbourne. Amongst true believers, it was an event not to be missed, and the only unpleasantness came from a few people who missed out on tickets. The organising and administration of the event was undertaken from my office and the profit went towards the Makin election campaign.

Nothing like it has happened since and it is hard to imagine such an event taking place 10 years after the end of the term of any of the Labor Governments that followed the Dunstan Government. Most people would be hard-pressed to remember much about the Corcoran, Bannon, Rann or Weatherill Governments, or anything that they achieved, except perhaps for the Bannon State Bank disaster. Later in 1995, again as a fundraiser, I organised a testimonial dinner for Don at the Norwood Club. More than 200 people attended and several speakers, including me, spoke of the Dunstan we knew. Don then replied with a characteristically generous speech, sharing the praise for the Dunstan decade with others. Sadly, no record of those speeches survives.

In August 1989, in defiance of the Labor Government's wages freeze, the domestic pilots' union made an ambit claim for a 28 per cent wage increase and backed up the claim with a strike restricting work to between the hours of 9 am and 5 pm. This led to domestic airline turmoil. Instead of Hawke exercising his legendary skills as a conciliator, he played hardball with the pilots. The RAAF was brought in to fly the domestic routes and international airlines were allowed to fly domestically to break the strike. There were no real negotiations and the employers announced that they were planning to sue the pilots' union and each member for damages. If successful, this would have led to a lot of bankrupt pilots.

This move by the airlines inevitably led to mass resignations from the union and to its collapse. The strike petered out towards the end of 1989, with most of the striking pilots losing their jobs and being forced to find work internationally. The upside was that international pilots flocked to Australia for work and the Hawke Government facilitated their easy immigration. The strike resulted in the deregulation of airline wages and conditions, a situation that greatly benefited Hawke's friend and mentor Sir Peter Abeles, who was the managing director and 50 per cent owner of Ansett Airlines. The other 50 per cent was owned by Rupert Murdoch. You might have thought that strikebreaking wasn't in Hawke's DNA. How wrong you would be, especially if Abeles and Murdoch were involved.

In October 1989, Julie and I went to Cairns for a ministerial conference, with the various ministers transported there in F28s because of the pilots' strike. After the conference we stayed at Port Douglas for a few days, at the Mirage Hotel. While in Port Douglas, we had dinner with an old friend from Adelaide, Tim Ferrier, who was selling real estate. The pilots' strike was causing havoc in Port Douglas – no tourists, no business and many bankruptcies. Over a few drinks, Tim described the problems the owner of one of the local tourist spots – Four Mile Beach Shack – was experiencing. Tim said that the bank was in the process of foreclosing on the owner and that the Beach Shack, a small bar at the southern end of the Port Douglas beach, was for sale on a 'take over the mortgage, and lease back to the vendor basis'. In effect the vendor just wanted the bank off his back.

Not to let a good opportunity pass us by, we bought the freehold for the small bar and leased it back to the vendor, as licensee and operator. Then in January the following year we travelled to Port Douglas for a week's break with the boys. We dropped in to see our investment, had a drink and all seemed to be fine. The rent was being paid. What could go wrong?

While there, we visited our friend Tim Ferrier, who was also the agent managing the property and collecting the rent and paying the mortgage. He reported that there were no issues and that fortunately the tenant was doing extremely well, with his brilliant new marketing idea, which had turned the business around. He explained that the tenant's 'brilliant idea' was jelly-wrestling once a month, whereby a large plastic swimming pool was installed in the empty carpark; it was filled with jelly and a few 'fat sheilas' were brought in from Brisbane as wrestlers. This 'entertainment' attracted up to 400 drinkers on a Sunday once a month.

Julie and I were totally shocked and I explained to Tim that this had to stop immediately since I didn't want my premises used for such sleazy purposes. I also emphasised that, apart from anything else, if this became public in Canberra, my ministerial career would be finished. Tim responded by saying that I may not be able to forbid this activity under the terms of the lease. Fortunately, however, the lease contained an incidental clause to the effect that the carpark had to be used as a carpark and for no other purpose.

Later in the week we visited the tenant with Tim and while there the tenant asked me if we would consider selling the real estate back to him. Yes, we replied, for a reasonable price. So, a sale took place, and everybody was happy, including Tim Ferrier, who received two commissions in about six months.

The Australian Government had an agreement for annual low-level consultations between Australian public servants and their counterparts in Papua New Guinea, which in 1989 occurred in early December. The purpose was really a training exercise for PNG bureaucrats. I was asked to lead the delegation. It quickly became apparent that the PNG side placed much greater importance on this annual event than the Australian side. In fact, I felt uncomfortable, in that the relationship was almost colonial. I was accompanied by Julie, my son Macgregor, my staffers, Chris Chappell and Robyn Geraghty, and an officer from Foreign Affairs, along with a contingent of bureaucrats from Canberra. Even 30 years ago, so-called law and order was problematic. My staff were not permitted to walk around outside the Travelodge, where we were staying in Port Moresby. Armed guards patrolled the hotel foyer and one night a minor invasion of so-called rascals, the local gangs, occurred.

On the trip we met the former prime ministers Paias Wingti and Michael Somare and the current Prime Minister Rabbie Namaliu, whose wife, Margaret Nakikus, became friends with Julie. They corresponded subsequently and Julie was devastated to hear that she had died of cancer some time later. One of the highlights was an amazing dinner at a beachside restaurant hosted by Margaret. Chris Chappell still describes the main course as 'the best garlic lobster I have ever had'. The main requirement of the visiting minister, as leader of the delegation, was to fly the flag and make a few vacuous speeches. Other members undertook meetings of substance and gave tutorials on aspects of government.

The PNG Government organised for us to visit Mount Hagen. We flew in over the mountains by light plane, fortunately on a day with clear sky. There was an amazing gathering underway, with maybe 500 people in attendance. The purpose of the gathering was to enable the newly elected local member of parliament to thank or reward his supporters or constituents. Hundreds of pigs were being cooked in pit ovens and the large, flat area was pungent with the pleasant aroma of roast pig, or *babi guling*, as it is known in Indonesia. After the roasting had been completed, each family was given a haunch or two and, with the prized pig on the heads of wives and dripping pig fat all over them, the families slowly departed from the festival with their booty.

We then visited the Australian War Graves Commission Cemetery at Lae, which resembled all war cemeteries, in being an immaculately kept facility with endless rows of headstones of mostly 18- and 19-year-olds. Some of my staff left crying, others, angry. As for me, my pacifism was reinforced and I was saddened at such terrible loss of life. We were also able to visit the Kokoda Trail. Finally, we visited Rabaul, at that time a beautiful city, which had been the capital of German New Guinea before the First World War and where evidence of the efficient German culture remained – straight, sealed roads, with grass verges, well-trimmed and maintained, and beautiful parks. Sadly, the town was later destroyed by a volcanic eruption. The visit to Rabaul was of particular significance for me and son Mac. My father, Mac's grandfather, John Mackie Duncan, had travelled to Rabaul in 1933 as a member of the team of three Australians who established the Commonwealth Bank branch in the town. It was a highlight of my father's life and one of the only two occasions he travelled overseas. Of course, we visited the old building that had been the Commonwealth Bank (although it turned out that the building was not the same one in which my father had worked).

Minister Dawkins had developed a policy to establish larger tertiary education units Australia-wide. In relation to South Australia, the plan was to maintain two universities, Adelaide and Flinders, with the Colleges of Advanced Education (CAEs) and the Institute of Technology to be incorporated into either one of the other universities. The Vice-Chancellor of the Institute of Technology, Professor Alan Mead, approached Neal Blewett, the Member for Bonython, who was the Minister of Health and a close Centre Left colleague of Dawkins.

Alan Mead pointed out that there was a university in the south, with Flinders at Bedford Park, while the city had the University of Adelaide, but there was no institution in the north of Adelaide. His argument was that the proposed plan created a further disadvantage to the depressed and deprived northern suburbs of Adelaide. The Institute of Technology already had a campus at The Levels and there was a CAE at Salisbury. Blewett was convinced by the argument and asked for my support for a third university. I immediately feared that this was a ruse to save the Institute of Technology as an independent institution. I supported the idea of a university in the north, provided that its administration was at The Levels. I insisted that the Institute campus on North Terrace be sold or bequeathed to the University of Adelaide. My rationale was that if the Institute buildings were sold, then the third university's administrative headquarters in the north would be secured. The disposal of the Institute campus was agreed in principle, and on that basis, I supported the proposal for a third university.

I hadn't counted on the guile of Denise Bradley, who would later become a vice-chancellor of the University of South Australia. The University of South Australia was established under South Australian legislation, with Australian Government funding. Under the arrangement, three SACAE campuses – Underdale, Magill and Salisbury – would become part of the new university, together with the Institute's campuses at City East, The Levels and Whyalla. The Adelaide CAE campus went to Adelaide University and the Sturt CAE campus to Flinders. The Institute building on the North Terrace campus was never transferred to the University of Adelaide but became the headquarters of the new university, which began in 1991. Alan Mead was appointed interim Vice-Chancellor on the casting vote of the new university's first Chancellor, John MacDonald, when the Interim Vice-Chancellor Selection Committee met to choose the new appointment.

The federal election was called for 24 March 1990 and I was re-elected, having the satisfaction of seeing off Daryl Hicks as the Liberal candidate. He was a former AFL footballer and someone with a significant local community profile. Following the successful 'Dinner of the Decade' fundraiser of the previous year, Terry Cameron, the ALP Secretary, decided to make no campaign funds available to Makin – one of the only two marginal seats Labor held in South Australia. The other seat was Kingston, held by Gordon Bilney, a member of Terry Cameron's Centre Left.

I returned to Canberra, looking forward to getting back to work on the ministerial agenda. My friend Frank Walker had been elected to the House of Representatives and things were looking good. But some political operators have long memories. Around 1986, Gerry Hand had told me that I'd 'upset Robert Ray. That exercise you guys ran winning the AWU in Victoria is going to cost you dearly. He has vowed revenge and Robert doesn't forget'. I didn't pay much attention at the time and, as I described, was elected to the ministry in 1987. However, during that period Tom Uren and Arthur Gietzelt from NSW were mainly running the Left Caucus, and I was elected with their support. By 1990, Brian Howe and Gerry Hand were more influential. Probably with Bob Hawke's knowledge, Howe and Robert Ray had done a deal, which, in effect, meant the Left would have one less minister if I was on the Left ticket. This would mean that Robert Tickner, who was last on the official Left ticket, would miss out if I was elected.

Those who had plotted my ministerial dumping had done an excellent job of keeping their machinations secret. I had sensed that something was going on. Of course, I had done my numbers and I couldn't see how I could lose. But I was counting Nick Bolkus in my list, the same Senator Bolkus whom I had supported for preselection for the Senate in 1981 and who wouldn't have been in the Senate without that support. He had been my close mate for more than a decade. We went on numerous holidays with our kids, including to Vanuatu. Although a small schism had occurred within the Left between the softs and the hard Left in the late 1980s, until that time there appeared to be no personal split between me and Nick.

Going into the Left Caucus meeting, Bruce Childs had asked for my reassurance that Nick would be on my side. I confirmed that he was, but I took note of his question. As soon as the ballot papers were distributed, I walked around the table, approached Nick and asked to see his ballot paper. He refused. I had lost by one vote. Brian Howe, who, in a rather Bannonesque fashion, loved to portray himself as a man of honour, did not escape my anger. Frank Walker continued to 'punish' him until 1996, when we both lost our seats. Nick, obviously comfortable with his betrayal of me, was promoted by Hawke to the Cabinet!

I had occupied the backbench in Opposition in the state parliament in 1980, and there I was again, but this time while Labor was in government. I was both angry and disappointed, particularly at the so-called Left comrades who had done Robert Ray's dirty work. I attempted to busy myself with electorate work and factional business in South Australia, my base. After a despondent week or so, I proposed to Julie that we go away for a few days, and we decided to go to Broome for a holiday. We had never been there and treated ourselves to eight days at Cable Beach Club Resort. When we returned to Adelaide, we were refreshed, and I had to come to terms with reality. Julie was still angry about what she saw as the unfairness, and more pointedly, the disloyalty of Bolkus, or as she dubbed him 'Nick the Knife'.

In May 1990, we decided to visit Mac in Germany; he was on Rotary Exchange Scholarship during a gap year, where he was being hosted in the small city of Walsrode, famous for its bird park. The father in the family was at the time the managing director of the Bayer Chemical conglomerate. We were flying to Turkey on Turkish Airlines and because neither Julie nor I had been to Turkey, we had decided to spend a few days in and around Istanbul. On the flight to Istanbul, we met a rich Turk of Greek origin, who became infatuated with blonde Julie and invited us to stay in his hotel and accompany him to Bodrum, where he had a massive outdoor disco that operated in the old Roman Halicarnassus. It was like a disco with circus acts, a Royal Show or a carnival at night in a huge stadium, with thousands of people milling around or dancing to disco music with fantastic strobe lighting.

Following our time in Turkey, we flew to Hamburg and visited Mac for a few days and then hired a car for a tour around Germany. Mac was thriving. The family had a son about Mac's age, and they had become friends and are still in touch all these years later. His hosts, who were very wealthy, were treating Mac as part of their family, taking him for holidays at their expense and leaving no stone unturned to expose him to the best of German culture.

This was also the time of the first Gulf War. Always basically a pacifist, I opposed the prospect of Australia sending troops halfway around the world to fight in Iraq. Many members of the Caucus, and particularly among the Left, were also concerned by this proposal. Hawke, to his credit, decided to hold a parliamentary debate on the matter, which enabled me to express my opposition to the war generally and to Australia's involvement, in particular. Whatever the issues and merits, it seemed to me that Australia had no place in this war. I took the opportunity to join a small band of members in opposing the government's resolution of supporting the war. Of course, the First Gulf War led directly to the Second Gulf War, which occurred after I had departed from the parliament. The wars were a shocking waste of lives, and as history demonstrates, completely unjustified.

My friend, Senator Margaret Reynolds, then based in Townsville, had responsibility for organising ALP efforts for the House of Representatives seat of Kennedy, which covered the town of Ravenshoe. She asked me to travel to Ravenshoe to be the speaker at the monthly branch meeting. I gave the speech in a hotel lounge and afterwards I spent some time meeting, speaking and drinking with the 25 enthusiastic members. During these pleasantries I shook hands with a man who had a rag wrapped around his right hand. I asked him what happened to his hand. He pulled off the rag to expose a bloody socket where his middle finger had been. He explained to me that earlier in the day he had been handling a bull and it had tossed its head when he was holding the rope attached to its nose through a ring, ripping out the middle finger on his right hand. I was stunned and asked whether he'd been to the hospital. He replied that he'd wanted to come to the meeting before he did. I told him he needed to get going to the hospital, also enquiring about the whereabouts of the finger, and was it painful? I asked these questions in rapid succession, indicating my shock. His laconic reply: that he wouldn't 'use thin rope in future'. I'm fairly confident that no one else during my political life had shown such enthusiasm to hear my pearls of wisdom!

After being dumped from the ministry, I decided that I needed some activities on the backbench to focus my mind. As I had recently been re-elected as the Member for Makin, there was no justification for feeling depressed. I had always dreamt of running a marathon, and at 45 years of age I felt that my options were closing. I completed the marathon in the surprisingly respectable time of 3 hours 36 minutes and 53 seconds. I suffered no ill effects from the run and assume that running the marathon probably helped my mental health at a time of considerable stress.

A highlight of 1990 was the release of Nelson Mandela from prison in

South Africa, a huge event for those of us who had been fighting apartheid since the 1960s. Only eight months after his release, in October 1990, Mandela visited Australia to thank the many Australians for their support, which had come from both the Australian Government and the many community groups that had sprung up in solidarity and were dedicated to raising funds to aid the struggle. At the time I was a member of the Nelson Mandela Foundation, of which Dunstan was chairman. Don visited Canberra first and then travelled to Sydney for Mandela's visit. While in Canberra, he used my office in the parliament as his base for the day. It was an exhilarating time. Mandela was viewed as a hero – as he should have been – and was welcomed everywhere with immense warmth. In my time in the Australian Parliament, I never experienced anyone who was as celebrated as Mandela. The occupants of the parliament mobbed him in a joyous outpouring of enthusiastic welcome, this response continuing in Sydney and reflecting no doubt the sense of achievement people felt in seeing the successful outcome of decades of struggle.

CHAPTER THIRTEEN
# The Keating ascendancy

The great event of 1991 was the arrival of my daughter Georgia, on 6 September. What a wonderful occasion that was. Her birth marked the culmination of years of effort for Julie and me to have a baby. Several miscarriages and a stillborn baby had preceded Georgia's safe arrival. Julie had gained some weight since the mid-1980s and eventually her doctor told her that if she wanted to have a baby, she should get fit and lose weight. This advice was not initially well received, but the doctor survived as Julie's medico and before long a fitness regime had been established that saw Julie fit and healthy during her pregnancy with Georgia. Julie used to say Georgia was conceived in her much-loved Tasmania, during January 1991, when we holidayed in Hobart.

Georgia's arrival was not without challenges. She was accompanied by *placenta previa*, which saw Julie in hospital for six weeks before Georgia's birth. Following the history of disappointments, Julie was understandably very anxious, despite stress not being particularly good for her health at the time. On the other hand, I was genuinely optimistic that everything would be alright, which it was. I remember this period as a time when 'team Julie and Peter' was operating at its best. She was worried, while I was optimistic, hopeful and capable of uplifting her often-low spirits. Being in hospital for six weeks was hard for Julie, who was normally extremely active – but the whole point of being in hospital was to rest and not move too much.

Julie brought the precious Georgia home to a nursery that Julie had prepared with love long before Georgia's birth. Georgia had little or no hair when born, which was a cause for alarm for Julie at the time; not surprisingly, Georgia eventually had beautiful hair, similar to Julie's blonde mop. Once Georgia was home and everything had settled down, we embarked upon what was to pass for our normal life while I was still in the parliament and Georgia was small. Soon after Georgia's birth, a 'Rolls Royce' Maclaren pram entered our lives, a pram that enabled a reasonable compromise between a restricted lifestyle for new parents and our usual social life. Georgia's first year of life was pretty much spent in a pram. She was taken everywhere possible – restaurants, parties and meetings. We dined out two or three nights a week and although Julie was a good cook, it was much easier to visit restaurants for socialising with friends than to cater at home. Peter Kellett and Gill Baker, Russell and Dana Wortley, Carene and Paul Evans, Mike Presdee and Gill Gower and so many others.

A duplicate of the pram was in Canberra for use during their frequent visits. Any restaurants that didn't welcome babies or children were quickly off the list, with a suitable letter from Julie to the editor of the local paper. This was before Trip Advisor. In later life, I have always avoided restaurants that refuse access to babies or children. As informal dining has replaced more formal dining, there are fortunately fewer restaurants with such restrictive rules.

This time of family happiness coincided with the beginning of the process of electing P.J. Keating as Prime Minister. In the wake of the shocking events surrounding Amann Aviation and the coastal surveillance contract, I had absolutely no time for Hawke; Frank Walker, an excellent judge of character, had no time for Hawke either. I hadn't supported Hawke for Leader against Hayden and my negative view of him had only been reinforced. I saw him as unprincipled and completely in the thrall of Sir Peter Abeles, whose knighthood, incidentally, was gifted by the individual now recognised as NSW's most corrupt premier, Robin (later Robert) Askin. Folklore has it that Askin, who was known to take bribes, decided he couldn't handle the name 'Robin' because it had been changed by the community to the nickname 'Robbin(g)'; hence, the change.

It was not difficult for me to identify positive characteristics in Keating. While I had plenty of arguments with him over policy issues, I saw one similarity between us. As Jim Snow in his book *Keating and his Party Room* commented: 'Popularity was less important to Keating than policies, which were vital to him'. From my time in the Dunstan Government, I had always seen my role as someone who implemented policy, rather than being a populist administrator. Paul never took his eye off the main game – the policy objectives – unlike Hawke, whose ego was always a failing.

The history of Keating's challenges to Hawke are now legendary and centred on an agreement that Hawke would resign as prime minister in Keating's favour after the 1990 election, the objective being to enable a smooth leadership transition. Keating had gained Hawke's agreement to this arrangement but had so little trust or faith in Hawke's word that he insisted on a meeting with 'seconds' as witnesses. Hawke, of course, had Abeles as his second, while Keating had ACTU Secretary Bill Kelty as his witness. The meeting, now known as the Kirribilli Agreement, was held at the prime minister's Sydney residence, Kirribilli House. The agreement, naturally, was a secret and its existence was unknown to the Caucus or the community at large, until towards the middle of 1991. As time went on, however, Hawke apparently became less enthusiastic about fulfilling the terms of the agreement.

By June 1991, the Caucus had become aware of rumours of a Keating challenge, with the media soon after beginning the inevitable speculation. Frank Walker had been discussing the matter with Laurie Brereton, Keating's factional ally and his chief numbers man. Frank and I had decided to support Keating some time before. Essentially, at that point, we were in the 'anyone but Hawke' camp. Later, when Keating was on the backbench after the first unsuccessful challenge and I got to know him better, I became a strong Keating supporter, as did Frank.

The first Keating challenge occurred in June 1991. The Left had discussed the matter at a meeting. With Gerry Hand and Brian Howe – both from the Left – strongly in the Hawke camp, it was assumed that the Left was behind Hawke. Much to the horror of some of the 'comrades', Frank and I announced that we were behind Keating and intended to vote for him in the Labor Party Caucus, regardless of any Left Caucus decision. Our position was viewed as a shocking betrayal of the group on a grand scale. Some were talking of expelling us from the Left Caucus, although this didn't eventuate. Our explicit intention to support Keating occurred without sanction and emboldened others to join us in this endeavour. Frank and I lobbied Senator John Devereaux, Wendy Fatin, Stewart West, Colin Hollis and a few others and eventually those four, along with Frank and me, voted for Keating in the first ballot. Andrew Theophanous claimed later that he voted for Keating but that is in some dispute. Without Walker and Duncan leading the charge, it is doubtful the others would have broken with the Left.

The practice in ballots was for two members of the Left Caucus to vote simultaneously and then show each other their marked ballot, an approach designed to ensure that no 'mistakes' were made. It had been introduced by Gerry Hand after it became public that in the Whitlam era Tom Uren from the Left and Senator Reg Bishop from the Right had an agreement to vote for each other in ballots, regardless of Left Caucus decisions. On this occasion we ignored the practice.

In order to settle the matter, Hawke, giving only a couple of hours' notice, called a Caucus meeting for the evening of 3 June 1991. He declared the leadership vacant, with a ballot to be held. Keating and Hawke nominated, and the result of the ballot was Hawke 66, Keating 44, portrayed by the media as a win for Hawke, but a good showing for Keating. For a Keating victory, 12 Caucus members had to be convinced to change their votes. After the first ballot, Keating resigned from the ministry and moved to the backbench. Some time after the first ballot, when Frank and I were dining with Keating, he intimated that, before the ballot was held, he had considered resigning from the parliament if he didn't receive a respectable vote. He didn't define what constituted respectable, although I asked him what it might be. Laurie Brereton, however, told me that without the Left votes taking Keating's vote into the mid-40s, 'He would have bolted'.

During the six months Keating sat on the backbench, the government seemed to drift: John Kerin didn't cope as Treasurer and the atmosphere in the Labor Caucus, and particularly the Left Caucus, was poisonous. I used to refer to Hawke as the 'reneger'. On the backbench, Frank and I had little to lose, so at every opportunity we highlighted and emphasised the government's failings and missteps, which was extremely irritating for the Hawke loyalists in the Left. The turmoil couldn't continue and finally Hawke called a Caucus meeting for Thursday 19 December 1991.

Hawke undoubtedly believed that he would win and that at that point he would have had the moral advantage, after two victories over Keating, to demand that Keating leave the parliament. If Keating had not resigned in those circumstances, he would have been portrayed as a wrecker, and with some justification. It wasn't to be, however, with the result of the second ballot Keating 56, Hawke 51. I'm not aware of all of those who changed their votes, and it doesn't much matter now. However, if the whole of the Left had voted as a block, Hawke would have won. The Left 'rats' again made the difference. Interestingly, if those members supporting Hawke because they were Cabinet ministers, ministers and parliamentary secretaries are considered, then Keating's real Caucus support was greater than the majority shown in the ballot result.

Several consequences flowed from Keating's victory. The Hawke loyalists were devastated but not rudderless. Robert Ray soon organised a delegation, consisting of himself, Kim Beazley, Brian Howe, Gerry Hand, Gareth Evans, John Button, Nick Bolkus and others. Essentially, they told Keating that if he attempted to remove *any* of the Hawke supporters from their positions, they would collectively destroy the government.

Ray, still displeased with me over the Victorian AWU issue demanded, 'and don't think of rewarding Duncan'. With Keating now in consensus-building mode, he agreed. Hawke resigned from the parliament to be replaced in the seat of Wills by Left independent Phil Cleary, a dedicated member whose politics were characterised by a commitment to progressive policies and diversity.

I had been blackballed, but not Frank, and Keating arranged to have Frank elected to the ministry as a captain's pick after the 1993 election, despite Frank having little support in the Left Caucus. Disregarding Ray's edict, Keating appointed me as a parliamentary secretary and apologised for the situation and asked me to choose my portfolio. I nominated Attorney-General and held that position until the government was defeated in 1996. I have never regretted supporting Keating and playing a role in his elevation. Prime Minister Keating reinvigorated the Labor Government and won an historic victory in 1993.

After our support for Keating in the first ballot, Hawke never spoke to me or Frank Walker again. Even at Gough Whitlam's memorial service, Hawke refused to shake hands. Correctly, he blamed me and Frank for leading the 'ratting' that had resulted in the split in the Left Caucus vote for him. Needless to say, we were also despised and vilified by the Left majority. On 27 December, I was sworn in as parliamentary secretary to the Attorney-General. Following Keating's election on 20 December, Julie and I flew to Adelaide for a short Christmas break and then returned to Canberra and back to work.

Upon becoming parliamentary secretary, I was given the usual departmental briefing and a copy of the parliamentary Question Time briefing book. I was quite surprised to find that a very wide range of issues were monitored, but not actively being pursued, in marked contrast to the very limited list in South Australia. The department had given suggestions to the Attorney-General on the matters for which I should have responsibility. Michael Lavarch, the Attorney-General, was quite flexible, and after the departmental briefing, I also made a few suggestions, with which he agreed. One of these was disability discrimination. I'd had a long interest in the area stemming from my time as Attorney-General in South Australia when I appointed the Bright Committee of Inquiry into the Rights of Handicapped Persons in the 1970s.

A departmental committee was set up to produce a draft Disability Discrimination Bill and, equipped with the draft, which had been made available to interested parties, we began a round of consultations. This issue quickly came to dominate my role as parliamentary secretary; the negotiations with interest groups over various drafts of the Bill were extensive and exhaustive. No one opposed the concept of an Act to outlaw discrimination against people with a disability, and the definition of disabled was generally agreed. It was likewise agreed that the Human Rights Commission should be the enforcing body. That, however, was about the end of agreement. The lobby or interest groups were not just the parties representing people with a disability but included a large range of groups seeking to protect their interests: employers' groups generally and charities claiming to be assisting the disabled were opposing having to deliver their services without discrimination. State governments as providers of schooling and transport services, as well as Australian Government departments, were all part of a long list of bodies demanding long compliance lead times before compulsory enforcement.

Arguments of proportionality were raised: if only one or a few people across Australia suffered from a particular disability, was it reasonable to require all providers to adjust their business or services to accommodate a very tiny need? If the government agreed to any such concessions, where should we draw the line? Likewise, if we agreed an exemption for bus operators until they replaced their fleets, why not a similar exemption for building owners? Or so the arguments went, interminably, and every time some aspect of the Bill was determined, it would be leaked from the department and another round of lobbying would occur. In addition, when I did make a decision, the perceived 'losers' would attempt to go to a higher authority, that is, Michael Lavarch. That said, after my experiences with Gareth Evans, and particularly John Dawkins, it was a delight working with Michael and his office, run by John Stanton, later the ACT Chief Minister. Michael always backed me and refused to act as an appeal court for lobbyists.

On the other hand, the lobby groups demanding more radical disability support would not countenance any delay in full compliance. It was a fraught situation. Take transport, for example, few buses were wheelchair-accessible in 1992. Quite simply, it was impossible to expect state governments and other transport providers to retire their existing non-complying fleets the day the Bill came into effect. The radical lobby groups believed that the Australian Government should simply subsidise these replacement fleets.

Eventually, the concept of justifiable hardship in relation to access to premises and services was adopted. That allowed state governments, for example, to obtain exemptions from providing wheelchair access to public transport until new buses, trains and trams had been introduced. I know this concession delayed the abolition of discriminatory practices by decades, but I have lived long enough to see the grandparenting aspects of the Act gradually washed out of the system. Access cabs have been introduced in all large cities and negotiations have gradually led to access cabs in most towns.

It is worth highlighting how developments in technology have resolved discrimination in some areas. Discrimination in telephone services was a nightmare in the drafting of the Bill. Special needs for the partially deaf and public phones at levels so that they were accessible to people in wheelchairs were major points of discrimination. Now the ready availability of inexpensive mobile phones with specialist apps and accessories has largely removed most of these forms of discrimination. Eventually a Bill was agreed with the widest support achievable and was taken to Cabinet and approved for introduction.

The Disability Discrimination Bill was in the public arena for its first reading by Deputy Prime Minister Brian Howe on 26 May 1992, and on this day and during the second reading speech, on 19 August 1992, the public gallery had a reasonable number of radicals who booed and generally disrupted the proceedings. Although the major disability groups supported the Bill, they were relatively invisible compared with the few making the noise. Since the Liberal Opposition generally supported the Bill, the protests from the radicals never amounted to much. I have never regretted the Bill, and with the benefit of hindsight, recognise that it has led to terrific improvements for people with disabilities. The aim of the Act was:

> To eliminate, as far as possible, discrimination against persons on the ground of disability in the areas of: work, accommodation, education, access to premises, clubs and sport; and the provision of goods, facilities, services and land; existing laws; and the administration of Commonwealth laws and programs; and to ensure, as far as practicable, that persons with disabilities have the same rights to equality before the law as the rest of the community; and to promote recognition and acceptance within the community of the principle that persons with disabilities have the same fundamental rights as the rest of the community.

The following anecdote describes a relatively recent event in the disability arena and is a reminder that governments and other service providers still do not accord disability discrimination the priority it requires.

On 10 December 2018, an inquiry led by retired District Court judge Michael Forde found that a multibillion-dollar contract to build new trains for Queensland had been flawed from the outset: none of the 75 new trains complied with disability access laws. The $4.4 billion New Generation Rollingstock project was undertaken in India by a consortium led by the company Bombardier. The Queensland Government had contracted the company to build the new trains but the contract neglected to specify that the trains had to comply with the *Disability Discrimination Act 1992*. It cost the government an additional $335 million to remedy the defects after the Human Rights Commission rightly refused the state government an exemption.

Looking back after almost 30 years, this reform is my most positive achievement during my time in the Australian Parliament and the one of which I am most proud. Disability discrimination reform had been an area of unfinished business from my time as South Australian Attorney-General. Now, whenever I see a bus tilt to allow a person in a wheelchair to board, or a mother with a pram enter or exit the bus or an access cab, I am pleased.

Effective decision-making and exercising ministerial responsibility require particular skills. I have never had any problem making decisions. I was good at reaching a conclusion, adopting and then enforcing it. Once I had decided an issue, I stuck to it, although not to the point of being irrational. Early in my parliamentary and ministerial career, I worked out two principles of good decision-making: don't be hasty in making decisions as other information may come to hand to assist you in making the right decision; and don't use the application of the first principle as an excuse for unnecessary procrastination.

In the recent past there has been an appalling tendency for ministers, both Labor and Coalition, to deliberately avoid becoming aware of unfolding events in the departments for which they are responsible, with some arguing that if a minister is unaware of an administrative issue within his or her department, he or she cannot be held responsible for errors or problematic areas. To this end, some ministers have even requested that they not be briefed by the public service head of their department or the minister's office on administrative problems. Of course, the Westminster tradition demands that the minister is responsible to the parliament for all that happens in their department, and this should remain the case.

The parliament has, despite politics, cut some slack to ministers who claim no knowledge of maladministration, as long as the minister acts proactively once aware of the problem, which is also appropriate. Perhaps as a result of the decline in Westminster ministerial responsibility in South Australia, an Independent Commission Against Corruption (an ICAC) was established, with powers to investigate corruption, which I believe is reasonable. What is very worrying however is that ICAC has additional powers to investigate maladministration. In the Westminster system, and for very good reasons, maladministration is traditionally the province of the parliament and its committee system. If a minister is incompetent, he or she should be dealt with by the parliament and if the parliament is incapable or unwilling to deal with him or her, the electorate should make its judgement at the next election.

During my time as parliamentary secretary to the Attorney-General, I had responsibility for the administration, but not the policy, of the Family Court. Sadly, the Family Court was then, and is now, a pale reflection of Lionel Murphy's vision. Contrary to what people generally believe, there is little wrong with the *Family Law Act 1975*. As a general proposition, the problems lie with the court. It was originally intended that the Family Court would be an informal tribunal. Unfortunately, apart from the Chief Justice, all the appointments to the original court were made by the Fraser Government. The court was captured by a bunch of status-seeking judges and its processes are now so complex that the average individual finds it impossible to navigate the labyrinthine system without a specialist Family Court lawyer, much less win without specialist legal representation. Even generalist lawyers shy away from the Family Court.

Matters of appeal simply went to a bench of three of the court's judges, usually including the Chief Justice. Tragically, this single-level court has evolved into a complex hierarchy, consisting of an appellate court, a general division, magistrates and conciliators, with the judges attaining federal court-level pay and status. When I was parliamentary secretary, the head of the court was Alistair Nicholson CJ, who was seen as friendly to the Labor Government and was mates with John Button and Michael Duffy. Before long I began to get some idea of how the court operated. Nicholson came to see me early in 1991 and his main complaint was that there were insufficient personnel to adequately staff the court to avoid backlogs.

Before my meeting with Nicholson, the Family Law Division of the Attorney-General's Department had briefed me on the administrative inefficiencies and the alleged empire-building activities of the court. The division officers suggested that I might like to visit the registry in Darwin and have discussions with the Northern Territory Law Society's Family Law Section. They also suggested that I might like to visit the Newcastle Registry and meet the resident judge. I arranged to visit Newcastle in the first half of 1992, soon after Nicholson's chat to me. Although I'm unable to recall the name of the Newcastle Family Court judge at the time, I do remember his telling me that he was intensely disliked by the Melbourne headquarters of the court. The basis of this dislike was his approach to the way he ran his court. His modus operandi was informality. He explained that, much to the disapproval of the legal profession, he refused to give judgements or make orders without the parties being present. His approach was to address the parties directly, in a manner they clearly understood. In instances of child custody accompanied by allegations of violence, whether physical or psychological by one parent of the other, the judge ordered that the children be transferred between parents at the local Relationships Australia office, with one of the parents to arrive half an hour after the other had dropped off the children.

This judge had almost no appeals or recurring appearances. People listened to the judge, recognising him as 'a tough bastard' and fearing another appearance before him. This approach worked like a charm and discouraged parties from using children in continuing domestic warfare with the other parent. Where there were arguments over substantial family assets, a more formal approach was needed, but this represented a tiny minority of the cases. That is how Murphy had envisioned the Family Court – informal and with no nonsense. Other registries across Australia, with their overly complex systems, involved large numbers of warring parties whose disputes lasted for years.

I discussed these issues with Michael Lavarch and he agreed that this was the approach the court should be taking, but believed that it would be almost impossible to turn things around at this stage: to address the problem, we would need to start all over again. Today the Family Court is unrecognisable when compared with the Murphy vision of an informal conciliator and inexpensive, readily accessible – hopefully – and mainly without the need for lawyers. What we have is the reverse.

Having experienced the Newcastle court, I then arranged to visit the Darwin Registry, to talk to the Northern Territory Law Society and my university friend John Waters, QC, who practised law in Darwin, where the problems were more administrative than judicial and possibly more manageable. I remember clearly that the visit occurred in August during the parliamentary break. That was a normal time for a visit, but later I wondered if the department had organised the timing deliberately. When I arrived in Darwin and met with the Law Society, I discovered that there was no permanent judge in the territory, despite there being enough court business to occupy more than one full-time judge.

Lunch with John Waters confirmed the situation, but he also supplied more detail about the judicial staffing of the Darwin Registry: it was staffed intermittently by judges from the Melbourne Registry, leading to a large backlog, which necessitated the scheduling of two judges. For a few weeks the court would be extremely busy as the backlog was reduced. It was well known, Waters explained, that, during the unpleasant wet season, a judge was rarely seen, but during the dry, which coincided with the Melbourne winter, the court was always staffed and busy. John suggested that, if I arranged a parliamentary question asking about the backlog in May, compared with September, this situation would be confirmed.

My next stop in Darwin was the registry itself, where I was not surprised to find that, as it was August, three judges were in town, two with their wives. Subsequent discussions with the department indicated that, in its view, the winter Darwin and Cairns circuits were allocated as favours for judicial mates in Melbourne. No doubt the Melbourne Registry had been informed of my visit to Darwin. On my return I sent a note to Nicholson asking for a briefing on the administrative arrangements applying in the Northern Territory. Back came a brief note and a request for a meeting. The explanations offered at the meeting were admirable in their complexity, being something along the following lines:

> Point one: If the government can provide the funding for a Family Court building in Darwin, the Family Court could find the personnel, but the lack of a building is a real problem and a deterrent to finding quality candidates as judges. My response was that a shortage of court accommodation was obviously not a problem, given three judges had recently been sitting, presumably each with a court.
>
> Point two: If a resident judge is required, the Family Court will require increased funds for this additional judge and accommodation. Well, I didn't respond with the obvious answer to the point about the additional costs of a judge but suggested that one of the existing judges be relocated there permanently.
>
> Point three: There were no suitable candidates available from the thin list of names from the NT Bar. My response? Later, when a list of new

Family Court judges was proposed, the matter was resolved with a suitable residential appointment to Darwin.

In my role as parliamentary secretary to the Attorney-General, I appointed a large number of marriage celebrants to ensure greater availability across the nation. Prior to this, a policy of appointment of one or two marriage celebrants per House of Representatives electorate had applied. When one marriage celebrant died or advised the department of his or her retirement, then a replacement would be appointed. The effect of this policy was twofold: first, it protected the businesses of existing marriage celebrants, who were able to charge for their services, and more celebrants meant less business for them. Second, the previous situation of fewer celebrants had ensured less competition for the churches in the race to serve the marriage market.

After my experience in appointing a large number of Justices of the Peace in South Australia in rather similar circumstances almost 20 years earlier, on this occasion I simply signed the marriage celebrant certificates and letters of appointment for those on the waiting list and had them posted, with a subsequent press release announcing the fait accompli. While there was a certain amount of muted opposition from the Civil Marriage Celebrants Association and the churches, their protests were all too late.

Prior to the 1993 election, Frank Walker, Garry Punch and I organised a hugely successful fundraiser at the Randwick Racecourse Convention Centre. The event, 'A Night With the Whitlam Government', was based on a similar event I had organised in South Australia in 1987 but which had celebrated Don Dunstan. Frank was part of the NSW Left and Gary, although having earlier been in the Left, was part of the Right, so the event was cross-factional and that was a key to its success. The three of us had been key backers of Paul Keating in the two leadership elections. The aim was to get all the old ministers who had served in the Whitlam Government together, and for true believers to have an opportunity to see, hear and speak to these ministerial veterans over dinner. We had an excellent response from the invitations to former ministers. Of the ministers still living, only John Wheeldon declined.

A few days before the event, I had a telephone conversation with Gough to brief him on the arrangements. After advising him of the likely former ministerial attendees, the following conversation occurred.

'And what about the leaders? Who's coming?', asked Gough.

'Well Paul will be there. Bill Hayden has declined, pointing out that it would be inappropriate for the Governor-General to be at such an overtly political function. We haven't heard back from Bob, but don't expect him to show', I replied.

'Ah Robert James Lee Hawke, longest serving Labor Prime Minister, but the only one never to serve in a *LABOR* Government', Gough replied.

An interesting and rare hint of what Gough Whitlam – with his booming trademark voice – thought of the Hawke Government. The event was a great success, raising around $80,000.

My friends, the two Michaels – Michael Deegan and Michael Knight, the latter the Labor Member for Campbelltown in the NSW Parliament – had gone to the US between May and June 1989 to attend the Campaign School run by *Campaigns and Elections* magazine. They also had numerous meetings in Washington, New York and San Francisco with various political consultants, with whom they formed longstanding relationships. These professional consultants were very generous in sharing their skills and experience with the two Lefty Australians. In Australia in those days, most election campaigns took place for the brief period before an election; that is, from the time of the issuing of the writs until polling day. Following the election, life returned to normal, with elections and campaigning forgotten until the next election. A small number of MPs, including Michael Knight, Frank Walker and me, had an ongoing interest in campaigning, despite having pretty busy day jobs. By contrast, the US had a professional campaign industry. In the US, apparently, campaign skills and knowledge didn't reside with politicians, or even with party officials, but with consultants who made their living from campaigning, given that at any time an election was due to be held somewhere in America.

What the Australian visitors learned in the US was the 'science of campaigning', some of which was technology-based and some strategic, and most of the concepts underpinning it were transferable to Australia. When the two Michaels returned, they shared what they had learned with Frank and me. I spent a day at Michael Knight's house in Campbelltown, for an extraordinarily useful and eye-opening tutorial. While I won't go into all the details, some of the general principles are worth highlighting, although they may seem obvious. In essence, the best approach was to use colour messaging and repeat the messages *over and over again*. Although the campaign team is sick of hearing a message, this doesn't mean every voter has heard it even once. Attack your key opponent as much as possible to reduce their base vote. Conduct professional, well-designed and executed surveys and be confident enough in the results of the survey to accept and rely on the results. Adopt a theme or slogan and endlessly use it. Include it on every piece of propaganda. On that point, I knew that my slogan 'Standing up for you', was working when a constituent who approached me on a Saturday morning street visit thanked me for standing up for the community and then asked for assistance with his neighbour.

Importantly, market the idea of ready access to the candidate/member. Never use 'them and us' language. Use large print because 40 per cent of the population have impaired sight. Of course, an important aspect was effective use of technology and direct mail. Go the extra mile. Stay under the radar of the mainstream media. Always act as if you are 10 votes short of winning – advice I, unfortunately, didn't follow in 1996.

All this advice, which I adopted in campaigning in South Australia, was way ahead of the Labor Party at the time. Party officials claim to have great knowledge of campaign techniques, but mostly that is not the case. One other great advantage of scientific campaigning is that it is possible to win elections without engaging with the mainstream media, specifically the Murdoch media. With the demise of newspaper reading and the decline in TV watching, direct communication with voters is becoming even more critical. In 1991, the Hawke Government was keen to ban television advertising for election campaigns and managed to pass legislation to do so, although the legislation was struck down by the High Court in 1992. No advertising on television would have meant greater focus on direct mail (which in the US was essentially leaflets, not letters). Because TV advertising for individual candidates is financially impossible in urban seats such as Makin anyway, the reinstatement of TV ads made little difference to local campaigning. In fact, the 'direct mail' approach was perfectly suited to a marginal seat campaign in a city seat.

CHAPTER FOURTEEN
# The 1993 Federal Election

On 3 March 1993 a general election was held and I won Makin, against a lacklustre Liberal candidate Alan Irving and basically without a swing of any consequence. By 1993, we had the electoral science working very well for us and had run an effective local campaign against the GST promised by John Hewson in the Liberal Fight Back policy. This victory was the 'One for the true believers', according to Paul Keating.

I was hoping to have been restored to the ministry, but it was not to be. The soft Left clearly had the numbers in the Left Caucus and were not about to elect me or Frank Walker as Left nominees for the ministry. Frank and I went to see Keating to press our collective case, pointing out that our problem with the Left arose partly from supporting him against Hawke. In addition, I still had Robert Ray against me from the Victorian AWU election of more than a decade earlier. Paul promised to support one of us as a 'captain's pick', but indicated that if he selected me, the Left and the Victorian Right might collaborate to defeat his pick and, in those circumstances, neither of us would be ministers. Frank and I considered the situation over dinner. I then offered to back out and support Frank. We advised Keating, and Frank was elected on Right factional votes. Frank never forgot my gesture until the day he died in 2012.

Frank Walker was elected to the ministry on 2 March 1993 and made Special Minister of State. In that position, he was given overall supervision of the design and drafting of the Native Title Act, which was to provide a framework for the granting of Native Title following the High Court finding in Mabo – that, at European 'settlement', Australia was already settled by Aboriginal and Torres Strait Islander people. Keating recognised that the legislation was extremely complex to draft, which is why he gave Frank overall supervision of the process. The interdepartmental committee dealing with the legislation had representation from Attorney-General's, Aboriginal Affairs, Administrative Affairs, Finance and other departments.

At the time, there was great fear, particularly amongst conservatives, about Native Title and its interplay with pastoral leases, and some of this concern also existed in the bureaucracy.

During the drafting of what became the *Native Title Act 1993*, Frank was staying in my house at Kingston, as he usually did, and every night we discussed its progress. It was high-stakes politics on a grand scale. We feared that some of the opponents of land rights, in an attempt to produce a Bill that would be struck down by the High Court, were collaborating with elements in the Aboriginal Affairs Department to support a land rights scheme that exceeded the scope of the High Court Mabo judgement. On two occasions we visited Keating to brief him on the dilemma. The quick-witted Paul Keating immediately saw the danger and ensured that Frank was afforded all necessary support and assistance. The outcome was legislation that granted land rights *and* did not fall foul of the High Court. Frank achieved a difficult balancing act. Sadly, because all the negotiations took place behind closed doors, Frank has never received the recognition he deserved – until now.

Frank Walker was the minister in charge of government advertising, and he appointed me as chair of the Government Advertising Committee, whose role was to approve all proposals for advertising expenditure. The committee had two purposes. One was a political purpose, which continues whichever party is in government, and that is to ensure that advertising contracts, which were awarded based on the artistic approach rather than a monetary tender, were awarded to advertising companies friendly to the government, where appropriate. At the same time, the committee had to ensure that groups supporting the Opposition were not getting favoured treatment by Opposition supporters in the bureaucracy. The committee's second, and equally important, purpose was to ensure value for money.

Advertising/public relations contracts were let according to the following framework. A government department would prepare a brief for the contract, and it would be circulated to several agencies, which would then develop an initial proposal for submission to the relevant department. Generally, the department would then prepare a short list of agencies to be invited to work up their proposal in more detail for presentation to the department and the Government Advertising Committee. Departmental bureaucrats naturally had their favourite agencies, and sometimes it appeared to the committee, that from the two or three proposals received by the committee one was superior to the other two. When these came before the committee, I asked to see all the proposals and, on several occasions, those that hadn't made the cut were clearly more worthy. In other words, the whole process was being corrupted.

On one occasion the Army proposed to spend a large amount of money for a marketing campaign to lift recruitment. Unlike most advertising contracts when the outcome is difficult to measure, this case was different, in that if the number of recruits increased significantly the campaign was gauged successful. The first proposals received by the committee were, in our view, either lacklustre or uninspiring, which prompted us to ask to see all the proposals. We selected the pitch 'Give yourself the edge', shortened to 'the Edge' later in the campaign and in individual advertisements.

The committee's selection provoked a huge argument with the military, but we insisted, and the campaign we adopted was very successful. As this debate was taking place, I asked for an estimate of the number of recruits the Army expected the campaign to produce. Although I have forgotten the actual figures, I do recall that, when the total expenditure for the campaign was divided by the number of additional recruits, it transpired that the military was planning to spend $50,000 per recruit, which prompted me to pose a serious question: if the Army was to pay each recruit a sign-on bonus of $25,000, would that not produce the requisite number of recruits and save the government half the recruiting advertising budget? I spoke to Kim Beazley, who at the time was Minister for Finance but who had an ongoing interest in Defence. Suddenly, the Army was taking the committee seriously. Beazley had obviously shown some interest in the committee proposal, although we lost that argument.

Between 1992 and 1993 the Royal Commission into the State Bank disaster in South Australia published its two reports. Premier Bannon claimed he had acted responsibly by remaining as premier until the report had been received. He then resigned, leaving his successor, Lynn Arnold, to deal with the remaining fallout and to face the wrath of the electors at the forthcoming December 1993 state election. I can't think of a worse political task given to anyone in my political lifetime. My friend Lynn was left to lead an election campaign in which the main task was to explain why a Labor Government, which had virtually bankrupted the state, be re-elected. He did a creditable job in impossible circumstances and Labor was reduced to a rump of 10 seats. The only thing to say about the outcome is that it could have been even worse.

On 7 May 1994, a by-election for the South Australian seat of Torrens was triggered by the death of the Liberal MHA, Joe Tiernan, only four months after he had won the seat in the 1993 state election with a two-party vote of 56.22 per cent. The plan had been that Lynn Arnold, Bannon's successor, would remain as Opposition Leader for a year or so after the 1993 election and then hand the leadership to Mike Rann, who, at that stage, was still portraying himself as an independent Lefty.

Lynn was exhausted and pretty rundown. We had a conversation about the Torrens by-election. He told me that the party considered that winning the Torrens by-election was impossible. Torrens was mainly within the boundaries of Makin, so I offered to run the by-election for Labor, on two conditions: first, that Robyn Geraghty from my office would be the candidate, and; second, that I was able to run the campaign without interference from the party office. The latter was mainly a reference to the inexperienced people running the Labor Party office at the time – and subsequently. Lynn agreed and I told him that we would win the by-election. I was confident of that because I believed that the voters had already taken the baseball bats to Labor over Bannon's State Bank catastrophe and would be ready to move back to more normal political support.

The ALP was virtually bankrupt after the state election and didn't provide any resources towards the campaign, but Robyn's husband Bob Geraghty, then secretary of the Electrical Trades Union, arranged for some funding from the union's national office. We ran a vigorous and positive campaign, supporting Robyn as a very good local community candidate. The Labor Party was not mentioned. The community was confronted with a choice between 'Our' Robyn, a local community candidate, and a stereotypical Liberal Party male candidate. It worked, with the Labor vote increasing by nearly 12 per cent. In two-party preferred votes, the swing was 8.63 per cent, which was a terrific outcome. The political class was stunned but believed the result to be an aberration, although when we repeated the feat in Florey at the 1997 election they conceded the effectiveness of our tactics.

The preference flow had obviously been critical to the outcome and if the flow had been reversed, Geraghty would have lost. One effect of this victory was that some in the State Caucus feared that, buoyed by the Torrens result, Lynn Arnold might have 'done a Hawke', and decided to stay on as Leader. That was never going to happen, but it demonstrates the impact the winning of the Torrens by-election had on the overall state political climate.

In September 1994, Julie and I were having a meal with Don Dunstan at his restaurant Don's Table, which had opened in Norwood earlier in the year. I was, no doubt, still delighted by the result in the Torrens by-election and discussing the result. Lynn Arnold was either about to resign as Opposition Leader or had already done so in favour of Mike Rann. It was in this context that the subject of Lynn Arnold as Leader of the Labor Party came up in discussion. Don expressed his disappointment in Bannon, whose elevation to premier had been supported by both Don and me as the replacement for Des Corcoran after the 1979 election loss. Don indicated that in retrospect, he wished that Corcoran's premiership had lasted a few years longer, meaning that his successor might then have been Lynn Arnold.

The year 1995 was the jubilee of the end of the Second World War and the Australian Government wanted to suitably mark the occasion, although it was felt that the word 'jubilee' was rather too celebratory to mark such a solemn occasion. The Minister for Veterans Affairs, the irrepressible Con Sciacca, named the occasion 'Australia Remembers', which was entirely appropriate. Con and his wife Tina were friends of ours, despite Con being a member of the Queensland Right faction and a Hawke supporter. It was decided that as part of the commemoration, each electorate would receive $200,000, via the local member, for expenditure on suitable commemorative projects. Many members unwisely, in my opinion, simply spent the funds on memorials. In Makin, I conceived the idea of an 'Australia Remembers' walking path along the Torrens River at Tea Tree Gully. The existing path was partly managed by the Tea Tree Gully Council, but needed surface upgrading, more trees, seating and signage. The council agreed to contribute funds and a beautiful walkway was created, with recognition for local Tea Tree Gully citizens who had served or sacrificed their lives during the war. My enthusiasm for Australia Remembers was not in conflict with my general pacifism. The Second World War was the only war in modern times that, in my judgement, could be justified.

The Australian election was held on 2 March 1996, and in my electorate of 85,000 I was defeated by 700 votes, although the swing in Makin was only four per cent by comparison with about 10 per cent across the nation. In Frank Walker's seat, Robertson, the swing was more than 10 per cent. On an overnight campaign visit to Adelaide, about 14 days out from the election, I had arranged for Prime Minister Paul Keating to visit Makin and make an unannounced walk-through at the Golden Grove Shopping Centre, just after it opened at 9.30 am. Keating would have been followed by the press corps during the visit, and if the response of the locals was seen as positive, it could have been something of a reset point for the election and for Paul, who, by that stage, no doubt knew that the polling was bad. I had arranged for ALP members and my supporters in the area to be doing their shopping early that morning. Some had even taken time off work to be present and Paul would have been guaranteed a warm welcome. He didn't need to speak, as it was just a walk-through and glad-handing event, with potentially good positive media coverage.

Unfortunately, Paul, who in any event hated meaningless shopping centre visits, had experienced an unfortunate incident during a similar visit in Peter Knott's NSW electorate of Gilmore during the 1993 election: the 'cunt from the cake shop' episode. Paul pulled the pin and refused to make the visit to Makin. I spoke to Paul's senior staffer, Bill Bowtell, whom I knew well, and he tried to change the prime minister's mind, but without success. I then attempted to speak to Keating himself, but he refused the call. I know what pressure party leaders are under during election campaigns, but I was very disappointed in Paul's attitude. I felt that he was equating my political judgement with the lamentable Peter Knott.

I was expecting this Australian election to be tough, but I never expected to lose. My belief in my capacity for victory was based partly on ego, partly denial of reality and partly on my knowledge of smart electioneering. What I didn't appreciate was how much the government's support had declined. Nonetheless, my friend Joan Bullock, a Liberal operator, had indicated that her party didn't consider Makin winnable against me and, as a result, none of their prospective highflyer candidates with personal money and support was lining up. In the event, the candidate was a local woman, Trish Draper. I had helped Trish as a constituent several times when she was living on unemployment benefits. The Liberal campaign was almost non-existent, and I was expecting a reasonable flow of preferences from the minor candidates. In this context I was feeling reasonably positive when I returned from Canberra a couple of weeks before election day.

I had always worked hard and done my best as a member of parliament and had achieved a great deal in my career. When I looked back in 1996, I saw a great body of work of which I could be proud. In Makin, I had assisted thousands of people and dozens of community groups. It may be the case that most of that work goes unrecorded by history but, in 1996, I felt great satisfaction in knowing what I had done and what had been achieved to make a difference to the lives of the community at large. I went into parliament to derive some satisfaction from undertaking good works and for no other purpose. I had few regrets and no feeling of being cheated by an ungrateful electorate. Makin was a marginal seat, meaning that, with a change in government, such seats change hands every so often.

The emotional shock of losing was quickly followed by the terrible sadness of dealing with the much-loved and totally loyal staff, who had lost their jobs and income, compounded by my feelings of having let them down. All of them were all incredibly competent people in their various fields and soon enough found new employment, which extended their skills and talents. Robyn Geraghty was already in the South Australian Parliament as the Member for Torrens and Frances Bedford was soon to be the very successful Member for Florey. They had both learned well whatever lessons were to be had from working for me, particularly my emphasis on serving the community. One great disappointment for me was never seeing Deirdre Tedmanson preselected for a winnable seat. In my opinion she was equipped with the ability and skills to have become premier; it was only the factional system or, more precisely, the emerging deal between the Right and the Bolkus Left that denied Deirdre the opportunity to serve the state and the people of South Australia.

Apart from staff, practical issues needed to be dealt with urgently. I had a parliamentary secretary's office in Parliament House, which was equivalent to a ministerial office. The office had to be cleaned out but with no paid staff, as all staff salary travel rights ended on election day. Cleaning out all the files and other detritus, accumulated over 13 years in the Australian Parliament, was no easy task and had to be completed before the declaration of the polls. Of course, the newly elected members were anxious to claim their offices and get to work. Julie and I undertook the mammoth task of sorting and cleaning. I remember that this work was assisted by Georgia, then about four years old, who was enjoying herself playing amongst the piles of paper and in the bins. The Department of the Parliament was only too anxious to provide us with wheelie bins for the material judged surplus to requirements, but harassed us to empty and return the numbered filing cabinets. Julie and I had to buy several filing cabinets and then relocate the files I was keeping to these new cabinets and transport them to our Canberra house in Kingston. A similar exercise had to be undertaken in Adelaide, with the accumulation of material from 25 years in two parliaments. Of course, my files from Elizabeth had not been culled properly in the years since I had ceased being the Member for Elizabeth and had merely been stored in the Makin office.

A priority for us was to determine the fate of the Canberra house, and that decision depended on whether I would run for Makin again at the next election. The house, which had four bedrooms, had also been the Canberra accommodation for Jim Hyde and Frank Walker, as well as for sundry friends and comrades passing through the ACT. If I was to run again, we would keep the Canberra house and rent it for, we hoped, the interregnum of three years. I was clearly the Labor Party's best chance of winning back the seat, although that might not have been the view of those running the South Australian Labor Party. As Dunstan had painfully discovered, it is amazing how quickly your power dissipates once you have made the transfer from rooster to feather duster. Nonetheless, I was pretty sure that the National Executive would have intervened to prevent any local move designed to deny me preselection. However, I was not sure that I wanted to submit myself to such an ordeal. I was exhausted after the election campaign and recognised that I was not in the best shape for making major decisions. My immediate realisation was that my parliamentary career was over, although I was only 51 and had plenty of working life ahead of me. Just how much I hadn't calculated!

Julie, by that time a lecturer at the University of South Australia, came up with the solution. We would take a few weeks off and travel to Europe and visit our friend, the former premier Lynn Arnold and his family, who by this time had relocated to Spain. Julie took leave and together with Georgia, who was just a bit too young to fully appreciate the visit, we headed off for what was, in anybody's terms, a well-earned rest.

To run or not to run again in Makin was discussed endlessly by me and Julie. She had probably had enough of politics by then and the endless grind of holding and finally losing a marginal seat, but typically she was careful not to allow her feelings to influence the decision-making. If I was to run again, I would need to establish a campaign office within six months and start the cycle of campaigning. Could I be sure I would win? Probably, given the margin and that Howard's deficiencies would have been exposed by then. In addition, I had little faith in Trish Draper's capacity to make speeches and felt that after three years her inadequacies would have been revealed. That said, I hadn't counted on the Liberal Party's astuteness in filling her office with minders. I wanted to continue what I considered my life's work – supporting the underdog and implementing decent policy to protect the environment and South Australia's lifestyle. Could I sit outside the action while I still had some enthusiasm and energy left? There was of course the further issue of whether I would be selected for the ministry even if I won Makin back.

I wasn't much interested in being in Canberra simply to make up the numbers if Labor won government. The new Labor Leader was Kim Beazley, no friend of mine in factional or personal terms, and I could expect no favours in that direction. With Labor in Opposition, would I be elected to the Shadow Cabinet? The prospects of getting onto the frontbench appeared bleak. I would be even less likely to have majority support in the Parliamentary Left than I had enjoyed in the recent past. In addition, my soul mate Frank Walker had also been defeated in the 1996 election – with an even larger swing against him. He saw no prospect of winning his seat back and was planning to seek a judicial appointment from the NSW Labor Government. Those cold Canberra nights appeared bitter indeed.

In the end, I decided against continuing with a parliamentary career.

CHAPTER FIFTEEN

# Post-parliament

As I explained, I expected the March 1996 federal election to be tough, but I did not anticipate losing. I was now forced to make a decision about a career after politics. Dunstan had provided a poor example of someone who had derived satisfaction from a post-parliamentary life, but on the other hand Lynn Arnold appeared to provide a more positive example. But what would I do? Foolishly, I hadn't made any plans for this contingency. I had believed in my invincibility as Member for Makin.

Although I was still a non-active partner of the law firm, after the excitement and achievements of being in the parliament, going back to legal work offered no attraction. Apart from that, there were real problems with the arrangements that would apply. I would have to earn my keep, and some of the firm's union clients were not factionally aligned with me, while my physical presence could potentially see some clients leave. Upon my return from Europe, I decided to sell my share in the law firm, a firm I'd successfully established 26 years earlier and which still bears my name. It was quite possible, if I'd expressed an interest, that the new Liberal Government would appoint me to the Federal Court. I was on quite good terms with Peter Costello, the new Treasurer, and it was likely the Libs would have offered me an appointment to protect Trish Draper. Financially, I didn't need to work and could have gone fishing, but that wasn't me. That I didn't need to work permitted me to move in a new direction: there were many small charities or organisations pursuing worthwhile causes in need of an executive but which couldn't pay market-rate salaries.

Julie and I had purchased a property in Hobart, which we considered might provide a second home following parliamentary life. Julie was a Tasmanian through and through and greatly missed the Apple Isle. She used to say she had sacrificed the life she loved for the love of her life. We fantasised about having a main house in Adelaide and another in Hobart, rather like other people have a holiday house at the beach. This, however, was all to occur after an orderly retirement for both of us, in another decade or so. Sadly, unknown to us at the time, Julie had less than a decade to live.

As I explained earlier, at the end of March 1996, the three of us flew to Spain to catch up with Lynn Arnold and his family. Getting away from Adelaide allowed us to escape the pall of the election loss on a day-to-day basis. It was always easy for us to go away at relatively short notice as we had no pets, a situation that Georgia raised in later life when attempting to illustrate her deprived childhood. Jim Hyde lived next door and looked after our house in Adelaide, and Kath and Sam, Julie's parents, looked after our property in Hobart. The Canberra house was easily locked up and left. Julie and I had spent time and money on Spanish lessons, encouraged by our Adelaide Chilean friends and comrades. Julie could just about converse. I, on the other hand, could utter only a few words.

We arrived in Barcelona to great spring weather. It was Georgia's first real trip overseas – she was aged just four. She was quite accustomed to air travel between Adelaide and Hobart, Canberra and Cairns etc., but this was a very big deal. In Barcelona, we wandered the famous La Rambla and visited a memorial to the International Brigade – the only political activity we undertook in Europe. We then hired a car and drove north to the town where Lynn and Elaine Arnold were staying while Lynn studied Spanish. The Arnolds were great hosts, generous and warm; Lynn, understanding the stresses of an immediate post-parliamentary life, was very supportive of me and my problem of how to fill the remainder of my working life.

We then travelled south, down the Mediterranean coast, visiting Valencia, beautiful Denia, Alicante, Malaga, Marbella and Gibraltar. We then cut inland to Granada, Seville and Cordoba, where we visited the cathedral built in the centre of a large and ancient mosque, which impressed me and Julie enormously as a great example of religious triumphalism. Then to Toledo and Madrid. From Madrid we went to Morocco, flying into Casablanca, which after the movie was a big disappointment. After this to Marrakech, where the pink city certainly lived up to its reputation as a wonderful desert city. Julie loved the four days we spent wandering around the streets at sunset or sunrise before or after the heat and lazing around the pool during the day. We were planning to go on to Fez, but unfortunately ran out of time. We then flew to Lisbon in Portugal or 'Portubul', as a very young Georgia pronounced it. Portugal was, I think, the highlight for Georgia. She already had a love of shoes and was in heaven when we bought her a pair of high-heeled espadrille shoes. It was then time to return home, rested and reinvigorated and having made some headway in the big decisions about my future working life.

I returned thinking that it might be possible to do some good works through business, by using my talents and my contacts. Some types of business obviously had positive outcomes for the community. At no stage did I consider setting up a consultancy to use my contacts to provide paid access to ministers. Similarly, unlike some ministers who used their time in office to do favours for interest groups in order to ensure jobs or board appointments following their parliamentary life, I never made any such arrangements. I believe this to be a corrupt practice and it should be recognised as such. If it is beyond prosecution under criminal law because of absence of evidence, then the law should be changed to ban ex-members and senior public servants from obtaining benefit from the private sectors in which they once operated. This ban would need to extend for 10 years after leaving the parliament or the public service. Tough, clear, and sensible.

I thought that, with my 'have a go', or as John Cornwall used to call it, 'crazy brave', approach, I had some special talents which might be of benefit to many businesses. I was a good problem-solver and decision-maker, rare skills in many quarters. My lifelong comrade, David Wilson, reminded me that 'good socialists should never become capitalists and rarely do so successfully'. I should have listened to his sage advice. My perhaps reckless response was 'if you're not prepared to be wrong, you'll never come up with anything original'. It seems that most often people with a crazy brave gene either fail dismally and burn, or reach great heights and soar. I offer John Cornwall, Don Dunstan and myself as the exhibits.

While overseas, Julie and I considered a suggestion Tim Ferrier had made back in 1989 about building units on our land in Port Douglas. After we had sold the bar back to the previous owner, Tim Ferrier had sold us a large house block in Davidson Street. We recalled that he had spoken about an architect or building consultant who specialised in medium-sized developments. We obtained his contact details and arranged to meet following our return from Europe in April 1996. After discussions with him, we commissioned him to design a unit development suitable for the property. Three months later, he produced draft plans for a 34-unit building and pool – 33 one-bedroom units for sale and a manager's unit.

While in Port Douglas, we had breakfast with the birds one morning at the Port Douglas Wildlife Habitat, which includes a butterfly area, giving Julie the idea of a butterfly as the symbol of our 'Freestyle Apartment' complex. All was going well, except that the off-the-plan sales had unexpectedly come to a halt and we started to panic. Tim Ferrier, who was unhappy that we were now using new Port Douglas-based sales agents, suggested that we might contact a firm of super marketeers in Brisbane for assistance with the sales. They were indeed super marketeers, agreeing to sell the Freestyle units on their terms, which included sole listing of all the remaining units and paying us our asking price for all the units. Furthermore, what they charged as commission was no longer our business. They contracted to sell the remaining units in four months. True to their promise, all units were sold within this timeframe. Their marketing approach involved full-colour full-page advertisements in Friday's *Financial Review*, a focus on a list of self-funded retirees and a 10 per cent income guarantee for two years. Prospective purchasers were flown, free of charge, to Port Douglas and we were told that everyone who took the flight became a purchaser. The original agents, who had been working to sell the management rights to Jason and Anne Moore, succeeded in making a sale and Jason and Anne are still the managers to this day. The original marketing material, still in use, tells the story: 'Enjoy heaven. Wander down Davidson St and find Freestyle Apartments with a large butterfly symbol out front.' It was our beautiful development, and we were very happy that we had achieved a high-standard development, where all players were satisfied. It made a very good profit, which, sadly, we subsequently poured into our dream of a plastic-recycling business, which at the time I believed would clean up the world's plastic-waste problem.

Lynn Arnold, by now head of World Vision, had offered to keep an eye out for any positions that might suit my talents. Early in 1997, he contacted me, suggesting that I approach Overseas Pharmaceutical Aid for Life (OPAL). A small charity, it had been set up by Geoff and Dara Lockyer, who although good people were struggling to get the organisation onto a stable footing. I contacted Geoff, who was expecting my call. All medicine packaging has a use-by date stamped on the packaging, after which it becomes illegal to sell the medicine – and of course outdated pharmaceuticals should not be used. About three months before medicine expires, the practice was for pharmacists to return the product to the manufacturer for disposal. What OPAL was doing was collecting these in-date, but short-dated, pharmaceuticals from pharmacies in Adelaide and, in effect, recycling them, mainly to Christian charities in small Pacific Island states. I met with Geoff and Dara Lockyer, and OPAL seemed like a worthwhile exercise. So, I agreed to become chairperson and became involved.

I contacted people I knew in the SA Health Department from my days as minister and identified the officer who had responsibility for ensuring that outdated medicines were not being sold or used. He seemed to be the starting point for exploring the future and was sympathetic. He was concerned that vast amounts of pharmaceuticals were being disposed into refuse collection or into sewerage systems by pharmacies and perhaps manufacturers, explaining that this was a major environmental problem, as well as potentially a health problem. He suggested that, if OPAL could set up a collection system for outdated or damaged pharmaceuticals, we could possibly collect short-dated medicines at the same time. This could be done for a small fee and would provide an income stream for OPAL. However, there was one further problem. He knew that before my time, OPAL had been sending expired pharmaceuticals overseas and that Geoff Lockyer had fraudulently signed declarations certifying that the medicines for export were in-date. If I could ensure no breaches in future, he was prepared to overlook past practices. I assured him that there would be no further breaches of the rules. To this end, I had a conversation with Geoff, who admitted to the breaches but viewed the situation very differently. He felt the bureaucracy was 'getting in the way of God's work'.

I was contacted by the Pharmacy Guild, which was being pursued by the Australian Government to set up a pharmaceutical waste-collection arrangement and saw OPAL as a potential partner in the provision of such a facility. It was becoming clear that there were two streams of possible development, the waste-collection stream with potential to provide an income stream, and the charity provision of short-dated medicines to needy people in poor countries. Could the two be married? I decided to give it my best shot.

Trish Worth, the Liberal Member for Adelaide, and a former pharmacist, was very keen on the undertaking and with her support a grant of $1 million was obtained from the Howard Government as seed capital, on one condition. The organisation to receive the grant had to be an amalgam of the Pharmacy Guild and OPAL. Given that I had written the grant application and that it was in the name of OPAL, either the Guild had more political power than I anticipated, or the bureaucracy had intervened because they didn't trust OPAL. I suspect the latter. In light of the conditional grant, OPAL and the Pharmacy Guild met and agreed to form a new organisation. Accordingly, a new body was established with a board, half of whose membership was nominated by the Guild, with the remaining half by OPAL, with myself as Chair. Geoff Lockyer was unhappy with this arrangement and sadly declined a seat on the board of the joint organisation. The aims and objectives of the new organisation were:

> OPAL Return Unwanted Medicines Limited is a national not-for-profit company with objectives to collect and destroy unwanted and out-of-date medicines in an environmentally friendly manner and to recycle the packaging; AND to source and collect in-date medicines from manufacturers and wholesalers for the purpose of humanitarian aid in Australia and overseas in compliance with World Health Organization and Australian Pharmaceutical Advisory Committee guidelines. Opal Return Unwanted Medicines Limited subcontracts Overseas Pharmaceutical Aid for Life Inc for its overseas aid program.

The national organisation, once established, progressed well. Sadly, OPAL and Geoff Lockyer, the originator of the whole idea, was left in Adelaide, battling with insufficient funds and OPAL eventually collapsed. I stayed as executive chair of the national body, Opal Return Unwanted Medicines Limited, until 2000, at which time it was well and truly established. It later changed its name to RUM (Return Unwanted Medicines) and sadly severed all connection with OPAL and Geoff's worthy dream of unwanted pharmaceuticals to the world's poor.

During our trip to Spain, Portugal and Morocco, we had encountered some fabulous restaurant precincts. In Denia, in Spain, we had visited a seaside restaurant precinct in which a number of separately owned and managed kitchens provided seafood and Italian, French, and Lebanese cuisine and operated side by side in buildings located in the large area abutting the ocean. The tables and chairs were set out in front of the kitchens, with the restaurant tables and chairs and waiters operated by an entity separate from the kitchens. The expansive menu had dishes from each of the kitchens, waitstaff took orders on hand-held computer monitors and the orders were delivered via Wi-Fi to the kitchens. When the food was ready to be served, the waiter collected the food from the relevant kitchen. In other words, people at the same table could eat seafood and Lebanese from different kitchens.

Following our return from Europe in the middle of 1996, I had the idea of attempting to establish a similar facility in Victoria Square in Adelaide, a part of the city that had never really taken off. Under the original plan, Victoria Square was to be the city centre, but it never attained that status. A department store had been established in Victoria Square but once the railway station had been constructed on North Terrace, Rundle

Street became the city retail precinct. The Hilton Hotel had been built on Victoria Square during the Dunstan Government and most government departments were in the vicinity. I concluded that it might be possible to successfully establish a restaurant precinct for alfresco dining, similar to the Denia facility, in the northwest corner of Victoria Square.

Adelaide's Mediterranean climate appeared suitable for large-scale outdoor dining, with gas overhead heaters providing a solution in cooler weather. Adelaide actually has few rainy days. I spoke to the Lord Mayor, Jane Lomax-Smith, who was enthusiastic. Victoria Square was jokingly referred to as 'the dead centre' of Adelaide and my proposal seemed to offer a real prospect of adding some life to the square. The idea appealed to my better instincts. It was a private business proposal that was designed to improve the ambience of Adelaide. I mightn't be in public life anymore, but I could still undertake good works. As part of the preparations necessary to get the project up and running, the Adelaide City Council upgraded the northwest corner of the square, basically to our specifications. We leased the shops abutting the precinct for the creation of four kitchens and we raised some funds. Fast-growing plane trees were planted, and the necessary restaurant furniture was ordered for a 400-cover facility. The special computer system crucial to the concept was ordered. Four leading well-known Adelaide restaurateurs were recruited to operate the kitchens and waiting staff were recruited and trained. All seemed to be in place. Paul Bennett, a friend of Julie's, was appointed as manager and John Kerr, from Tasmania, became the cuisine manager to ensure quality and cleanliness of the highest order. Unfortunately, he resigned to return to Tasmania six weeks before opening, after we had been paying him for almost a year.

The *Advertiser* had covered the plans and the development in a fairly negative manner from the outset: 'Roadworks on Victoria Square disrupts traffic' and so on. While its coverage included commentary on whether the council should be supporting this type of development, there was no recognition that the project would add life to Victoria Square, or that at last there would be a facility taking advantage of Adelaide's Mediterranean climate.

The precinct opened in September 1997, and we were expecting to have a good spring and summer season to set us up financially. The first two weeks of income and patronage were above budget, and we were getting really good reviews. Although the technology had some teething problems, we seemed to have the various issues under control. On the third Friday following the opening, Paul Bennett was able to arrange for the Tasmanian Symphony Orchestra, which was in Adelaide for a concert series, to give a free prom concert in the precinct at lunchtime. We were very excited at this prospect and advertised the event widely. The weather turned out to be perfect. Unfortunately, our planning for the event was disastrous. The orchestra had been advertised as playing between 1 pm and 2 pm. We hadn't insisted on bookings, nor did we make any arrangements to stagger the arrival of guests. By 12.45 pm around 50 guests were seated in the restaurant precinct, with the number increasing to 400 by 1 pm, with many more prospective diners milling around. The orchestra was great. That was the best thing that could be said about the whole day. The restaurant systems collapsed, the kitchens ran out of ingredients and patrons were criticising the waiters unstintingly. It was hard to get a drink and people left without having eaten.

The word 'catastrophe' comes to mind. On the following day, the *Advertiser* reported the fiasco on the front page with a 'we told you so' tone. The business, which we'd called 'Round the Square', never recovered. As people in the industry know, the rarest commodity in the restaurant business is a second chance. People are not forgiving, and the precinct never recovered from that single disaster and the bad publicity it generated. If I had not been involved, perhaps the headlines would not have been so large or so negative. To add to our woes, that spring turned out to be quite wet.

The project struggled on, but within a year it was obvious that we had to cut our losses, and the precinct closed. Friends and comrades who had invested lost $350,000, and Julie and I a similar amount. Paul Bennett was down $100,000. The Commonwealth Bank had lent the company $300,000 and held a chattel mortgage over the fittings. The bank auctioned off all the tables and chairs, umbrellas and computers and there was nothing left for the shareholders. I am still devastated at the losses made by friends. Most were generous in their response, but a few, understandably, were unforgiving. So, my dream of developing an innovative alfresco dining space for Adelaide disintegrated into a financial mess. The *Advertiser* and the *News* danced on the grave of Round the Square, with Colin James reporting in the former on 13 August 2002, 'people invested after being guaranteed a minimum return of 10 per cent'. I don't know where that figure had come from and it had certainly never been promised.

As the 1997 state election approached, the Labor Party was dysfunctional: it was short of funds and was still suffering the electoral drag caused by the State Bank disaster, although Mike Rann, by then Leader of the Opposition, was doing a good job attempting to unite the party. The former head of the Drug Squad, Sam Bass, was the Liberal Member for Florey, one of the state seats within the boundaries of Makin, my former federal electorate. Following the last general election, Florey needed a swing of more than 11 per cent for a Labor victory. A member of my former staff, Frances Bedford, was seeking preselection and because nobody else was much interested, Frances became the candidate. I was thrilled by this, as I thought Frances was a great local candidate, with a real chance of winning.

Running a successful campaign against Bass had two side benefits. Years ago, Sam Bass had attempted to discredit me when I was Attorney-General. As a sergeant in the Drug Squad, he had led a raid on the home of my senior private secretary, Peter O'Brien, an incident described earlier in the book. The election provided an opportunity to exact a small revenge. In addition, Bass had earlier offered me an arrangement whereby he promised not to campaign against me if I returned the favour. He had breached the agreement in 1996 by campaigning for Trish Draper.

Bass didn't believe he could lose. The general polling was showing a swing against the Liberal Government of about three per cent. An amount of more than 11 per cent looked to be impossible. But we set about applying the smart electioneering processes that had worked earlier. Frances had an engaging personality and was hard working and enthusiastic. (Frances, who describes herself as 'my prodigy', was one of the group of friends, along with Julie, who provided domestic and other support for Don Dunstan in his last months.) She let me get on with running her campaign, as campaign manager, without interference. Her corflute posters were colourful and very much in evidence, but corflute posters have never won an election. Their purpose is to present the candidate as warm and to give the voters a feeling of familiarity, and we achieved both.

Sam Bass had attempted to amend John Howard's gun legislation to allow semi-automatics to continue to be available throughout Australia. We produced a cardboard cut-out pamphlet, about 400 mm long with a photo of a very nasty-looking Sars special semi-automatic gun. The slogan 'Sam Bass wants these guns on your streets' was devastating in areas where there were large numbers of voters with children. Furthermore, Bass had attended a Parliamentary Speakers' conference on the Pacific Island of Nauru, an obvious junket since he wasn't the Speaker. Capitalising on this, we distributed a postcard with a cartoon of Bass sunning himself with a cocktail and bearing the message 'This is the postcard Sam Bass should have sent to you from Nauru, to thank you for paying for his junket'. By this stage, Bass was feeling under siege and stupidly allowed himself to be photographed with the postcard, complaining that it was unfair. Really? The local free newspaper ran the story with a photo. We were getting traction. We then produced a pamphlet called 'The Free Travel Times', which implored the voters to 'bring the frequent flyer down to earth, put Sam Bass last'. Finally, a card was distributed listing 'Three (bad) things Sam Bass has done', and on the back 'Three perks Sam Bass will qualify for if re-elected. Don't reward the rorter'.

We also paid particular attention to the Independents who were running. People often ignore the impact a candidate's personality can have on third-party decisions on preferences. Frances Bedford is a genuinely nice person, which is immediately obvious when you meet her. Sam Bass didn't seem to present as well, making it easy to convince the Independents to preference Frances on their how to vote cards. The two-party swing to Labor was 12.3 per cent. For every five Independents, or third-party votes, she received approximately three preferences and Bass only two. We didn't know that Frances had won on election night, but it was looking pretty good. Ultimately, Labor won by about 500 votes. It was a stunning outcome and left the political class utterly astonished and somewhat in awe. Joan Bullock, a Liberal MP, told me that people in the SA Parliament on both sides had been saying that if Duncan is running the campaign none of us are safe. Quentin Black, the Labor candidate for Hartley, who lost by a small margin, claimed the one mistake he had made was not to have Peter Duncan as his campaign manager.

Some talk of an appeal to the Court of Disputed Returns circulated, but it came to nothing, although Bass took our comrades and supporters Geoff Roberts and Ken Case to court, claiming defamation over pamphlets they had authorised. We provided Geoff and Ken with legal support and the matter eventually ended up in the High Court, where we finally won, with Stuart Littlemore, QC, as our barrister. The court case bankrupted Bass.

This election win – seeing Bass off and Frances elected – was the high point of my career as a marginal seat campaigner. In the 1997 general election for Torrens, Robyn Geraghty, whose campaign I had managed, gained an additional 12 per cent swing on top of the swing we had achieved in the 1994 by-election. Graham Richardson described me as the best marginal seat campaigner in the country and I am delighted to take such plaudits ... even from Richo (one hand clapping).

At the 1998 Australian election, the singer–songwriter John Schumann, a friend at the time, was considering running as an Australian Democrat candidate. He wasn't sure which seat to choose and sought my advice. John was reasonably well known in South Australia and was obviously a star candidate for the Democrats. The only problem with John was his ego, and because of that he was reluctant to take advice. Initially, he wanted to run in Kingston. When I explained that he needed to choose a safe seat and preferably a conservative-held seat, he believed that I was attempting to dissuade him from running in a seat where Labor had a chance of winning. Eventually, after about two weeks and several conversations with me and Julie, and probably others, he finally understood that he needed to run in a safe seat, take votes from the incumbent and win by coming in second and then rely on preferences to get over the line.

He finally decided on Mayo and then asked me to be his campaign manager. We sat down and I tried to explain the many problems with that proposition. While I was delighted to support him, I realised that if my involvement became public it would have sunk John's campaign. The incumbent, Alexander Downer, would have portrayed the Democrats as a Labor front. Another problem for John was that his confidence had him believing that his popularity would sweep him to victory. Julie and I and Frances Bedford gave him a tutorial on campaigning. I don't know how much sank in, not a lot, I suspect. However, before I committed to becoming his campaign director, I convinced him to undertake a survey. We did the survey 'in house' by training some supporters. The polling had the desired effect: five per cent of the individuals surveyed had heard of John Schumann; Redgum, his band, rated much better but the band's name wasn't going to be on the ballot paper. John had been having some issues with other band members at the time and the survey came as a tremendous shock. I suspect he thought of John Schumann and Redgum, rather than Redgum, featuring John Schumann. The survey, however, introduced a bit of reality, at least for a time. I agreed to provide strategic advice for him but refused to formally be his campaign manager. I specifically told him not to tell the Democrats of my assistance. I think John was happy to keep our secret. It meant he was able to take credit for whatever advice and material we provided. He knew of my difficulties with sections of the Labor Party, but despite that, John just couldn't understand that if I campaigned for him and it leaked, I could be expelled from the ALP.

The relationship bubbled along, with meetings between me, Julie and John and no other members of his team. I think we finally convinced him that, strategically, he needed to poison Downer's standing in order to reduce the Liberal first preference vote. John's inclination was to run a campaign boosting himself. He couldn't see that wasn't a winning strategy. The only successful strategy would be one that reduced Downer's first preference vote down to a percentage in the low 40s. Everybody hates negative campaigning because it works. We put together pamphlets for his use and Julie wrote press releases and copy for the printed material, mainly getting stuck into Downer. John still wanted material starring himself and wasted scarce resources doing so. Another initial problem was convincing the Labor candidate not to campaign too vigorously. The critical issue for Labor in terms of defeating Downer was to come in behind Schumann, and some work behind the scenes achieved that objective.

One of our team went to the public meeting of the One Nation candidate, who, according to our polling, was doing well. We discovered that the candidate, Lea Peacock, had a campaign that was little more than an idea and a box of stationary. One Nation had no on-the-ground organisation whatsoever. Our man (who shall remain nameless) generously offered to assist in the campaign and also offered to have how to vote cards printed, both of which offers Peacock readily accepted. The selected preferences were supplied by candidate Peacock. Unfortunately, the printer made a mistake, placing Schumann above Downer on the how to vote card, which, furthermore, did not arrive until the Friday night before polling day, meaning, happily, that it was too late to have them reprinted. Peacock was so relieved by the arrival of the how to vote cards that the 'mistake' was soon forgotten.

On election day, One Nation workers were in evidence at all booths and One Nation gained a respectable 7.33 per cent and passed about 65 per cent of preferences to Schumann. One Nation preferences normally split 55 per cent to the Liberals. All in all, it was a fun campaign. In the end we were short of fewer than 3,000 votes – or the fewer than 1,500 voters who needed to change their vote, a small number from the nearly 90,000 votes cast. More focus on attacking Downer might have changed the result. The fact that Mayo was in play for a non-Liberal candidate was demonstrated in 2018 by the Independent Rebekha Sharkie winning the by-election and subsequently holding onto the seat. Whatever the case, we gave the Downer dynasty one hell of a fright.

On 28 July 1998, my mother Phyllis Margaret Duncan died. She had lived a long life and she died relatively peacefully, spending her last few years in a nursing home, now referred to as an aged care facility. I had looked after the administrative arrangements, and I think that her time in the nursing home was happy enough, as she had friends there with similar interests. In later life, she suffered from epilepsy, although it was quite well controlled. All in all, Phyl was an excellent mother, giving us a great start in life. With the benefit of hindsight, I can see how my mother, an intelligent and sensitive person, had her life constrained and constricted by the 1950s culture – to which she subscribed – that a woman's place is in the home. My only criticism of her was her desire to impress those around her. For example, even in the nursing home, years after the event, she would still introduce me to residents or guests and the family of residents as 'my son the Attorney-General', although I do also recognise that she was proud of her son. I understand that if my father had lived for another decade or so, my mother may have been a different person in her later life. Like so many wives during the 1950s, she saw her role as an appendage of my father. I don't think that she ever recovered from the loss or adjusted to living her life alone after he died aged 57 in 1971.

In November 1999, the Australian Government contacted Opal Return Unwanted Medicines to determine whether it would accept a contract, at very short notice, to travel to East Timor to re-establish the central pharmaceutical facility in Dili, which had been looted and burned by the Indonesian militia prior to the arrival of INTERFET, the international peace-keeping force led by Australia. We were delighted to accept. I had been a supporter of Fretilin from the outset and saw Whitlam's tacit agreement to the Indonesian Government's invasion as an appalling betrayal. Astonishingly, Prime Minister Howard – of all people – was attempting to right the terrible wrong inflicted on the East Timorese people by the international community, and particularly Australia. Here was a chance to play a small role in the turmoil that was unfolding.

With the contract signed by mid-December, Geoff Lockyer and I headed for Darwin with cases packed with medicines, a small refrigerator and sundry other equipment. We planned to stay for five weeks. We caught an RAAF flight from Darwin and arrived in Dili, not knowing what to expect. The disarray was shocking. We stayed for a few days on the hotel ship that had been anchored in Dili harbour to accommodate UN personnel, and then moved to the shipping container hotel that an enterprising Australian had managed to construct within a few weeks of the arrival of the INTERFET troops.

The Central Pharmacy building was a burned-out shell, with the rafters gone and only the walls standing, although fortunately the steel shelving attached to the walls was still in place. It was a terrific time to be attempting to achieve something worthwhile in Dili. Our contract allowed us to order building materials from suppliers in Darwin and have them consigned to the RAAF, which was running an air-transport service from Darwin to Dili. Delivery only took 48 hours. After calculating what was required, we contacted a hardware supplier in Darwin and ordered timber, paint, corrugated iron roofing, nails and guttering and sundry other materials. Cement was available in Dili from Indonesia. Within a few days, we had a team of East Timorese builders. They were not skilled in Australian terms but were well able to undertake the building work needed to an adequate standard. We made excellent progress and had a room with pharmaceuticals available within three weeks, completing the building work and opening the facility within five weeks. Geoff stayed a further two weeks to receive the pharmaceuticals ordered earlier and to hand over the facility to local pharmacists, identified by us during our stay. Notably, with the collapse of the local society, the original staff of the central pharmaceutical facility had simply disappeared. This had been a great and satisfying project for my post-parliamentary life.

While working for OPAL, I met Malcolm Barnes, who had a factory adjoining OPAL's Adelaide premises. With a very likeable nature, Malcolm was a farmer and a greenie, a rare combination. He owned a sheep station, Mt Bryan, near Oodnadatta, as well as a very large 10,000-hectare wheat property on Eyre Peninsula, near Wudinna. Barnes had inherited these properties from his father, along with a large share portfolio. Unreliable rainfall meant that the Wudinna property was in marginal wheat-growing country but the approach his father had taken – using the income from the share portfolio – enabled a wheat crop to be planted each year.

Malcolm had wanted to extend his business activities into green industries and had invested in a number of projects, which included a start-up road-building business using rubber recovered from old tyres, as well as a process called Omnipol, by which unsorted or comingled waste plastic could be processed and then used to manufacture useable products, for which there was good commercial demand.

In late 1996, Malcolm introduced me to the Omnipol inventor David Horne and invited me to become chairman of the fledgling company. In retrospect, I foolishly agreed. Julie and I also invested money over the next few years, probably amounting to over $1 million. I am not sure of the exact amount as I no longer have access to the books recording the amounts. Although Omnipol appeared to us to be a great potential business, everybody associated with the company underestimated the capital requirements, and it was always undercapitalised. I asked the obvious question about whether patents had been applied for, and over the next few years poured a great deal of money into patent applications, realising that the business and the process had little value without a patent. Eventually, provisional patents were obtained, just prior to the business going into receivership.

A further problem was whether the company was to be a plastic-recycling company or a manufacturer of Omnipol machines. We decided to focus the business on manufacturing the actual machines, with an associated small business manufacturing plastic product at Gillman. We would use the model plant to show the process to prospective purchasers of Omnipol machines. In retrospect, that might have been a mistake at that stage in the development of the business. Furthermore, there were major structural and personal problems within the company. David Horne, understandably, felt that the whole project was his baby. He only had 34 per cent of the company left at that stage and wasn't inclined to see his shareholding diminished further, while Malcolm Barnes had 50 per cent but was only prepared to sell any shares in a float, which in 1997 was a distant prospect. Julie and I saw Omnipol as an example of outstanding Australian technology, one also with great potential to protect the environment. We thought that it would be a travesty if the usual pattern was followed, whereby great Australian ideas are bought and further developed overseas. We were happy to invest funds, but not without proper protection of our money by way of a substantial shareholding. However, this appeared impossible to achieve in the circumstances.

After the company had drifted from one financial crisis to another, I had the idea of forming another company in which Julie and I could have a shareholding. Omnipol Australia was formed and was given the rights by Omnipol Pty Ltd to use and develop the technology, which it did. The former was the company intended to be floated onto the stock exchange. So, with this unsatisfactory corporate structure, we invested and for a while the group was financially stable. I became a director, and our family company became a shareholder in Omnipol Australia, when it was formed in January 1997.

I had met another Malcolm – Malcolm Turnbull – through Neville Wran, when they were in business together and I thought that he might be a useful contact for exploring the start-up funding possibilities for Omnipol. I arranged to meet him at his office, and he was generous with his time and gave me some useful suggestions about contacts. I much appreciated the assistance and thought that was the conclusion of our contact. I was therefore surprised to receive a phone call from him a few days after our meeting, in which he invited me to lunch next time I was in Sydney. About three weeks later, we met for lunch at Forty-One, an exclusive French restaurant in the Chifley Tower. Over lunch Malcolm explained that he was interested in seeking ALP preselection for Newcastle, where the long-serving member Allan Morris was retiring at the next election, in 2001. He claimed to have considerable support in the ALP (through Neville Wran, I suspect) but that he'd encountered a problem in the form of the local plebiscite and that the Left was very influential and expected to win the preselection.

I explained to Malcolm that what he was asking was almost impossible. Although I still had considerable influence with the NSW Left through my friends, including Frank Walker, the issue was that the NSW Left was culturally wedded to local plebiscite preselection. In my judgement, the NSW Left would be unlikely to allow an attempt to be made to subvert a local vote. I asked Malcolm about joining the Left to obtain its support in the preselection, but this suggestion appeared to ruin his lunch. I had no further contact with him over the matter. He obviously decided to stick with the Liberal Party, a decision which served him well in terms of opportunity.

I returned to Timor in late 2000 and on the flight from Darwin I happened to be seated next to John Sanderson, the head of the Australian military at the time of INTERFET. I knew him from my parliamentary career days and congratulated him on the excellent outcome, particularly the way the Australian troops had rounded up and stopped the Indonesian-trained militia infiltrating from West Timor. He explained that the troops had been:

> greatly assisted by the US, which moved a low-flying, heat-seeking satellite to hover over the border ... and that our platoons had computer monitors showing on heat maps where the militia was operating, and we were able to jump on them as they crossed the border, before they were able to disperse. The militia activity fizzled out in a couple of weeks.

I asked whether he thought the Indonesians realised what was going on. His reply: 'No, and they probably still don't'. His response is particularly interesting in light of subsequent comments from the US Government on their support for the operation, which I assume is what Sanderson was referring to: 'The United States offered crucial logistical and intelligence resources and an "over-horizon" deterrent presence but did not commit forces to the operation'. Finally, as Bill Clinton announced on 11 September 1999, 'I have made clear that my willingness to support future economic assistance from the international community will depend upon how Indonesia handles the situation from today'.

A few months later, in September 2001, we made visits to Indonesia and the Philippines on behalf of Omnipol. What is now the South Australian Water Corporation was vying for a contract to manage and operate a large part of the Jakarta water supply, and we had been introduced to the person in charge of the project, Peter Von Steigler. He spoke Bahasa; was a Muslim for business convenience; and knew all the players in the Jakarta business and political jungle. He was generous with his time, and I suspect he believed I had more political clout back home than was actually the case by that time. He introduced us to several prospects to purchase Omnipol machines and educated us to the realities of doing business in Asia:

> You have to pay. Nothing gets done here without grease money, known as administration fees ... We probably can't win the Jakarta water contract because the decision makers here want the grease up front; and there is no way that I can get money for that purpose out of the South Australian State Government.

Omnipol had a grant from the Australian Government of $100,000 to assist in establishing a sales office in Indonesia and we were getting some valuable help from the Jakarta Embassy staff. I shared their enthusiasm that Indonesia provided a great investment opportunity for Australian businesses, particularly in relation to upgrading the Indonesian services sector. Sadly, that remains the case – unmet need and a capacity on the part of Indonesians to pay for the services that Australia is undoubtedly able to supply. In many respects, Indonesians at the government level and others, particularly outside Jakarta, do not appreciate the need for improved services. The quality of transport, communication, government services and power supply is often poor, and Australia could meet a need on commercial terms.

I had been invited by the Australian Ambassador to a barbecue on the night of 9/11. The ambassador and I, and several others, were on the roof garden of the Embassy, enjoying the ambassador's hospitality when his mobile phone rang. He told us that a plane had flown into the World Trade Centre. A television set was immediately produced, enabling us to watch the carnage on CNN. At that point, it was believed that the event was an accident. Within a few minutes, however, it became clear that it was an attack from some opponent of the US. The ambassador apologised and withdrew to his 'situation room', leaving us with the feeling that a third world war may have begun. CNN soon disabused us of the idea that it was a nation state attack, but the ambassador's initial response gives a hint of what must have been happening in Washington in the first few minutes after the attack. Urgent communications with Moscow, Beijing? I have never had any difficulty in answering the question: Where were you on 9/11 2001?

On an earlier visit to Indonesia, we had met Ross Taylor, the West Australian Agent-General in Jakarta. The entrepreneurial West Australian business community was much in evidence across Asia. The WA Government, recognising Indonesia as the centre of commercial opportunity in Southeast Asia, had moved its Agent-General office from Singapore to Jakarta at a time when the SA Government was unwisely privatising SAGRIC, the agricultural extension service, and maintaining an Agent-General's office in London.

Ross Taylor was impressed by Omnipol technology. He put us in touch with a Western Australian company with a contract to operate a large landfill outside Manilla. We flew to Manilla, visited the facility and met the executives. What they had operating at the landfill was a large sorting line, where the refuse, having been brought in on trucks and dumped into a hopper, was fed onto a conveyer belt, from which rag pickers, who were seated under shelter from the weather, were systematically sorting glass, paper, metals and, potentially, plastic for resale and recycling. This was very different from the usual Asian landfills, where trucks dumped refuse onto the rubbish pile as rag pickers scrounged the piles for anything of value amid the vile stench and acrid smoke. Again, we had a very positive meeting and left confident that an Omnipol sale was in the offing. If that was to be the case, there was no shortage of plastic in Philippines. Recovering and reusing the plastic had the additional benefit of extending the life of the landfill by reducing the quantity of refuse entering the facility.

In January 2002, just before Omnipol collapsed, I had visited the Governor of Bali to discuss the possibility of selling the Balinese Government two Omnipol machines. He was very keen and although very busy, attentively sat through the eight minutes of the Omnipol video. He then indicated that he wanted to purchase the machines and called a Chinese Indonesian, Mr Yeo, in from an ante room. Mr Yeo was introduced as the governor's assistant, and it was he who would look after all the details of the sale. At that point, I left the governor's office with Mr Yeo, who suggested that we have a coffee. Over coffee Mr Yeo made it clear that he was in fact the governor's partner. The conversation that ensued came as a surprise, with Mr Yeo first indicating that the governor was very keen on Omnipol, but price was a problem. 'Oh, here we go', I thought. 'We are in for a negotiation in which Omnipol will get screwed.' Imagine my shock when Mr Yeo then explained that our price was too low and that we needed to consider additional factors, for example, 'the administrative costs that we need to meet'. His solution was that we invoice his government 'four million for the two machines and reimburse me [Mr Yeo] 1.8 million for the administration fee'.

Well, that couldn't have been any clearer. We pay a whopping bribe, and we get the contract. There was only one problem. Aside from the moral aspect, the criminal law in Australia, with which I am passingly familiar, provides heavy sanctions, including gaol time, for bribing officials of foreign governments. The law covered Mr Yeo's proposal to a 'T'. I responded by rejecting the bribery proposal and suggested instead that maybe Omnipol could treat him as our agent: we could sell the machines to him at our normal price and that he could sell them on to the Balinese Government at a price of his choice. Nothing doing. It was his proposal or nothing. I went back to Australia empty-handed to find a collapsing business.

While I undoubtedly had made the right decision, if I had agreed with Mr Yeo's proposition, I would have returned with a substantial deposit and Omnipol would have survived. I wonder how many others in business in my position would have made the same decision. I felt this dilemma particularly keenly later, when the media was relentlessly implying that I had lined my pockets. What an irony it was that the reason for the collapse, at that point, was my reluctance to act immorally and illegally, rather than the opposite.

In 2000, two years before the Bali negotiations referred to above, work had been proceeding with the building, shipping and installation of two machines to fill an order for Gerry Michard in Wichita in Kansas. Michard was a retired trial lawyer who wished to leave a mark on his home city and saw Omnipol as that mark. Gerry understood the rather long lead time required for us to build, freight, install, test and then train operators for the machines. It was not a great problem as he needed time to find a factory and arrange a supply of plastic waste. The Wichita machines were built and operated in Adelaide and then completely disassembled and packed in containers and dispatched. When the forwarder advised that they had passed through US customs and were on the way to Wichita, my son Jock and I flew to Kansas, on 28 February. Jock had worked for Omnipol in Adelaide and was the most technically savvy of our staff, apart from David Horne, one of the company's shareholders, who had declined to go to Wichita because he didn't like flying. Just for clarity, we had many machine operators, but they were not skilled on maintenance. Once there, Jock began to install the machines in the factory Michard had leased in Wichita.

Later in court documents, Michaud claimed that the machines had been incomplete on their arrival in the US. While it is true that we had to source some piping and metal foundations, this was simply to enable the machines to be installed to the specific requirements of Michaud's factory. In addition, one of the machines had to be modified to fit under a factory roof beam. Before I returned to Australia, Gerry took me on a tour of Wichita and to lunch and lobbied me about obtaining the rights to manufacture machines in the US. After eight weeks, Jock had successfully installed the machines and had them operating and was training Michaud's staff. He must have worked virtually around the clock; he did a fantastic job, overcoming many difficulties.

About 10 days later, I received an email from Gerry complaining that the machines were not producing the quantity of product guaranteed in the contract, which specified that each machine would produce 1,000 kg of product per hour of operation. I returned to Wichita, where Gerry again lobbied me about manufacturing rights. The machines' performance hadn't dampened his enthusiasm. In relation to the complaint, we agreed to have an engineering consultant test-run the machines and report. It is worth noting that the machines were still being operated while I was in Wichita and that there was a huge build-up of the resultant plastic products – they were making plastic railway sleepers for light gauge railways in mines and for decorative walls in gardens.

A consultant was identified and appointed. After his test, he reported that, from eight one-hour test runs of each machine, one machine had averaged 986 kg output per hour and the other machine 980 kg. I accepted those figures and spoke to the designer David Horne, who advised that the machines could be modified to increase the output, an option I then offered to Michaud. He refused and began to raise the issue of the loss of profit over the life of the machines, which he claimed amounted to millions of dollars. Of course, this was legal nonsense, but the discussion was again couched in terms of his obtaining the manufacturing rights. Finally, I left Wichita with no resolution and with Gerry threatening to go to court.

In my view, we had made three mistakes in our dealing with Michaud. In terms of increasing the size of the machines, David Horne the designer should have built each machine a bit larger, but this was not a big issue, as technically they could have been scaled up without difficulty. I doubt legally whether that amounted to a fundamental breach. Second, I didn't get a release signed when handing over the machines, which would have provided some further defence to Michaud's claims. Finally, we had not provided an operating manual. That was clearly our legal responsibility but was not our 'fault', in that we had contracted an Adelaide-based technical documentation specialist months before to write the manual and he had let us down. We had paid a large deposit and couldn't easily change to another supplier.

Despite Michaud's threatened legal action, he remained in touch by telephone, advising me of his steps towards suing Omnipol. His strategy was clearly to apply pressure until we agreed to sell the machine-manufacturing rights for the US, Canada and Latin America. His next move was to appoint solicitors in South Australia and to issue a claim for $16.4 million. At the time the *Advertiser* reported the quantum as $16 million and the *News* $14.8. This ridiculous claim was based on the alleged loss of the $2.2 million purchase price and losses of profit for the life of the machines.

What Gerry Michaud didn't appreciate was that in claiming $16.4 million, Omnipol was forced to advise the National Bank of his claim. The facility we had with the National Bank required the directors to advise the bank of any unusual occurrences in the business. Malcolm Barnes and I met our contact at the National Bank and detailed the court action. I explained that the action had no legal merit and was no real threat to the business. Our contact thanked us for the information. We left the meeting believing that there was no problem, but 10 days later we received correspondence from the bank seeking immediate repayment in full of all funds owing to the bank. That was not a fatal problem for Omnipol or Omnipol Australia. At the same time, however, using the information that had been provided in relation to Omnipol and Michaud, the National Bank foreclosed on Malcolm Barnes, and this had a cascading effect. The bank was intending to take over Malcolm's shares in Omnipol, which were in excess of 50 per cent. I hadn't been aware of the details of the bank's relationship with Malcolm. Apparently, his overdraft or facility had been increasing over the years and although the bank was well secured, the bank was at the end of its patience and took the opportunity to end the Barnes relationship, with the obvious catastrophic consequences for Omnipol, its staff, creditors and the Duncans.

In January 2002, I was in Sydney with a firm of Initial Public Offering specialists, preparing a float of Omnipol to occur mid-year. They had a private investor who was proposing to inject $2 million to clean up the balance sheet before the public float. Everything was looking good, but how quickly things can fall apart.

Other creditors, becoming aware of the National Bank foreclosures, moved quickly to appoint liquidators in the case of Omnipol and receivers in the case of Omnipol Australia. I am sure that Gerry, on the other side of the world, was unaware of these developments as they occurred. However, the chain reaction he had set off had the opposite effect from that he intended: the technology was sold to the large French water and waste conglomerate, Lyonnaise des Eaux. I'm unaware of the price achieved, and I have no interest in knowing, as the whole episode is still too raw and painful.

Lyonnaise des Eaux was owned by the French Government until privatised in 1987 but had maintained close contact with the government. In effect, it is a corporation that operates under French Government protection. I understand that Omnipol technology is being used in the US, the UK and France in the production of so-called 'plastic wood decking'. The value of the technology is demonstrated by the following media quotation at the time of the collapse.

> Omnipol liquidator Mark Tonzing of Bruce Mulvaney and Co said yesterday that he expected to sell the technology interstate or overseas for several million dollars. He was optimistic this would enable the Commonwealth grant to be repaid and other debts to be cleared. The technology really is world class, I've no doubt it will sell for many millions of dollars as there is a huge international interest. What is a shame is that because of what has happened with the company, the people who came up with the idea and put money into the business are going to be left with nothing. (*Advertiser*, 19 July 2002)

Terry Plane, former Bannon staffer and no friend of mine, quoting the liquidator Mark Tonzing in the *Australian* of 19 July 2002, said 'It was not so much poorly managed as having insufficient working capital'. On 24 July 2002, the receiver of Omnipol Australia, John Irving, noted that 'The assets appear to be valuable', referring to the equipment standing idle at the company's northern Adelaide plant.

Julie and I had no shareholding in Omnipol Pty Ltd and only a minority in Omnipol Australia so we can hardly be considered the key players. Malcolm Barnes had that honour. But I had the biggest headline by far and the media sought to blame me for the problems, hinting at corruption, even though there was absolutely no evidence of any such thing. Of course, the Australian ethos of a fair go was never in sight in the Murdoch media's attitude towards me.

The time I had spent working on the Omnipol project amounted to years and years of unpaid work and, of course, we lost large amounts of our family capital. Anyone who has stood at a landfill and watched an avalanche of plastic waste pour out of a compactor truck – containers, bags, packaging, bottles, yogurt tubs and so on – understands what a massive problem it is. At least in landfill all of it is buried, unlike the plastic in the oceans, which is rapidly destroying the marine environment. But, well before the disaster, when I tried to explain the truth about burying all the plastic, and that we had a solution in Omnipol, many people didn't want to hear.

Plastic waste is not valuable, and it never has been and never will be without government intervention (although there have been amazing changes since that time). But of course, the makers of plastic – in many cases, the world's largest oil and gas companies – have no interest in recycling plastic as this would diminish the demand for new plastic. The fossil fuel industry spends millions of dollars each year fighting against plastic recycling while telling the public they are working on the problem.

With my involvement in Omnipol, I was attempting to do something about the plastic waste catastrophe confronting the world, and South Australia – and the Adelaide *Advertiser* – was attacking me. The fact that an American, who wanted to seize great Australian technology, had destroyed an Australian small business with great potential was never mentioned in their coverage. In fact, the SA Government itself should have considered funding or operating the Omnipol process. There was certainly adequate social justification for doing so, but such a move would have been condemned viciously by the *Advertiser* and the rest of the media as dangerous socialism.

I found the collapse of Omnipol overwhelming and devastating to the extent that, in around April 2002, I could do little more that lie on the sofa in our house in a foetal position. I was particularly shattered by the staff not being paid for work undertaken and losing benefits that were due to them. Our friend Dr Maurice Asz came to see me at Julie's request and out of my hearing told her that it would be better for my health if I left Adelaide for a while – suggesting Bali. This episode now reminds me of Bill Shorten saying that, when he woke up the morning following his loss in the 2019 election, the first thing he considered doing was travelling to Bali, sitting under a palm tree and drinking Bintang. I wonder now if that was the sort of thing Dr Asz had in mind? So, two days later, Julie took me to Melbourne and put me on a plane to Bali. At Melbourne Airport, she bought me the *Lonely Planet Guide* for Bali and Lombok. I don't think I had heard of Lombok before then. On the plane I read the *Lonely Planet* guide, which informed me that Lombok was 25 years behind Bali. I had been to Bali before, and it had bad memories involving Omnipol. I had the idea that if I was to avoid a nervous breakdown, I should go to the quieter place. Two days later I took a slow ferry to Lombok.

Since the Omnipol disaster, many people have commented that it was a great project but before its time. In my view that is just not true. We were just hopelessly undercapitalised, and Malcolm Barnes and David Horne were not prepared to diminish their shareholding or control to enable a much-needed injection of capital. As a result, Omnipol collapsed and the technology was bought by an overseas conglomerate, the very thing we had all wished to prevent. At least Gerry Michaud, who had inadvertently caused the demise of Omnipol, was denied his desire to obtain the technology and the manufacturing rights.

In truth I don't suppose any of this matters now, but at least in telling this story I have the chance of placing on record what really happened and why we considered that it was so unfair. My collapsing health meant that I had little opportunity to deny the mainstream media narrative or to defend any of the Michaud matters in court. Of course, with Omnipol's liquidation and receivership, the Michaud action died. The National Bank sold up Malcolm Barnes's properties and he died some time later in a Bangkok hotel. I do not know any other details. Julie sold our much-loved Adelaide house, paid off our debts and, in an extremely stressed state, moved to Tasmania with Georgia.

In my view, the Australian Government and the state governments should have much more proactive policies to assist in the commercialisation of Australian technologies. In addition, more thought needs to be given to just how disadvantaged Australian corporates are in their attempts to conduct business in the third world, where bribery is endemic. I am not advocating that we weaken our laws criminalising bribery of public officials in other countries, but Australia could do far more to help to strengthen law enforcement in the third world and thus assist in levelling the playing field.

In my earlier Australian business career, I had been involved in the very successful establishment of what became South Australia's largest industrial law firm, Duncan and Hannon; I was instrumental in the start-up of radio station 5AA, of which I was a director for many years; we had successfully developed Freestyle Apartments in Port Douglas; and prior to that a small redevelopment in Battery Point in Hobart. However, the unsuccessful attempt to enliven Victoria Square as a restaurant precinct and the failed early start-up business for recycling plastic waste, Omnipol, became the media's only focus. Unsurprising, I suppose.

CHAPTER SIXTEEN
# LOMBOK AND JULIE'S DEATH

I arrived in Bali with a business visa that allowed a three-month stay, after which I would be required to leave Indonesia. In other words, it couldn't be extended within Indonesia. After two nights in Bali, I took a slow and ancient ferry to Lombok, arriving at Lembar port around midnight to discover that there was no readily available transport to the tourist town of Senggigi, where I was planning to stay. A number of touts were hanging around, offering transport at outrageous prices. I eventually took a car for $40. I later discovered the price should have been $10.

I checked in at Windy Beach Cottages, which I had found in the *Lonely Planet*, staying in a grass hut at $8 per night, with no hot water, until I had to leave Indonesia. No one could contact me except Julie. I read and walked/ran up the road and slowly recovered. I was restricted by not having transport. A local gigolo, Berry, who had 'found' me, offered to sell me a 125 cc motor scooter, which I bought and started riding. I had almost never ridden a motor bike previously, but soon mastered the skill. After three months, I had bought a motor car and also organised for licences for the bike and car from the Indonesian police.

I was learning fast that corruption was the only way to survive in Indonesia. I turned up to the police licensing division to obtain the licences on my own. I sat in a room for the test with a written exam paper ... in Bahasa Indonesian. Not surprisingly, I failed dismally. Disappointed with that experience, I told Berry, who laughed and explained that for $100 he would get me licensed – and he did.

In July 2002, when my three-month visa had expired and I was required to leave Indonesia, I decided I would ride the motor bike across Lombok and from there travel variously by bike and ferry to Dili, via Sumbawa, Flores and West Timor, to the Timor Leste border and finally to Dili. In retrospect, this elaborate plan was clearly evidence that I was still not myself. However, off I went and after many long days of travel

I arrived at the Timor Leste border, where I was told by the Indonesian border police that I couldn't take the motor bike out of Indonesia without a police permit; I would have to obtain it in Atambua, a ride of 25 kilometres, retracing my steps, which I reluctantly did, eventually locating the police compound.

The police were good natured and were interested in this crazy Westerner riding a small motorbike across Indonesia, with one of the police officers speaking good English and helping me to fill in the form for the bike exit permit. I was getting the feel of Indonesia and when they asked me where I had come from, I stood up wiggled my hips in a sort of dance – or party mode – and said 'Senggigi'. For the uninitiated, Senggigi is viewed as the last outpost of Western civilisation, going east in Indonesia. Senggigi would be known as 'Singgigi' if locals understood the play on words in English, as it has nightclubs and booze, in other words, a party town. The cops cheered my dance, and I was suddenly amongst friends. One question on the exit permit application form required details of the 'blue book'. I had never heard of a blue book. The police explained that in Indonesia vehicles have registration papers *and* ownership papers, the latter known in English as the 'blue book'. I telephoned the bike vendor Berry, who cheerfully advised me that he hadn't as yet paid out the bank, which had a chattel mortgage over the bike and that the bank held the blue book. He did, however, have a photocopy of the blue book, which he faxed to the Atambua police. Berry spoke to one of the cops and for a payment of 500,000 rupiah, or $50, I was issued with an exit permit and was back on the road.

Assuming that I was now legal for the purposes of leaving Indonesia, I decided to visit the Timor Leste enclave of Oecussi, on the basis that I may never have the opportunity to return. I arrived at the border to find that it was staffed neither by Indonesian border police nor Timor Leste officials, so I simply passed through and continued on to Oecussi – which turned out to be a sleepy uninteresting dusty backwater. After a little more than an hour, I returned to the border, which by this time to my surprise and shock was staffed on both sides. I assume that the Timor Leste border police had been having a lunchtime siesta earlier and now they merely waved me through. The Indonesians, however, who spoke no English, were less accommodating and eventually, at my request, telephoned the Atambua police. I was able to speak to the officer who spoke English, who clarified that, as it was Friday, the border staff had been praying during my first border crossing. I suspect that, feeling embarrassed at having left the border unattended, they also waved me through without passport stamps, other documentation or payment of any 'administration fees'. When I finally reached Dili, I checked into the Shipping Container Hotel, where I had stayed when working with OPAL.

Since I knew people at the hotel and others from my earlier time there, I decided to stay for a few days. I paid a visit to the Australian Ambassador, whom I had met in 2001, and then visited my friend José Ramos-Horta, at that time the Timor Leste Foreign Minister. We had first met in the late 1970s, when he was Fretilin's external representative based in Australia. He told me he longed for the 'simpler days' in Australia, when the struggle for independence was underway, and that he was sick of the bickering amongst the Timor Leste leadership that was then occurring – bickering that subsequently led to his serving as Timor Leste's Prime Minister.

The long ride from Lombok at the beginning of my journey prompted my decision to ride only as far as Kupang in West Timor for the return trip and from there consign the bike by Pelni ship to Bali, Pelni being the Indonesian Government's inter-island shipping line. I would then fly from Kupang to Lombok via Bali. On my return visit to Kupang, I went to the Balibo Cemetery to pay my respects to the five Australian journalists who had been killed by the Indonesian military. In Kupang I found a shipping agent and consigned the motor bike to Benoa Harbour in Bali, on a ship leaving in seven days. I then flew back to Lombok, timing my return flight to Bali to accord with that of the ship delivering my motor bike. I arrived at the port at the designated time to find that it was four hours late. Fortunately, I had rented a car and was able to sleep in it for a while. When the ship finally berthed, at about 1 am, I presented the foreman with a copy of the cart note. After some delay, he informed me that my bike was not on the ship, which, given the late hour and how long I'd been waiting, provoked my wrath. A boy who was part of the stevedore gang then explained to my Indonesian friend (who was assisting me in the bike-retrieval process) that there was a Honda bike in the ship's hold but that it was going to Surabaya. I demanded to be taken onboard to check, and found my bike. It had been mistakenly placed with cargo bound for Surabaya. I retrieved the bike and returned to the hotel.

Earlier that day, I had learnt another lesson about living in Indonesia. When driving the hire car, I had pulled up at a set of traffic lights, possibly stopping on the white line, crossing which is illegal. A police officer nearby caught my attention and indicated that I should go through the lights and then stop, which I did. In the conversation that followed he gave me a lecture and asked for a bribe of 50,000 rupiah, which, being a good law-abiding Australian citizen, I refused to pay, his response being, 'Ok Pak [Mister], lock your car and come with me'. I was taken to a police station on the back of his motor bike. I sat on a wooden bench at the station for two hours. I didn't encounter the traffic cop again and finally was told to go on my way. For not paying the small 'administration fee', I was fined three hours of my life and was forced to take a taxi from the police station back to the hire car, a trip costing me 40,000 rupiah. There is an assumption in Indonesia that all Europeans are rich. White faces are viewed as an ATM and are often targets for 'administration fees'.

During the riots in Indonesia in Christmas 1999 and into 2000, and particularly those in Lombok in which Christian and Chinese-owned property was burned and numbers of people were killed and injured, the police largely stayed on the sidelines. As a result, after things had returned to 'normal', the small Catholic community in Lombok decided to facilitate the entry of young Catholics into the police force. Money was raised and each year several candidates had their entrance fees paid. The new officer would later return his or her entrance fee to a pool, which would then enable more Catholic candidates to join Indonesia's police force. Notably, the Christian churches in Lombok are clustered around the police barracks in Ampenan and also the TNI (Military) headquarters in Mataram. This strategic location is, of course, an attempt to ensure protection in case of civil unrest.

Returning from Timor Leste with a new visa and having decided to spend more time in Lombok, I rented a cottage behind the Melati Dua Hotel in Senggigi's main street. I paid a year's rent – about $3,000 – and began to learn the mysteries of being a householder in Indonesia. The tenant is responsible for all repairs and renovations, regardless of how the problem arises or whether it is structural. If white ants eat the rafters and the roof or ceiling collapses, it is the tenant who meets the cost of repairs.

In July 2003, during my time at the cottage, Julie and Georgia paid me a visit and it was wonderful to see them. To this point Julie had been protecting me from the turmoil in Adelaide, but had decided that it was time for me to be made aware just how much damage had been done financially and to my reputation. It was hardly surprising, but so unfair. We had done our best to promote and develop great South Australian technology and had failed. We had done so against the backdrop of a massive negative publicity campaign waged by the *Advertiser* and other SA media. Julie told me she had heard that the Australian Liberal Government had referred the Omnipol disaster to the Australian Federal Police (AFP) and that, if that was the case, they might want to interview me. I wasn't surprised when, some time later, Julie informed me that the AFP wanted to interview us both in Australia.

I had been planning a trip to Australia in the near future and Julie had told them that we would be happy to meet officers in Hobart, where she was living by that time. Subsequently, Julie and I were interviewed by the police, in 2004, and we left the interview believing that was the end of the matter. It is worth noting that the substance of the interview related to how the monies had been spent. For example, a cheque or a bank transfer ledger would be produced and we would be asked to match expenditure to particular transactions. I felt that we were able to answer all the questions adequately. Interestingly, the later charges against me were unrelated to any of these, indicating that our answers had been satisfactory.

Prior to the visit by Julie, a Channel 7 team had travelled to Lombok looking for me. I had no intention of assisting *This Day Tonight*'s ratings, and basically made myself scarce. The crew stayed for three days. One night as I returned home on my motor bike after being at a friend's house, I called my security (*penjaga* or *jaga*), who indicated that people were waiting outside my gate. I told him to open the gate to enable me to drive straight into my driveway when I arrived home. Paul Makin, an Adelaide TV doorstop 'journalist', jumped in front of my bike and was knocked sideways. Before he could recover, I was inside and the security man had slammed the gate.

Prior to coming to Lombok, the Channel 7 crew had been given the incorrect information that I was in Jakarta, staying at the Jayakarta Hotel. This is where I had stayed in 2001 while working for Omnipol, but I hadn't been there since. As reported in the Australian media at the time, while the crew were in Jakarta staking out the hotel, they caught Terry Cameron, a member of the South Australian Upper House, walking out of the hotel arm-in-arm with a young Indonesian woman.

The small cottage I had rented was perfect for me and all seemed to be going well. However, after I had been living there for seven months, the landlord, who was a woman, indicated that she was resuming possession and would refund three months rent. I said that I was staying until my lease expired. A few days later, while I was out having a late-afternoon drink, my Indonesian friend Abak rushed into the bar and in broken English explained that the external doors and gates had been removed by the landlord and that all my possessions were exposed to the elements. The remaining five months rent, paid in advance, was retained by the landlord.

The following day I moved into a two-bed room unit at the Holiday Resort apartments, which at about $10 per day was relatively inexpensive. Following the riots at Christmas during 1999 and 2000 and the 9/11-induced recession, the tourist industry in Lombok had become very depressed and remained so – as well as the Lombok economy at large – until 2008–09.

In July 2003, Julie and Georgia came to Lombok for three weeks to escape the Hobart winter and the ongoing stress associated with the Omnipol failure. About this time, I discovered that she was being assisted in her dealings with the fallout by Garry Sampson, a well-known member of the Adelaide establishment, who given his past misadventures could be well described as a black sheep. This was going to end badly. I gently warned her but by then Sampson was embedded into our affairs. He ended up exploiting her further before she died.

We had a magnificent holiday together, wandering all over Lombok, eating out and enjoying new friends. We were discussing some future arrangements, whereby we could live partly in Hobart and partly in Lombok. We knew people who lived part-time on an outback station and part-time in Adelaide and so we thought that some similar arrangement between Lombok and Hobart could work.

Four months later, in November, Julie was diagnosed with terminal cancer and telephoned me with the news. It was the worst day of my life. I believed that her cancer was basically stress-induced and that it was my affairs that had caused stress – I still believe that and also that I should have been the victim of stress-related cancer rather than Julie. Initially, she convinced herself that she could beat the disease, although it eventually proved not to be so. Prior even to her cancer diagnosis, I considered that we had been exposed to all the worst stresses and pressures that life could throw at us but Julie's death was a tragedy of immeasurable proportions.

Julie and Georgia, along with Garry Sampson and one of his sons, visited Lombok on 1 February 2004, Sampson naturally coming at our expense. Although his visit was not particularly enjoyable, there was one positive aspect, in that his son and Georgia undertook a diving course. Although they were way below the legal age for diving in Australia, this was no barrier in Indonesia. This was a piece of minor good fortune because Georgia was diagnosed as a type 1 diabetic late in 2005 and subsequently was unable to dive.

Early in the year, after Julie and Sampson's visit, Randall Ashbourne, a gay journalist friend, came for a visit to check out how I was coping.

Despite my terrible experiences with the Adelaide media, 'journalist' and 'friend' are not mutually exclusive words in my lexicon. There are many decent journalists. Randall was enchanted with Lombok and fell in love with a ketch, *Evening Star II*, which was owned by a friend of mine, Dooley Marshall. Dooley had the idea of operating a dive-tour business from Lombok to Bali to Labuan Bajo in Flores, with the 'dive tourists' living on board. He had bought one suitable vessel, *Nugaroo*, and another vessel, the previously derelict *Evening Star II*.

*Evening Star II* had come with an interesting history. It was a wooden ketch of about 100 feet and had been built for Brian Burke's WA Labor Government, to be used as a 'gin palace' (another one) during Australia's defence of the America's Cup. Since such an expensive toy could hardly be justified by the state government, it was ordered by the WA Education Department as a sail training vessel and was fitted with cabins below deck. The main deck was luxuriously appointed. Within a couple of years, expensive sail training had become unfashionable, and *Evening Star II* was dry-docked, enabling Dooley to buy it in a derelict state. He repaired and renovated the vessel himself and brought it to Lombok.

Randall returned to Australia, and a few weeks later came back to Lombok with the intention of buying the ketch. I introduced him to Dooley, and they reached an agreement for its sale. It was estimated that it would take up to six months before all the paperwork had been completed and the transfer of ownership finalised. To accommodate this six-month hiatus, I was asked if I would live on the ship for that time, as an honest broker and a protector of the interests of both parties. I agreed. Randall paid $20,000 deposit and I moved on to the yacht. Sadly, a few months before the sale was finalised, Randall was diagnosed with emphysema, which eventually killed him. Considering the diagnosis, Randall sensibly decided that he could not take up the lifestyle he had planned on the yacht and the contract was broken and the deposit forfeited.

In April 2004, while I was still living on board the yacht, Julie and Georgia visited Lombok for the school holidays and stayed on *Evening Star II* with me. We had a lovely time, with more of a maritime flavour than usual. The ketch had a tender, and a boat man, available for my use. We sailed to the Gili Islands and to the Secret Gili Islands, to the south-west of Senggigi, selecting restaurants on the basis of their location on the waterfront or beach. It was great fun getting off *Evening Star II* onto the tender and then leaping out of the tender onto the beach in front of a restaurant. Georgia loved the nautical romance.

Julie had studied Classics at university but had never visited Egypt. I, on the other hand, had been to Egypt on two occasions. It was her wish to see the Nile and the Valley of the Kings before she died. At that stage, she was remaining optimistic that she would beat cancer and live on, but was also realistic, recognising that if we were to go to Egypt, it needed to be soon. We didn't have much cash and Julie had spoken to her parents, who with their usual wonderful generosity had offered to pay the cost of the trip down the Nile, on a first-class boat, which had a doctor on board. The trip was organised to begin on Monday 24 May 2004, when I was to meet Julie and Georgia in Singapore to catch a flight to Egypt.

There was one problem. My passport was with Indonesian Immigration and was awaiting a new Indonesian visa. I had advised my immigration agent that I needed the passport back by Friday 21 May, so that I could fly to Singapore two days later. The agent shared this knowledge with Immigration, who saw an opportunity for a large 'administration fee'. Not surprisingly, my passport was not returned by the Friday, causing me a great deal of anxiety. The agent reassured me by explaining that Immigration opened on Saturdays and all would be okay. On the Saturday, I found the agent and I accompanied him to Immigration in Mataram. At the office, I told him to forget about the visa, just get my passport back. He then spoke to the Immigration officers, who apparently said that I still couldn't get my passport back because it was locked in a safe and that the senior officer who had the key was in East Lombok. By now I was in full-on panic mode and demanded that the senior officer be brought in. Finally, the real agenda was made clear: he would come back but only for an administration fee of 20,000 rupiah, around $2,000. I became really enraged and refused to have anything more to say to the agent and returned to Senggigi. I then telephoned Julie and explained what had happened. She was justifiably furious with me. The phone call ended with her saying she would cancel the tour, which was covered by travel insurance, using her health as the justification.

I began to feel very sorry for myself, believing that nothing was working for me, that I was 'poison' and had caused Julie the stress that had induced her terminal cancer. Around midday, I decided that I could no longer cope. I went to a pharmacy, bought 100 Phenobarbital tablets and returned to the boat. I was alone on board. I went to my cabin and took all the pills. I wrote a letter to my friend Bert, an Australian I had met in Lombok, informing him that the 13,000,000 rupiah in cash in my suitcase under the bunk was for him. I was found about 4 pm, by a local expat, who had come on board to fish. The rest is history. I survived and my magnificent wife Julie flew to Lombok a few days later. I recovered without apparent permanent damage. The letter to Bert had disappeared, as had the 13,000,000 rupiah. There was only one person who could have done that – the person who found me. I presume he assumed that, as I was going to die, I would not need the money, nor would I be around to act as a witness against him.

Many friends and others have since asked me if I regret attempting to end my life. In terms of the terrible, horrible, experience Julie endured as a consequence of my actions and all the heartbreak I caused for friends – and, of course, the fact that I wouldn't have been part of Georgia's life – the answer is yes. But they were not the issues for me on that fateful Saturday. At the time I felt I had let Julie down once too often and that everything in which I was involved inevitably fell apart. It is also obvious that I wasn't acting rationally in my anguish. It is easy now to see my actions as selfish and self-centred, which they undoubtedly were. But at the time, I just couldn't cope anymore.

By the second half of 2004, Julie had accepted that the cancer was incurable and that she was going to die. Despite being devastated, the 52-year-old Julie was determined to make the most of her remaining life. I was living under a pall of misery. She was heartbroken that she would not be able to share more of Georgia's life and to provide a mother's guidance as Georgia grew into adulthood. Julie, in typical style, planned Georgia's future as much as she could. She and Georgia came to Lombok for Christmas on 15 December and stayed until 7 January. It was obvious that this was going to be Julie's last visit, even if she managed to survive for a few more months, and we were determined to have the best holiday we could in the circumstances. We walked up a river to swim in a waterfall. We sat on beautiful beaches watching fabulous sunsets. We went to the Gili Meno bird park, where Julie, to her delight, was photographed with beautiful birds perched on her arms. Julie, who was taking Endone for the pain, pushed herself to her limits. It was her wish that we go to places with Georgia in the hope that Georgia would remember an active, enthusiastic Julie to the last: the Julie before she was sick. That was the image Julie wanted to leave her daughter, not that of a debilitated and bedridden mother. We cuddled at night as always, and I still treasure the memories of those nights. She was thin and delicate, not the robust Julie we all knew.

We discussed Georgia's future at length, and Julie's memorials, which she was planning in great detail. She was intending to have songs played that reflected the members of her family: for Georgia, Bryan Adams's 'Everything I do I do it for you'; for Julie, Edith Piaf's 'Non, je ne regrette rien' (No Regrets), Nora Jones's 'Come away with me', and Helen Reddy's 'I am woman'. For me, it was Rod Stewart's version of Tom Traubert's 'Blues' (Waltzing Matilda) and 'Desperado'. At that stage she was adamant that she did not want me to return to Australia, and particularly for her memorials. People have probably forgotten what a big headline I drew at the time, and how biased and unfair the coverage had been in Adelaide. Julie was worried that my presence at the memorials would divert the focus to me and transform a private and sad occasion into a disrespectful media sideshow.

Julie, Georgia and I went to Bali for a last farewell before Julie and Georgia returned to Australia. I last saw her at Bali Airport, before they went through immigration. Georgia took a photo of our last tender embrace. I still have the photo, which shows two people overwhelmed by inconsolable sadness. Although I was consumed by feelings of incredible guilt about not returning to Australia with her – not to be beside her as she died – I was fulfilling her wishes. Julie wanted me to remember her as she had been, not as she was when dying. While I have received a great deal of criticism about these decisions, at the time I was doing as she had requested. I spoke to her almost daily before she died five weeks later, on 21 February 2005. When she had visited me in Lombok in December 2004, she had brought three bottles of Pike's Clare Valley Riesling, our favourite, and asked me to drink them on the day/night she died, and I did. She had urged me not to be sad, but 'to remember the good times, the happy times'. Julie had left me but she is always in my heart. We had been together for 26 years. We had enjoyed great love but had endured more sorrow and heartbreak than most.

Before Julie died she wrote me a letter, to be given to me after her death:

> I love you, Pete. I wish we could have lived out our years together – sitting in the rocking chairs on the veranda – forever. I miss you and need you. Cancer stopped all that – not business. Know that you had 25 years of my life – because I love you, take each day and each week now and remember me fondly with love. Smile when you think of me. Think of my generosity and my cuddles. Try to forget the bad things – when you think of me, think only of what is wonderful and what was good. Do not cry for me – that is done. Yes – I would do it all again. I would marry

you, were that an option. I love you. Don't hide from what has happened Pete. You must accept we got it wrong. But always know that we loved. Remember those many quality moments to ourselves. Carry me with you in your heart each day, always love me specially – know that I loved you. Read this knowing I die loving you. Smile – think of me cuddled safely in your arms so no one can harm me anymore. Have me there with you each moment.

Love me Pete as I always loved you. Julie.

Julie had also written a piece to be read at her memorial, an extract of which follows:

The South Street years in Hobart followed – and it's not an address . . . It's a way of life . . . I really did have the most fun imaginable. It was legendary. And just when it seemed that it couldn't last forever . . . Peter Duncan came into my life – at a lunch one day in Hobart. The next time he saw me . . . he asked me to marry him (he had taken me to Sydney for Lionel Murphy's 60th birthday and he was very, very sorry the Hilton hotel did not have twin beds). After spending just 20 nights together – we did just that – married. My wedding day was full of love and very little ceremony. Darling Kimmy married us at Taroona, surrounded by our closest family and those close friends who could make it, and my exciting life of travel and politics began two days later on a flight to Greece. It wasn't all a bed of roses. I endured about a dozen election campaigns. Our travel was usually to the second or third world. (That's what you get in the Left). And at first step – parenting was a challenge, but hey – I've ridden the Speaker's elephant in Kandy, Sri Lanka, seen Uluru ceremonially handed to its rightful owners, eaten duck brains at a banquet with one of Mao Tse Tung's right-hand soldiers, met presidents and princes and kissed an awful lot of babies. I accepted that in a big marriage there is only room for one big job. I was once told there's only room for one-and-a-half people in any marriage, but my working life is still special – because it was full of such very special people. Forget the professions, journalism students really are the most challenging and intelligent at the university – and I met more than my share. So many of them have been with me for life and during this last challenge – so many of them I love. How lucky is that?

Peter was far too brave in politics. With a passion which left us somewhat in its wake, he did nearly to the end follow absolutely what he thought was right. It would've been so easy, so cushy had he chosen to be like the pack. And in some cases, the media showed no clarity at all. Peter had already been branded – even before I met him. He was on the agenda as a passionate radical – oooh dangerous. And that for passing some of the best legislation that the country has ever seen. Things that cost so little, like laws for gays, women, consumers, tenants, used car buyers, vagrants, laws that abolished hanging, made rape a crime in marriage and forced the advertised average of 50 matches into a box. Legislation which left him forever labelled as dangerous, but which was never seriously changed, and which has been quickly broadly adopted nationally. I could only admire.

Peter's vision in business was so typically good. Shame his luck didn't match. He wanted to turn Adelaide into an alfresco dining city, clean up the environment – and help foster good people into politics. I know that. I lived with him, and I heard his inner thoughts and dreams. That's why so much of what we had was diverted back to the cause and not where I wanted it – into painting the mission brown bedroom walls in Gibbon Lane, that wonderful home of so many.

The destruction of Peter has been such a great sadness to me – and I and many of you have our thoughts about the impact this had on my health.

In the end he did make mistakes and this hurt and he paid for it dearly – with his own mental unwellness. Those who doubt it – look at my emotions till the end. Peter was the love of my life and I know he loved me; and, of course, Georgia and the boys beyond the scope of his own words.

Peter is not here today by agreement between us – but no one should doubt our love for a moment.

After Julie died, I was in frequent phone contact with Georgia. In the May holidays, Georgia visited me in Lombok, accompanied by Julie's brother, David Badcock, returning via Singapore, where they visited the night zoo, which much impressed Georgia. She seemed to be coping with the absence of Julie, but I could sense from her joy in seeing me and also her need for reassurance that maybe her coping was probably a bit superficial. After all, she was only 13. The three of us had a lovely time before she returned for the next term. One thing that was going well in her young life was school. She was managing well, had made some good friends and loved the Friends School in Hobart. On her return to Hobart, she was diagnosed with type 1 diabetes. The bad news just kept coming.

Late in May, I almost had another visitor – Peter Kellett, who was heading for Europe to lead a walking tour. He had decided to divert to Lombok to see how I was getting on. Coincidentally, I needed to leave Indonesia to renew my visa, so instead we arranged to meet in Singapore for two days. He had been the MC at Julie's memorial in Adelaide and described the memorial in great detail for me. He was such a good loyal friend and I miss him greatly. For the first Christmas without Julie – a sombre occasion – Georgia joined me in Lombok. Our Christmas lunch was celebrated at a long table at the Taman Restaurant at Senggigi, with about 40 local friends.

I am no longer a member of the ALP and that is generally a matter of regret. My membership of the party expired after I had relocated to Lombok, but before it had, I asked my son Jock to attend the Labor Party office and renew it. It was normal practice for people who were members of long standing to forward money by cheque by mail or in person through a third party. This was even done in the case of new members in bulk – that was called branch stacking. My application was simply for one membership of a well-known member in good standing. In an example of factional pettiness, Ian Hunter, who became a member of the Upper House in the SA Parliament, but who at the time was working in the South Australian Labor Party office, refused to accept the fees offered on the basis that I was no longer living in South Australia. Don Dunstan had no such problem with his party ticket when living in Victoria. In retrospect, while I am somewhat sad about no longer being a member of the Labor Party, I am now in a position to criticise without restraint some elements of policies that have been developed across the past 30 years and more.

CHAPTER SEVENTEEN
# A NEW LIFE

In January 2006, during the school holidays, Georgia and David Badcock came to Lombok. David stayed in the Mascot Hotel. Georgia had decided to learn Bahasa Indonesian and I arranged for Mili, a young local woman from Setangi village, to give her lessons. She was about Georgia's age and Mili and Georgia became friends.

The lessons, which were costing $10 per hour, soon became opportunities for Georgia and Mili to go out on my motor bike, visiting shopping centres and other attractions. Georgia justified this unorthodox method of learning by claiming that she was learning Bahasa by osmosis while hanging around with Mili. I couldn't really object. The Duncans have a poor record in language use and learning. I had studied Latin for two years at Gardenvale Central School in Melbourne. During the first year, when the focus was partially on Roman history, I managed to pass. In the second year, when the study moved to Latin language learning, I failed dismally. In the 1980s, Julie and I had attempted to learn Spanish, but the attempt petered out before I reached conversation level. Finally, in Lombok, I tried to learn Bahasa Indonesian. About 15 expats had enrolled in a group lesson organised by my friend Derek Pugh, who was then the principal of the Lombok International School. Unfortunately, the local Indonesian teacher's method of teaching was to exclude the use of English from the classroom. The result was a great deal of frustration and a dropout rate that saw the whole exercise collapse after about three weeks. Not a great record.

In February, my great friend Tom Kelly came for a visit, and we wandered around Lombok as I showed him the sights. Waterfalls, beaches, bars, restaurants and a massage or six. I met Tom, one of my many ex-Catholic friends, through Dr Greg Woods, who had worked with me in Adelaide in 1977. Over the years I have discovered that ex-Catholics make great comrades and friends. Tom really enjoyed himself, prompting us to plan a trip together, specifically to Thailand during the month of Ramadan. After an incident at a local restaurant I had discovered that it was wiser for me to leave Indonesia during Ramadan.

In 2004, Don Storen, whom I had known in Adelaide, turned up in Lombok. Although I wasn't aware of this at the time, he was on the run from the Adelaide Lebanese mafia. He decided to stay in Lombok and one day sought me out to offer me, as he described it, 'the deal of the century', which in essence was that he and I rent the Taman Restaurant for $1000 a month. Storen pointed out that he had no money and would be relying on me to buy the stock and fittings. He explained that he had extensive involvement in the hospitality industry in Adelaide and was proposing that he manage the restaurant. Given that I was doing little more than attempting to recover my mental health and believing that I would not be involved in any serious way, I agreed.

Storen turned out to be a hardened criminal and some little time later was jailed for six years and eventually deported back to Australia. That left me running the restaurant, whose lease was in my name. The owner, however, chose for reasons not relevant in this context to evict me and lease the restaurant to another person. This individual was prepared to pay five years rent in advance as opposed to my monthly arrangement. I then decided to sue the owner, Ian Henderson, for loss of profits over the term of the five-year lease. I might not have known much about the restaurant and hospitality trade but I did know something about the law and the court system – even in Indonesia.

After about four years, the Indonesian Supreme Court ordered Henderson to pay $US180,000 damages. He had no money and the court ordered an auction of the premises. Puspa, my partner by then, and I were the only bidder at the auction and we bought the restaurant and land for just a little more than the amount of the court judgement. A very satisfactory outcome. Later, when Jetstar began flying from Perth to Lombok direct, and tourism in Lombok was booming, Puspa and I decided to build a hotel on vacant land at the rear of the restaurant. As I explain later, we opened Taman Unique Hotel in May 2018, two months before the terrible earthquakes of that year.

The local government attempts to restrict the availability of alcohol, along with food, during the day when Indonesian Muslims are fasting during Ramadan, and live music during the evening. All the massage parlours are closed and the karaoke bars shut. Every year prior to Ramadan, the Taman Restaurant receives a letter from the governor advising that live music can only be played between 8.30 and 10.30 pm during Ramadan. The band usually plays between 7 and 11 pm. The restaurant is located in a tourist area and the tourists usually dine between 7 and 9pm. Having a band play at 8.30 pm was virtually useless in terms of attracting customers. Early on during my time in Senggigi, I suggested to the manager that the band should continue its normal practice – play from 7 pm. I told him that if there was any trouble he should instruct the band to play the Indonesian National Anthem – 'Indonesia Raya'.

On one occasion when I'd gone off to Thailand for my annual escape from Ramadan, I had a phone call from the manager. Two police officers had arrived after a complaint from the local mosque about the live music. The band had played 'Indonesian Raya' over and over and eventually the cops had left. Ah, a great victory, I thought, until the next night when I received another phone call, this time to advise that a truckload of armed police had arrived and had taken over the restaurant, terrifying the guests. The police told the band players that if there was any more trouble their equipment would be confiscated.

When I met Puspa she had a friend Ita, a distant relative by marriage. Ita's eldest brother – and the head of her family following the death of the father – had discovered that Puspa, who was divorced, had a small amount of money. Ita's brother had eight Are (a measure of land in Indonesia) of beachfront land, north of Senggigi. The brother claimed to need money urgently and offered to sell four Are (about one acre) to Puspa for a very cheap $2,500. Coincidentally, that was about the amount of money Puspa had in total. The money was handed over and she was given a signed receipt. These transactions had occurred before I met Puspa. When Puspa proudly took me to see her land, I asked to see the title. Puspa explained that she didn't have a tile and the transfer was being managed by a *Notaris* (Indonesian equivalent of a solicitor for these purposes). When she told me that she'd been waiting eight months to receive the title, I suggested that we visit the *Notaris*. Eventually we identified the *Notaris* – she didn't have a name for him – and went to see him. He explained that the transfer couldn't occur because Ita's brother doesn't have a KTP (an identity card). When Ita's brother was asked for a copy of his identity card, he confirmed that he didn't have one; he had lost it. It is illegal in Indonesia to be without an ID card. The transfer of the land couldn't go ahead without the ID card and the money was gone. I asked 'John' Dory, a police officer known to me, whether he could help. Dory then contacted Ita's brother and advised that a complaint had been made that he had no KTP.

Ita's brother immediately produced his KTP. Dory photocopied it and gave the copy to us, which we in turn passed on to the *Notaris*, who, once his fee had been paid, processed the transfer and delivered the Certificate of Title to Puspa. As an aside, some time before the title was delivered to Puspa, she saw Ita's brother socially and he actually asked her for an extra 25 million rupiah for the land, on the basis that he hadn't meant to sell it so cheaply.

Puspa's land was eventually quite a good buy and, along with the other four Are owned by Ita's brother, would have made it a nice small hotel site. One day, while at the ATM, I met my friend Bert, who at the time was in a relationship with Ita. Bert told me he was about to withdraw five million rupiah to lend to Ita's brother, who needed the money urgently because a family member was in hospital. I quickly told Bert that we wanted to buy the adjoining piece of beach land and that I would pay a five million rupiah deposit that day. So, I withdrew the money rather than Bert and we both went to Bert's house, where Ita's brother was waiting. The brother was not happy to see me and when I made my proposal, he rejected it and left. I had saved Bert five million rupiah, about $500.

Peter Kellett, Georgia and I had planned a visit to Laos and Cambodia to see Angkor Wat in September 2006, but, without giving us much notice, our friend Mike Presdee decided to make a visit from the UK to the Antipodes. Instead of heading straight for Australia, he came to Lombok to see me and Georgia. Peter joined us in Lombok and we all had a great few days before heading off to Cambodia. I had visited Angkor Wat previously, with Julie, but it was great to be back, wandering around the labyrinthine temples with Georgia and PK. The highlight of our visit to Laos was the old capital Luang Prabang, which is absolutely a must-see for any tourist.

We then flew to Kuala Lumpur, with PK and Georgia returning to Australia, while I met up with Puspa, who had been looking after the Taman Restaurant. We travelled to East Malaysia, staying at Kuching and taking a cruise boat for a day trip up the Rajang River. When coming around a bend, we encountered a live-aboard boat, which I assume had been cruising up and then down the river. As we passed the boat, an Australian voice yelled to us, 'Anyone come from Australia?' When I replied with a 'yes', the response was 'How's Collingwood doing?' You can't get away from the scourge of Aussie Rules football, even in East Malaysia.

Georgia came to Lombok in the May school holidays, and, as usual, it was great to see her. She was coping pretty well and doing okay at school, despite all the stress she'd endured so early in life. She had managed to deal with the Omnipol disaster, which, at the time, she couldn't really understand; her father partially disappearing from her life; being uprooted from her home in Adelaide and separated from her Adelaide friends; moving to Hobart; being enrolled at a new school; moving into a new house; and making new friends. Then, to cap it off, her mother became sick with cancer and died in February 2005. Julie and I had agreed that, after she died, the best arrangement for Georgia would be for her to live in Hobart with Holly, her cousin. Holly and her family moved into Julie's house in Hobart. Contrary to what many outsiders thought, I was still pretty fragile. I had only made one visit to Australia after moving to Lombok in 2003. I had visited Julie and Georgia in Hobart and had gone nowhere else. Even then I had become very depressed and had seen a psychiatrist, who prescribed antidepressants. After a two-hour session, in which I detailed all the horrors, the psychiatrist advised me to go back to Lombok and continue to recover, which he thought would just take time.

Georgia and I had decided to spend part of the holidays visiting Indonesian Papua. We flew to Jayapura and stayed there a couple of days. We applied for visas to travel around the country and experienced the usual difficulties with Indonesian Immigration. Eventually, after a day or so of stress and frustration, we flew to our final destination – Wamena, a valley in the highlands – where we stayed for three days. Georgia loved it. She has always had sophisticated tastes and relished the rich culture of the country. Because everything required in the valley had to be air-freighted in, the region has very few vehicles, meaning that we mostly walked in and around the town. However, we did manage to locate a local man with a car. With no roads connecting the valley to the rest of Indonesian Papua, we decided to drive the length of the valley, driving east on the first day and to the west on the second, each leg being around an hour return trip. On both occasions, locals hitched a ride, travelling on top of the car (literally!). We drove until the road petered out and then turned around and drove back. At the end of each of the roads, the altitude increased and the view over the valley was spectacular.

There was no mains power in the township, only generators, many of which were shut down, which meant that we generally had early nights. We would have a late-afternoon snack, find something to drink and head back to the hotel for a cold shower. Georgia wasn't too keen on the cold showers, nor the fact that the only food available was the local cuisine. The amazing tropical fruit bought from the central town market, fried bananas and fried vegetables became our staple food. Hot frying kills any germs, which otherwise would have caused trouble for our stomachs, used to a more Western diet. Georgia really enjoyed buying the local goods, particularly the penis gourd, or *koteka*. We bought some, which we intended to use as joke presents, but we inadvertently left them on the return flight. We often laugh at what the hostesses must have thought when they found this bag of long phallus-like items. Georgia was most disappointed at the loss and also that many other handicraft pieces she had bought could not be shipped home to Australia due agricultural quarantine requirements.

Indonesians are racially distinct from Papuans and it was easy for us to distinguish between the two groups. While there were numbers of Papuans in police uniform, the overwhelming membership appeared to be Indonesians. The TNI, the Army, was very much in evidence and out on patrol, not just in or near barracks. The soldiers appeared to us to be Indonesian to a man (no women). We didn't see any signs of civil unrest, although we were there for a short time only. We did speak to some Papuans, including a schoolteacher who spoke some English. From that conversation, I gained the impression of a territory under military garrison. In my opinion Indonesian policies are not working, and a complete rethink is necessary. The future government of Papua has a long way to go in determining whether it continues to be part of Indonesia or under some other administrative arrangements.

September was Georgia's sixteenth birthday, and she was planning a party in Hobart. She was enthusiastic for me to be there, and I was keen to come. I took a flight from Bali to Melbourne on 3 September 2007, only to be met by the Australian Federal Police at Melbourne Airport, where I was served with a summons. I accompanied the officers to the Moonie Ponds Magistrates Court, where I was bailed to appear in Adelaide at a later date with permission, in the meantime, to go to Hobart for Georgia's party.

The party was a great success. I took on the role of supervising the allocation of very modest amounts of illicit alcohol to the under-age kids, a bad practice no doubt and roundly condemned by some when it was revealed. However, happy punch was better than the binge drinking that might otherwise have occurred outside on the street. Georgia thoroughly enjoyed the party, her first real social outing on her own account. I think Georgia would have been a bit of a laughingstock in her social circle, without the happy juice or spiked punch.

I was furious with the AFP and the way I had been intercepted on my trip to Hobart. The Australian Consul-General in Bali had an AFP officer attached at the time – Paul Hunniford. I had met him several times in Lombok and had specifically asked him if the AFP still had any interest in me. He had indicated that the investigations arising from Omnipol had closed. Moreover, if the AFP had wanted to charge me with any offences, they only needed to ask me to return to Australia to answer any accusations against me.

AFP officer Hunniford's presence in Lombok on several occasions was the result of a joint operation between the AFP and the Australian Secret Intelligence Service (ASIS) at the time, seeking intelligence on the people smugglers who were working out of Lombok and Kupang and sending refugee boats to Australia. The AFP had set up a front organisation called Concord Services, which initially had a shopfront and offices, supposedly selling pearls, in Senggigi Plaza. It was absolutely a Keystone Cops operation. At one stage they had five or six officers working out of the premises. Collectively, they appeared to have little to do apart from playing golf and drinking, and they spent most of their time in Lombok hanging around with local expats, who were the last to know about, or have intelligence on, people smugglers.

The Senggigi expats largely kept to themselves and had little to do with the locals, who actually might have had information about people smuggling. Very few of the Concord Services spooks – all men – spoke Bahasa Indonesian. Within a week of the pearl shop front being established, its identity was revealed, probably as the result of my smelling a rat and sharing my reservations and joking about it with other local expats. A couple of days later, Ralph Blewett, a somewhat crazy expat, visited the Concord shop/office, jumped the counter and entered the inner offices. Before he was bundled out, he noticed the extensive computer systems and communication equipment. Not the sort of equipment that a pearl company would normally have needed. Ralph also indicated that there was no large safe, which he not unreasonably considered would be essential for a pearl retailer. Thus the existence of the AFP operation was revealed, and then sensibly the pretence of the pearl operation was dropped and the agents began to be seen around Senggigi in company with local Indonesian cops. The operation closed after a couple of years.

In 2007 my son Jock and his partner Toni announced that they were planning to get married in January 2008, which in terms of timing was a disaster for me. The Adelaide *Advertiser* of the day viewed me as public enemy number one. My Sydney barrister wanted me out of Australia, until the trial, which was not scheduled until late in 2008 or even in 2009.

On the few occasions I had returned to Adelaide, the *Advertiser* published my every move as a headline and reprinted their version of the whole sorry series of events leading up to the AFP charges and the court case. In September 2007, I was charged with 'making an untrue statement in application for a Commonwealth grant and with dishonestly causing loss to a Commonwealth entity'.

When in Adelaide for the court appearance in October 2007, I had a coffee with Jock to explain the problem and pointed out that the media might even turn up at the wedding, transforming it into a media circus. I told him that in the circumstances I thought it would be better if I didn't attend the wedding. He was not happy with this, pretty much accusing me of being timorous by allowing the *Advertiser* to dictate my decision. For a few years thereafter, my relationship with Jock was on ice. Happily, it has recovered, and Jock and I are again close. Jock and Toni have an excellent relationship: she is a terrific partner and an exceptional mother, and Jock has become a great father to his three lovely daughters. Another disappointment for Jock in relation to his wedding was that Georgia had booked and paid for a school trip to Vietnam, which clashed with the date of the wedding. Georgia was seriously torn and explored every option to enable her to be in two places at the one time. None of the options worked and eventually she had to choose between the wedding and the trip. I think it was the toughest decision she had been forced to make up to that time. Eventually she decided to go to Vietnam. I don't know how Jock felt about her decision. Georgia's absence was obviously exacerbated by my absence from the wedding.

After I returned in Lombok in mid-2007, the court case was never far from my mind. Every morning when I woke up, it was hanging heavily over my life. It was a welcome diversion therefore when, in June, my friend and former senior private secretary, Jim Hyde, and Georgia came to stay. Jim had been always great company and an eternal optimist despite living with HIV/AIDS. He lectured me about my miserable state of mind and before long had me laughing. As a teetotaller, he urged the alcohol-dependent members of the expat community in Senggigi to change their ways.

In October 2007, after Georgia's birthday party in Hobart, I had proceeded to Adelaide and arranged to appear in the Magistrates Court. I wanted to be bailed to enable me to return to Indonesia until the District Court jury trial which, given the length of the court lists, was unlikely to be heard until the second half of 2008. This proved to be more difficult than I had anticipated. The AFP opposed the granting of bail with a condition allowing me to return to Indonesia, arguing that I was a flight risk. When AFP officers had indicated that they wanted to interview Julie and me in 2004, we had made ourselves available and cooperated fully. I had flown from Lombok to Hobart to meet with them. I made the point to the bail court that I had a business in Indonesia and couldn't be away from it for a year or longer. The prosecutor then claimed that he was totally unaware of my business. I then invited the AFP to contact its officer, Paul Hunniford, in Bali for confirmation. After an adjournment, the prosecutor returned, claiming that the AFP had spoken to Hunniford and that he knew nothing of my business activities. Straight lies. Fortunately, the magistrate was having none of the AFP's hardball and granted bail, allowing me to return to Lombok until the trial. Of course, the *Advertiser* was having a field day with this, with its 'Duncan a flight risk' headline.

A further aspect of the bail hearing was disappointing to me. It was part of the AFP case that I had left Australia to avoid the legal consequences of the Omnipol collapse. As I explained earlier, I was seriously depressed and mentally falling apart. Julie had asked a friend of ours and a GP, Maurice Asz, to visit our house and to give Julie advice on what we should do about my mental state. He confirmed that I needed to get away from the daily stress, suggesting, 'go to Bali or something', which of course is what I did. In support of the bail application, I had asked Maurice to give evidence to that effect but he refused on the grounds that he was not my GP at the time he had advised the trip to Bali. He also explained that his giving medical advice to another doctor's patient could be viewed as unethical and might get him into trouble with the Medical Board. Hardly the act of a friend, but then he was a Collingwood supporter.

The media, particularly the *Advertiser* and the *Australian*, had delighted in Omnipol's collapse. The headlines essentially had me absconding with pockets full of cash, while my political opponents were mumbling darkly about fraud and other actions of dishonesty, with the media frenzy inevitably leading to the Australian Coalition Government asking the AFP to investigate the Omnipol collapse. After trawling through the Omnipol books, they found no fraud or financial misconduct. The only pathetic charge that they were able to bring amounted to a claim that Omnipol had received a grant from the Australian Government on condition that the government would be advised if there was any change to the ownership structure of the company. The charge was that a change in the shareholding had occurred and had not been notified to the government.

As I had signed the documentation for the grant as a director, I was potentially liable.

The reality was that, in the last days of the company, before it was put into administration, I had attempted to inject our last $50,000 into the business to pay wages and rent. Omnipol was still expecting at any time to receive a $210,000 deposit on a machine that had been sold to a company in the Philippines. The plan was that the $50,000 would then be repaid. Julie had been unhappy with this unsecured arrangement and Malcolm Barnes had agreed to mortgage some of his shares to secure the $50,000. An agreement to that effect was drawn up and signed. In addition, a share transfer had been drawn up and signed so that Julie and I could have registered the share transfer without further action by Malcolm if the $50,000 had not been repaid. Somehow the agreement covering the transaction had been 'lost' and all that remained was the signed share transfer. On the face of it, ownership of the shares had passed to me and Julie, or our company, although the share transfer had not been registered. On its face, the presumed transfer breached the grant agreement with the government, in that it had not been notified of the transfer. This appeared to the AFP to be a clear-cut case, which would have me imprisoned for a few years with what little was left of my reputation completely destroyed.

I knew that the $50,000 had been paid as a loan and was furious that the loan agreement had 'disappeared'. However, there was one other source of written evidence which might enable me to prove my innocence. Omnipol had used a MYOB accounting package and those records would show that the $50,000 had been recorded in the company books as a loan. But there was a problem: when the AFP uncovered copies of all the documents they intended to rely upon to prove their case, the MYOB discs were not listed. My solicitor then sought the MYOB discs, only to be informed that they hadn't been produced because the prosecution would not be relying upon them since they had been corrupted in some way. We then demanded that the discs be produced, with the judge making an order to that effect. Despite all their technological expertise, the AFP claimed they had not been able to open the discs.

My Sydney barrister fortunately knew an old gentleman who was one of the original founders or engineers of the MYOB system, so I went to see him at his home in Campbelltown and was able to tell him my story about our great Australian technological innovation going offshore. Given the struggle that MYOB had undergone to get established, he was sympathetic and promised to do everything he could to access the information on the discs. To my enormous relief, he, or the engineers at MYOB, were able to open the discs and give me a hard copy certified as a true record. It showed that the $50,000 had been recorded as a loan. I thought I was in the clear and that the AFP case would collapse. But no, the prosecutor continued with the case, wasting four days of court time and that of my legal team.

The upshot was that on 11 November 2008, the jury retired and after 15 minutes returned a not guilty verdict, and that should have been the end of the matter. Well not quite. The *Advertiser*, which had been headlining and front-paging the story of the trial for months failed to report the not guilty verdict in its printed edition. The 'not guilty' verdict was only available in the online edition. I had only managed to survive this horrendous ordeal through the tremendous support of my lifelong friend David Wilson, who acted as my solicitor, and my Sydney friend, Tom Kelly, who had helped me to find a suitable Sydney barrister and who had come to Adelaide to support me during the trial. I am forever in their debt.

Sadly, on 10 July 2009, my friend Mike Presdee died. He and his first wife Margaret had migrated from the UK to Elizabeth in the early 1970s, where I had met them through the Labor Party branch. They were both schoolteachers at the time and became great friends and friends of my circle of friends. They divorced and moved back to the UK. Mike always had great faith in my capacity to win elections and was always very dismissive when I was crossing campaign T's and dotting I's and worrying about the last vote. He came to Australia several times to help with Makin election campaigns and used to tease me about wasting his time because I never lost. Unfortunately, he didn't come to Australia for the 1996 election, at which I was defeated.

Mike had met his second wife Gil Gower after he returned to the UK and through regular visits to Australia she also became friends with me and Julie. They were even married at our house in Gibbon Lane, North Adelaide. It was a great event, which we were delighted to host. Gil was, of course, devastated by Mike's death. I had stayed with her in Canterbury in April 2010 and was marooned there for a few days when the English airports were closed by the volcano eruption in Iceland. Mike and Gil's daughter Hanna is one of Georgia's friends. Gil was subsequently elected to the Canterbury Council as a Labour Councillor and served until she died in 2019. Their deaths remind me of the adage, don't worry about old age, it doesn't last very long.

CHAPTER EIGHTEEN
# A LAWYER ONCE AGAIN

In late 2008, I received a phone call from Australia from a person I didn't know, who said something along the following lines:

> Hi, you don't know me, but I am a friend of Lee Rush, the father of Scott Rush, a drug mule who is one of the Bali Nine. Scott is currently on death row. I have researched your history, Peter, and I need your help. Can I visit you in Lombok to explore what we might be able to do to get this bloke's death sentence reversed?

I had maintained a long history of opposition to the death penalty and was appalled by the Indonesian legal system and the government's determination to enforce the death penalty. I agreed to meet this individual and he visited a couple of weeks later. After a briefing, I agreed to help. By that stage, it looked as though it would be very difficult. The first and most obvious issue to be addressed was the legal contract between Scott Rush's Indonesian lawyers and the Australian lawyers assisting, which had to be terminated. The Australian lawyers probably weren't doing much more than running a watching brief and were no doubt doing so from good-hearted motives and probably *pro bono*. They did not have sufficient cultural sensitivity, however, to realise that a white face watching proceedings in an Indonesian court was likely to have an adverse impact. As for the Indonesian lawyers from Bali, they had a 100 per cent fail rate. Rush's sentence had increased from 20 years imprisonment to life imprisonment, to the death penalty imposed by the Bali High Court on 6 September 2006. With such a track record, the Bali-based lawyers hardly engendered any confidence in the outcome of an appeal that they might launch in the Indonesian Supreme Court.

I agreed to become involved to assist in getting Scott Rush's death penalty reversed. I had high-powered and well-connected Jakarta-based lawyers advising me over various other matters. I contacted them and they agreed to become involved. However, they couldn't do so until the Bali lawyers had been removed from the court file. When the Bali lawyers heard that they were being sacked, they were not happy, probably due to both the loss of the money they had been receiving from Scott Rush's parents and supporters and the loss of status, as well as the publicity that had arisen from representing a party in a high-profile case. Scott Rush, of course, was the client and not his father or my new acquaintance. The Bali lawyers went to see him in the gaol. Initially, he was inclined to remain with his current lawyers. It took a visit from Scott's father to reverse the decision. Even then, the Jakarta lawyers were extraordinarily careful in initial dealings with Scott, fearing that they might encounter ethical problems.

It is important to understand how Indonesian lawyers handle relationships with their clients. First of all, the client signs a General Power of Attorney in favour of the lawyer. Cancelling that arrangement requires a deed signed before a *Notaris*, for these purposes, the Indonesian equivalent of a JP or Notary Public. A deed cancelling the Power of Attorney therefore had to be drafted by the Jakarta lawyers, who, in doing so, were acting unethically. Then the document had to be brought to Bali and a *Notaris* booked and paid to visit the gaol. Finally, the Jakarta lawyer couldn't try to attempt to see Scott in the gaol, as at that point he was not Scott's lawyer. Nothing is simple, but finally the new lawyers were on the court file and the former lawyers off the file – but not before they produced a final bill of costs associated with this process.

Another problem was Scott Rush's attitude. I have never met him, but by all reports he was a young punk who arrogantly thought he knew best, regardless of his dire predicament. He resented assistance in a surly offhand manner and appeared to have few regrets over the decisions he had made, which had ruined his life and that of his parents. He had already been in trouble with the law in Australia and was probably using drugs.

When aged 18 or just 19, he had started visiting Bali with apparently no visible means of paying for the visits. His parents, good upstanding Catholics, sick with worry and assuming the Bali visits involved untoward behaviour, spoke to an Australian lawyer friend, who suggested to Scott's father that they should approach the Australian Federal Police and ask them to prevent Scott from leaving Australia. There is some confusion about whether the AFP agreed to do this, but in any event that contact tipped off the AFP to the drug run. The AFP subsequently advised the Indonesian police of the details. Knowing that these matters involved drugs, the AFP clearly breached the government policy of non-cooperation with foreign governments and agencies over law-enforcement matters where the potential penalty in the foreign country is death. Chan and Sukumaran, the ringleaders of the Bali Nine, with some justification from their point of view, blamed Lee Rush for their predicament, on death row.

The Jakarta lawyers began to prepare the appeal to the Supreme Court, taking great care in their approach; for example, they advised against seeking a reduction in sentence to 20 years, fearing that the court might simply reject such a reduction and leave the death penalty in place. The alternative was to seek to have the death penalty overturned and replaced by the next most serious penalty in the Indonesian criminal code – life imprisonment. That became the strategy. On 10 May 2011, the Supreme Court reduced Scott's penalty to life imprisonment. There is currently some confusion over whether this penalty is for life or can finish administratively after a reasonably long prison term has been served.

The present strategy is to leave the situation as it is until Scott has served near to 20 years and then attempt to have him paroled or released. Three reasons underpin this approach. Firstly, Indonesian courts or prison authorities are unlikely to be sympathetic to a release unless a substantial amount of gaol time has been served. Secondly, a long gaol time will have allowed Rush to have demonstrated good behaviour over a longer period. In his initial time in gaol, he didn't demonstrate exemplary behaviour and thus didn't assist his cause. Finally, the Bali Nine engendered a strong emotional response amongst ordinary Indonesians. Although the drugs were headed for Australia, that detail was largely overlooked in Indonesia, where the Bali Nine were just seen as entitled expats who 'got what they deserved', with the intervention by the Australian Government not helping in that regard. The execution of Sukumaran and Chan was overwhelmingly popular in Indonesia. As far as Scott Rush is concerned, after a substantial amount of time has passed, his chances of being released and quietly returning to Australia increase if there is less political background noise.

This process kept me and the friend of Scott Rush's father occupied during the two or three years between my early involvement and the Supreme Court decision and subsequent events. It entailed the friend making several trips to Indonesia for consultations and meeting me in Australia on two occasions. Likewise, I went to Jakarta on several occasions to meet with the lawyers, with the lawyers travelling to Bali several times to meet with Scott Rush. During that time also, the prison authorities had the opportunity to report to the Supreme Court on Scott's behaviour, which, as I said, hadn't always been exemplary, and we had to ensure that the reports on his behaviour were positive.

We heard in November 2010 that the Supreme Court was working on a draft judgement to reduce the penalty to life imprisonment. While this was great news, it wasn't as yet a judgement and we couldn't share the news with Scott for fear that he would broadcast it around the prison. Finally, in May 2011, the Jakarta lawyers received a copy of the formal sealed judgement. We were overjoyed, and I was delighted to have successfully steered the strategy to save someone's life from the firing squad. I had become involved in this issue because it was the right thing to do. I didn't get paid for my services, except for a few free meals. That said, the satisfaction was well worth the stress. I had often thought of how I would feel if we had failed, and Scott Rush had been forced to face an Indonesian firing squad. We went to Penang for a few days to celebrate.

Andrew Chan and Myuran Sukumaran were executed by firing squad on 29 April 2015, along with several other expatriates, also convicted on drug charges. They should not have been given death sentences; the death penalty is never justified, full stop. Chan and Sukumaran were two of the ringleaders, although the other two ringleaders appear to have escaped penalty. Clearly, the ringleaders should have been given higher levels of punishment than the drug mules, and, on any view of the legal principles involved, the fact that the Indonesian court system at various times treated some of the mules and the ringleaders equally is clearly wrong.

Andrew Chan and Myuran Sukumaran did an excellent job of convincing many naive people in Australia that they had reformed in the decade they spent in an Indonesian gaol. Chan allegedly became a devout Christian, while Sukumaran became an artist, apparently giving lessons to other prisoners. I have no direct knowledge of Chan or his activities in gaol, so I will not comment. I am aware however that in 2013 Sukumaran threatened Scott Rush in Kerobokan Prison, where they were both incarcerated at the time. Sukumaran blamed Rush and his father for his death penalty because Rush senior had informed to the AFP. Sukumaran believed that killing Rush would extend his life while the Indonesians prosecuted him for murdering Rush.

We took the threat seriously and initially arranged for a Balinese prisoner, who was the boss prisoner, to provide protection for Rush, although we recognised that this wasn't a satisfactory solution and immediately sought to have him moved to another prison. Scott Rush again caused problems, initially refusing to sign a request for transfer. I have no direct evidence, but I suspect that his reluctance to be moved was related to the availability of drugs in Kerobokan prison. In 2014 he was successfully transferred Karangasem prison. I understand that he is comfortable enough in the smaller prison and that his behaviour and demeanour have improved.

Between 2005 and 2009, Australia and Indonesia were actively engaged in negotiations to establish a prisoner-exchange treaty. The negotiations were near agreement some time in 2009 and I considered that this could have provided a partial solution to the problem of Scott Rush and the other Bali Nine prisoners, who were incarcerated for life. Of course, that was on the assumption that we could have Rush's sentence reduced from death to life imprisonment. I approached the Australian authorities asking them to ensure that indeterminate sentences were included in the agreement. I was assured that they would be but was advised that the agreement had stalled and that no movement was likely in the short term. At the time the Australian Government was partly motivated in its attempts for a prisoner-exchange treaty by the position of Schapelle Corby. She had a high media profile in Australia and had always maintained her innocence, despite a fair bit of evidence. Schapelle had a significant number of supporters in Australia who believed in her and who were lobbying members of parliament and the government in support of the proposed prisoner swap agreement. The irony of this was that Schapelle did not wish to complete any of her sentence in an Australian prison. When a friend of mine who lived in Bali and who visited Schapelle asked her if she was looking forward to the prisoner swap agreement and finishing her sentence in Australia, her reported reply was 'no fucking way'.

There is a great deal of misinformation in the West about Asian prisons. My experience is limited to my visits to three Indonesian prisons and a couple of police prisons, so I will restrict my comments to Indonesia. Prisons anywhere are pretty horrible places and most people I know are proud of the fact that they have never been inside a gaol, even as a visitor. I started visiting prisons as a young lawyer in Adelaide and they are very depressing places. The Indonesian prisons I have visited were grossly overcrowded; however, if a person wanted to pass their time with as little trouble as possible and had a small amount of money to buy food and to pay 'administrative fees', they would be not too badly off in relative terms. By way of example, a friend of mine in Lombok was unjustly sentenced to five years imprisonment and I visited him monthly, until his release and deportation to England. He had a small space at one end of a community platform bed, where he had a mattress and a small wooden partition to separate him from the next prisoner. He bought food from outside the prison, played tennis most days with prison officers and other prisoners, had a mobile phone for most of his time inside and read his way through my library. He managed to stay healthy and had no real problems during his stay.

In 2011, instead of going to Thailand during Ramadan, Puspa and I decided to visit the Middle East and East Africa. We flew to Istanbul, where we met up with David Badcock. We then flew to Israel, where we joined a bus tour of the biblical sites. As an Indonesian Christian, Puspa saw a visit to Palestine similarly to the way Muslims see Haj visits to Mecca. Several of the fellow travellers on the bus tour were committed US Christians. Imagine my response when, as we travelled from one site to the next, one of them began to read pieces from the bible that related to the various sites. I entertained myself by asking the guide difficult questions about Israel's treatment of Palestinians, for which she had no answers. Puspa, anxious to get back to her cats, then flew back to Lombok. David and Tom Kelly, who had joined us, and I flew to Nairobi and then visited Tanzania and Zanzibar. Finally, we flew to Addis Ababa in Ethiopia, which I had long wanted to see. Without qualification, Ethiopia is one of the most interesting countries I have visited and is a greatly underestimated tourist destination.

In May we received the new Taman Restaurant Certificate of Title. After refurbishing and restaffing, Taman Restaurant and Deli reopened in late June. We were heading into the June to October tourist season, and all was looking very positive. Business was picking up and the minor mistakes that had occurred during our first time as restaurateurs were not repeated. We owned the freehold, had no rent to pay, no mortgage and were doing good business.

Just before Christmas that year, I travelled to Melbourne to see Georgia and while there visited Springvale Crematorium, where my father John Duncan's ashes had been interred. This visit proved to be a matter of great good fortune, as the operator of the crematorium had lost touch with our family and had planned to remove my father's ashes at the end of 2011 – two weeks away. I signed all the necessary paperwork, and the ashes and the brass plate were consigned to my sister for interment with my mother's ashes.

Then came the terrible news that my dear friend and comrade Frank Walker was fading fast. Frank was dying from cancer and I had last seen him in Sydney earlier that year (2012) for lunch with Greg Woods and Tom Kelly. I decided to visit him one last time and flew to Sydney. Frank was stoic and facing the inevitable with a typical Walker approach: if nothing could be done, worrying was no solution. Frank died on 10 June. I stayed for the state funeral, where he was appropriately farewelled. Our adult lives had followed similar paths. We had both been ministers in our respective state governments and in the Australian Government and we had both experienced personal tragedy. In Frank's case his two sons committed schizophrenia-induced suicide and in my case Julie's premature death from cancer. We had both left a body of good public works, of which we were rightly proud.

The positive event of the year was my son Mac and Tanya's wedding on 1 July, in New York City, a very grand affair. Initially, I was hoping that Puspa would accompany me to the US for the wedding; however, it proved to be extremely difficult for an Indonesian, even a Christian Indonesian, to obtain a visa to the US. Georgia, David Badcock and I attended, and David and I decided to go on to Cuba followed by Ghana and Liberia. Obviously, an extensive tour.

In early September I went to Adelaide to farewell yet another friend and comrade, Frank Blevins, also dying of cancer, which had advanced to his spine. I saw him at home in North Adelaide and he was suffering shocking spasms of pain. He died on 7 September, a few days after I had visited him. I hope his death was due to a sympathetic doctor ultimately increasing the level of morphine he was receiving. The pain Frank endured gives lie to those who, in opposing euthanasia, claim that palliative care can always relieve pain. No one should have to experience the pain that Frank was suffering when I saw him. Frank was one of those people of his generation I describe as working-class intellectuals. Other South Australian examples are Clyde Cameron, Mick Young and Bob Maczkowiack, all inherently smart people who, because of lack of opportunity, never had a formal education. Frank rose from merchant seaman to become deputy premier of South Australia. Frank could have achieved more in his political life, but sadly his period in parliamentary life mainly coincided with the ultra-cautious Labor Government of John Bannon. I saw him often when he was a minister and he aired his frustrations privately to me; however, he was too loyal to the Labor Party to complain publicly, which on his death led people to praise his loyalty, rather than his achievements.

In late September, my friends Tony Reeves and his partner Kamala Shakti visited. It was great to catch up with an old mate and one of the true characters of our generation. I have great memories of the visit, now tempered by sadness over his death, which occurred in Jogja two weeks after his visit to Lombok. I first met Tony in the mid-1970s, and later in the decade he visited Adelaide to obtain my support to incorporate the Shirley Brifman papers – relating to Abe Saffron's role in police corruption in New South Wales – into SA's Parliamentary Hansard. We had remained in contact over the years as he fought battles to save Sydney's built environment and expose the police corruption that fed off developers and 'sleazy peelers' in Sydney and Brisbane. He had the unique claim to have assisted in the establishment of two Royal Commissions – the Moffitt Royal Commission into Police Corruption in NSW and the Fitzgerald Commission in Queensland. A great life well lived and an individual I was proud to call a friend and comrade.

In early 2013, the Qantas subsidiary Jetstar announced that it was planning direct flights from Perth to Lombok, an announcement the tourist industry in Lombok had been anticipating eagerly for over a decade. I decided to go ahead with a plan to build a hotel on land we owned at the rear of the Taman Restaurant. My idea was to wrap the hotel around the rear of the restaurant. The building would be a tight fit on the available land but complied with the Indonesian plot ratio. My hotelier friend, Don Neil, had advised me that, unless we were planning a six-star plus hotel, we needed to have at least 20 rooms otherwise the hotel would not be booked by tour groups and travel agents. He also explained that we needed to be able to accommodate a medium busload of tourists. Our architect produced a design that contained 25 rooms, as well as a swimming pool, deck and bar on the top level. Initially, my plan had been to build the rooms and to add the pool later, but Georgia, by then an interior designer – and who was visiting at the time – sensibly explained that the hotel, without the pool, lacked the wow factor enabling it to be photographed for marketing purposes. I agreed and we planned to build 15 rooms, the public areas and swimming pool deck and bar in the first phase. So, with all the government approvals in place and a builder contracted, on 23 October I breached my Indonesian Immigration visa by undertaking some physical building work. I turned the 'first sod'.

Our builder for the structure, my friend Mel Higgs, recommended that, because we were in an earthquake zone, we should insert Kevlar needles into the cement mix to ensure it had maximum strength. When the horrendous earthquakes occurred in 2018, the hotel and the pool were undamaged.

Having recently had Georgia staying in Lombok, I hadn't planned to visit Australia for a few months, but sadly, that wasn't to be. Kath Badcock, Julie's wonderful mother and my mother-in-law, died just after Christmas, and I headed to Hobart for the funeral on 30 December 2013. She was in her 90s and had lived a great life, with the sad exception of Julie's premature death. Kath had always been generous and caring, both to friends and the extended family. My friend Peter Kellett flew to Hobart from Adelaide for the funeral and my son Jock came from Alice Springs, such was people's regard for Kath. At the funeral, all of Kath's grandchildren presented a eulogy, as did I and her son David Badcock. Despite the sadness of the occasion, it was really good to catch up with the Badcock family and I enjoyed their company. Of course, it was, as always, great to see PK, who, unknown at the time, was soon to be diagnosed with cancer.

I returned to Lombok in early January. The South Australian election was due in March 2014, and I had booked to visit Adelaide to coincide with election day. In the meantime, there was much to do with the hotel fit-out and finishing. Hundreds of decisions had to be made on everything from indoor plants to the style of sheets. Once these decisions had been made, orders had to be placed and arrangements for timely delivery organised.

On 10 March, exhausted from this rush of activity, I flew to Melbourne and on to Adelaide a few days later. Campaigning for the state election was not going well, and it was likely that Labor would lose. The standard line was that Labor's potential loss was attributable to its having been in office for a long time. In my view, if a political party continually renews itself and its policy, there is no reason why it couldn't govern for the long term. My belief is that the Labor Government was failing as a result of the idiotic, misnamed 'fair elections' legislation, which had been introduced by the Bannon Government. This legislation necessitated a redistribution of electoral boundaries after each election and required the Boundaries Commission to redraw the boundaries so that they reflected the percentage of the two-party vote received by the major parties at the previous election. In other words, if the vote from the previous election was replicated on the new boundaries, the party with the largest share of the two-party preferred should win a majority of seats. Such a system inevitably discriminated against the government of the time, which held the marginal seats. If a party had good marginal seat members and good marginal seat campaigning, it could hold those marginal seats. Bannon's legislation ensured that after each election the boundaries were changed to make the marginal seat boundaries more favourable to the Opposition. The point had finally been reached where the Liberal Party was almost guaranteed victory even before the campaign had started, based on the boundaries.

The strategy pursued by the Labor Party since the 1980s had been to avoid spending money on safe Liberal-held country seats. Inevitably, the result was that the Labor vote in country areas had collapsed and the Liberal vote across the state was more than 50 per cent. Premier Weatherill had recognised the danger, as well as the inequity, and changed the legislation, but it was too late. The die was cast, and Labor was going to lose convincingly. I had recognised this problem for a while and could see no future for the Labor Government if it continued with a conventional approach to the campaign. Jay Weatherill had been a fair Labor Leader and certainly deserved to be re-elected when compared with the Liberal Opposition, which was not much more than an incompetent rabble – the truth of which is on display daily.

I had always been friendly with Nick Xenophon, who, like me had been a previous editor of *On Dit*. Although Nick started as a Liberal and became an Independent, in my judgment he was the best parliamentarian and political leader in South Australia of his generation. In policy terms, he was a Playfordian socialist figure in the best sense of the term. Behind the marketing hype was a smart political brain and he very clearly had South Australia's best interests at heart. The problem for Nick was that he had chosen a path as an Independent and although he had lifted the vote for his micro party to approach 25 per cent, his capacity to increase it further was doubtful. He was planning to run a slate of candidates at the state election and, based on receiving a percentage of the vote in the low 20s, was hopeful of winning several seats in the House of Assembly. It was likely that these seats would have been mainly at the expense of the Liberals. However, Nick failed to understand his fragile supporter base. He was strapped for resources and had not conducted any internal polling, which would have identified that his support was very much based on the theme of 'keeping the bastards honest'. As soon as the *Advertiser* began to portray him as a serious contender for government, his support started to collapse. If he had restricted the Lower House candidate numbers to not more than around eight, he would have dispelled the idea that he was seeking government. Unfortunately, he had almost no party organisation and was attempting to organise almost everything himself. Potential candidates were coming out of the woodwork and Nick, not recognising the problem, felt that the more Lower House candidates the better his party vote would be in the Legislative Council.

I was in contact with Nick and could see some opportunities for Labor in this semi-turmoil. What if Labor did a preference swap with Xenophon? It might have meant that several candidates were elected to Nick's party, but almost certainly it would have ensured the Liberals didn't obtain 24, the majority of seats. Of course, that would have created a parliament where no party had a majority of seats in the Lower House and Xenophon held the balance of power. What would Nick have done with that power? Although at university he had been a Liberal, years of exposure to real politics in Canberra and Adelaide had changed his views. I had several conversations with him and understandably he had no intention of making any commitment to support any party in government before the election. Given that he was attempting to attract both former Labor and Liberal voters, any such commitment before the election would have been political death. Nonetheless, some agreement with Xenophon seemed the only path available to avoid a Liberal Government.

In the meantime, I was communicating with my friend Quentin Black, who had deep roots in the Labor Party power structures. We thought that it might be possible to organise some arrangement whereby a minority Labor Government was elected. However, Quentin's suggestions were rejected by both the Labor Party office and the Labor Government. The convenient argument was that Xenophon couldn't be trusted in any preference swap. I proposed an arrangement whereby, in several seats, a Xenophon how to vote card would be registered with the Electoral Commission allocating preferences to Labor over the Liberals and vice versa in some other seats. This approach would allow Xenophon to continue to show balance between the major parties. The trick would have been to have Labor benefit in the marginals and the Liberals in safe seats. In the event, Labor refused any deal. Perhaps some in the party were prepared to lose office to gain the opportunity to elect a new Labor Party Leader rather than to hold government, admittedly in a minority position.

On election day, Xenophon's party was wiped out, Labor lost the election, Premier Weatherill resigned, and the less-than-inspiring Steven Marshall became premier in a majority Liberal Government. That left me ruing what had happened and contemplating what might have been. Nick had made a disastrous mistake in nominating so many candidates, which left him open to the charge that he aspired to become premier. In my opinion he would have been an excellent premier, but that of course was never on offer. Sadly, Nick Xenophon has now been lost to politics and to public life in South Australia. Labor, in effect, forfeited an election it might have won as a minority government. Irrespective of the circumstances, it is always better for Labor to be in government than in Opposition. I still ponder over whether certain elements in Labor were comfortable with losing in the expectation that Labor would win in 2022.

It had been our practice for some years to have a Melbourne Cup lunch at Taman Restaurant. Unfortunately, this event ended in tragedy in 2015, with our friend Danny in a coma, and his death a few days later. He had left Taman in his car with his wife and baby daughter and gone home after the lunch, arranging to meet some friends later at La Chill bar. After dropping off his family, he headed south towards La Chill, this time on a motor bike, missed a corner and hit a wall. Danny was the son of my friend and old comrade Bob Hogg, who at one stage was the National Secretary of the ALP. Bob and Danny's mother Caroline flew to Lombok but nothing could be done to save Danny. I felt dreadful about Danny's death, given that he'd spent time eating and drinking at my restaurant. Melbourne Cup Lunch 2015 was the last time we ever held such an event at Taman Restaurant.

I had been in Lombok in 2004 when a serious earthquake occurred and was well aware that Lombok was on the ring of fire, with the danger of an earthquake always present. On 29 July 2018, six weeks after the hotel's opening, a major earthquake struck. It was one of three 6+ on the Richter scale over the next 10 days and one of dozens to hit Lombok over the next month. Our hotel, a four-story construction with a pool on the top level, was virtually undamaged by all of the earthquake activity. Given the damage elsewhere, it was an amazing outcome. As an indication of how violent the earthquakes were, I was having an afternoon nap in one of the hotel rooms when one of the big earthquakes struck. The TV shot off the wardrobe and flew across the room towards me as I lay on the bed. The limit of its electric cable halted its flight and the TV crashed to the floor. Although the hotel was undamaged, that incident had a deep psychological effect on me.

Our two-storey house near the hotel was badly damaged, including major structural damage. Since we had not built the house, we had no knowledge of how well it had been constructed and whether or not it was earthquake-proof. I was concerned that after the first big earthquake it had been weakened and might collapse if subjected to further strong activity. For the next few nights Puspa and I slept in the carport, with the car parked on the street. The incident in the hotel with the afternoon earthquake meant I couldn't sleep there. The hotel was one of the safest buildings on Lombok, the damage assessor who had arrived to help with insurance claims soon deciding that Taman Unique Hotel was the safest place to stay. He became our only guest for three weeks, after all of the tourists had fled.

Around 10 days later, a 7+ Richter scale earthquake occurred as Puspa and I slept in the carport. We ran into the street to watch the house 'rock and roll' in the moonlight. It didn't collapse, although if it had, so also would have the flimsy carport where we were sleeping. Puspa and I decided to stay for the remainder of the night in our car, parked in the middle of the street. Aftershocks continued throughout the night and I could see the ripples of energy passing through the ground across the bitumen surface. Intellectually, I knew that earthquakes occur through a build-up of pressure and once the pressure is relieved, calm is again restored until the build-up of pressure again, years later. That knowledge was not of any use that night and by the next morning, I was suffering serious phantom earthquake syndrome. A car door banging, or Puspa turning over in the bed, was enough to have me running for the door. I still haven't completely recovered.

Meanwhile Georgia, who had come to Lombok a few weeks earlier to consider taking over the management of the hotel, decided to return to Melbourne. Of course, I was sad and disappointed, but didn't blame her for a second. She was looking sunken-eyed and terrified, and escaping was the best solution. Puspa and I decided to move into a small hotel that consisted of standalone grass huts and this seemed to me to be the safest place in the terrible circumstances. After a month there and some repairs to our house, I was able to return to the villa, still in shock, but much better than a month earlier. I didn't really start to recover properly until after I travelled to Australia in November that year. In the meantime, across the northern half of Lombok was injury, damage, devastation, destruction and death. Unknown numbers of people had died, thousands were injured and most of the houses in North Lombok were uninhabitable.

Contrary to some opinions on social media, I thought that the Indonesian Government did a pretty good job in dealing with the disaster in the immediate aftermath. The day after the first big earthquake, I counted more than 30 ambulances with Surabaya number plates travelling north on the main road past the Garden restaurant, which was an amazing achievement. They had been requisitioned; driven to the ferry port at

Banyuwangi; ferried to Bali; driven across Bali and ferried to Lombok, all in fewer than 24 hours. Credit to the government when due and given that this is Indonesia, an amazing effort. August was the dry season, with little likelihood of rain. Nonetheless, vast numbers of tarpaulins appeared within a few days to provide shelter for those who had lost their homes and protection for unroofed buildings. For our part, initially we bought a tonne of rice, rented a truck and consigned the rice to a badly destroyed village in North Lombok. Financially, the timeframe for us was terrible. Having just finished and opened the hotel, we were short on money; however, we survived. I wrote to my friends in Australia asking them to help the Senggigi community and several responded very generously and about $26,000 was raised. I then deliberated on what should be done with this money. I could have bought large amounts of rice and that would have been valuable, but would only have represented short-term assistance. I wanted the money used for something more tangible. One reason that the flimsy houses had collapsed was a lack of steel reinforcing in the cement.

I decided to buy steel reinforcing and allocate it to people in the Senggigi village. We purchased the steel, had it delivered to the driveway of Taman Unique Hotel and organised for the staff of the hotel, who knew the people of Senggigi, to undertake the distribution. Overall that arrangement worked well. As far as I know, it was equitable, non-bureaucratic and sans corruption. One of my staff later told me that the head of the village was unhappy that he wasn't in control of the distribution. I was also told that, within a few days, there was a thriving secondary market in steel reinforcing, as people sought to turn the steel reinforcing into cash. What can you do?

The earthquakes had profoundly affected us, with the following email sent to a friend describing the situation at the time:

> We are still ok. We are staying in a little one-storey hotel with bamboo walls and a grass roof. (I used to say such construction was a fire hazard.) I slept properly last night, for maybe the first time in a week. There was another 5+ earthquake at 9 am but we hardly felt it. I have emptied the rooftop pool at Taman Unique Hotel. I am suffering phantom earthquake psychosis and that is probably compounded by Parkinson's. I have closed the hotel and restaurant from tonight. No tourists, no money.
>
> I feel unable to shake off the suspicion that a unique malice has singled me out. I don't feel that particular misfortune has come my way

but rather, that my star has dimmed with age as the stars of others have brightened. The consequence is that my decision-making is not what it used to be.

...

After a bit of stability and the monster 2013–14 season when Jetstar was flying directly from Perth, we started hotel building. The real basis for that decision was that the hotel business would feed the restaurant and help overall viability. In addition, what else was I to do with my later life and income except to travel and piss it up?

So, we struggled and managed to open 15 rooms in June. We were on track for success and to raise the remaining $70,000 to finish the last 10 rooms. Puspa and I managed to stay in the hotel just a few nights and Georgia likewise.

I always worried about Muslim extremist riots, Bali's Gunung Agung or Lombok's Rinjani volcanos blowing and closing the airports, the occasional earthquake etc., but 117 earthquakes in the past 30 days? WTF!

My plan was to finish the hotel, get some trade on the books and sell. Well, the hotel is still in good shape and so is the pool. The restaurant has minor damage, and the deli needs structural work. The architect says the house is structurally OK but needs major work on infill walls.

But I'm 74 in five months, where to get the energy to go on?

There will be no tourists for months and even then, why will they come to Senggigi? There are better ruins to be had in Greece (thank you for the quote, Gough).

The government does not have the sense to kickstart tourism by subsidising direct flights, which is the only way to restart tourism quickly. If you can fly Hong Kong to Lombok for $200 return the tourists will come.

Then again, have the earthquakes finished or when will they? No one knows. There is no geological measuring of the pressure between the Asian plate, which is being subsumed under the Australasian plate. The recent set of earthquakes might have relieved pressure short-term or might be a precursor to something bigger. One local geologist speculates that over time, the north of Indonesia is likely to see a substantial expansion of land mass as the seabed rises higher than sea level under pressure from the plates. Again, who knows?

In the middle of all this turmoil, Jim Hyde, my friend and former senior private secretary when I was a minister in the Australian Government, had a massive stroke and was in a coma. After a few days his family decided to turn off life support. Jim, an amazing and committed person, had been close to me for 30 years. He had lived with HIV/AIDS for decades, but that was not what killed him.

Many years earlier, in 2003, I had joined the Lombok Hash House Harriers, part of the international Hash House Harriers, a walking/running club or, as the slogan has it, 'a club for drinkers with a running problem'. In Lombok, members would drive to a parking area where the run was to start and we would run or walk through the jungle or rice paddies. The runners would follow a paper trail for an hour or so, or longer if walking, and end up back at, or near, the parking area. The trail was usually about six kilometres in length, and with the typical Lombok terrain it was usually very hilly. After the run everybody gathered for a few beers. Once Puspa and I had got together, we participated in Hash twice a week at sites across Lombok. When in Lombok, we rarely missed a meeting. It was Puspa and my 'thing' and we enjoyed it, not merely the exercise, but also the friendship with other Hashers and being able to visit parts of beautiful Lombok, which otherwise we might never have seen. The Hash club in its heyday had well over 200 active members, both men and women.

Puspa and I hashed until I severed my left Achilles tendon in July 2018. I had, by then, completed 980 Hash meetings. I wanted to reach 1000 but after my Achilles had been repaired, I feared that at the age of 75 the rough terrain was too dangerous, and I didn't want to run the risk of further injury. Sadly, I have ended my active hashing days. There must be something about my foot, as I was born with a twisted left foot on the first day of the last year of the Second World War, in Richmond, Victoria. My baby foot was straightened after I had worn a plaster cast for three months.

I had decided to travel to Australia to have the Achilles operation but encountered a problem with that plan. My five-year Indonesian visa was being converted to the equivalent of a permanent resident visa. I had paid the fee in June and was awaiting the visa, which should have taken no more than six weeks. It dragged on and on, and I was getting really annoyed with the agent. When Jim Hyde died in Australia, I was unable to go to the memorial service on 27 August, because the Indonesian Immigration Department still had my passport. I met with Immigration, and they said of course I could have my passport back but that I would lose the $2,000 fee I had paid and, furthermore, when I returned to Indonesia, I would have to apply for a five-year visa and wait five years before again applying for a permanent residence visa. That is what I call being over a barrel. I had no choice but to sit it out with a severed Achilles.

By November 2018 I was in Australia and, while I waited for the operation, I went to stay with my dear lifelong friend Peter Kellett at his farm at Kangarilla. Peter had terminal cancer. We had a fantastic time together, but it was a time that had a tone of finality about it. Of great sadness was the fact that he was unable to drink red wine. In a generous gesture, he opened his oldest and best reds for me to savour. During these few days we revisited the highlights of our lives both together and apart. He was an exceptional cook, and each night produced great meals. I saw him for the last time in Flinders Medical Centre before I left for Melbourne and then to Hobart for recovery. Sadly, he died on 27 February 2019, and I returned to Adelaide for his funeral. Thanks PK, you were such a great friend.

After the Achilles heel operation, I found running difficult, but on my return to Lombok, I found a way to keep fit. Near my house in Senggigi there is a relatively steep concrete path that runs up a hill. I started climbing that hill at walking pace every morning, accompanied either by Puspa or her maid. I have been doing that ever since. As a result, I am now quite fit for a 76-year-old (2021). While staying with Tom Kelly and Linda Funnell in Sydney in June, I was officially diagnosed with Parkinson's Disease. Tom nursed me through the shock with good wine and Linda sustained us with exquisite food. The Parkinson's has made little progress and I'm not on any Parkinson's-related medication – a good outcome in the circumstances.

I had conceived the idea of developing a long tourist walking track across Lombok, following my earlier Hash House Harrier experiences. I had walked various sectors of the Heysen Trail in South Australia, and of course such trails exist in other countries. Tasmania has the Overland Track, which has been an important part of the development of tourism in that state. As far as I am aware, there are no internationally recognised trails through tropical rainforests. Lombok had a unique opportunity to fill this gap.

Fifteen years of Lombok Hash House Harrier membership have provided me with many occasions to walk and run over most of western Lombok and see the wonderful terrain – the rainforest and the abundance of rivers and waterfalls. This experience led me to the realisation that the essentials for a world-class trail already existed in Lombok. I decided to introduce the concept at a Lombok Tourism seminar sponsored by the Australian Government and held in April 2019. The concept was well received at the seminar, particularly the idea of local people benefiting by being trained and employed as guides, obtaining employment in local hotels and other service positions or developing small business activities of interest to the trekkers.

A few months after my operation, on 26 February 2020, I dragged myself over a difficult seven-kilometre section of the trail – and I survived. I wanted to be able to claim that I had walked part of the trail, the concept of which I had inspired.

Bob Hawke died in May 2019, with a memorial in Sydney announced for mid-June. As a minister in his government, I was sent a VIP invitation. I flew to Sydney and Georgia flew up from Melbourne to attend the memorial as my partner, and I arranged for Tom Kelly to attend as one of my former staffers. As readers will already know, I had little time for Hawke, attending the function in the Sydney Opera House mainly to catch up with friends from my political life and to be part of what inevitably was going to be a great political and cultural event. On both counts it was a resounding success. I returned to Lombok a couple of days later, and soon after Tom Kelly and Linda Funnell paid a visit. While they were here, my old comrade Bob Hogg and his partner Maxine McKew visited, and we had a couple of great catch-up dinners. Bob and Maxine and Danny's mother, Caroline Hogg, have been regular visitors to Lombok since Danny Hogg died, helping Danny's widow Izzy with a project and seeing their sweet granddaughter Java.

Later that year, in October, I attended the Golden Jubilee of my graduation as a Bachelor of Laws from the University of Adelaide. I went to the function not for the ceremony but to catch up with many of the old friends with whom I had studied more than 50 years before. Don – my hotel advisor – and Annie Neil came to Adelaide, and we spent a great day showing them the delights of the Clare Valley.

I spent the period of the COVID-19 pandemic usefully, I hope, reflecting on my own life and writing down these reflections and memories. Looking back, I feel quite contented to leave this life, whenever that may happen. Having said that, I am in no rush. I'm over the hill, but still able to climb it every morning. Recently, one of my friends, when enquiring about the progress of my writings, asked me if I had reached the stage in life where I didn't buy green bananas anymore. I was able to reassure her that, although my life is fading and that the optimistic vision I once held is dimming, I still buy green bananas! On reflection, it is the case that the man I used to be is becoming a fast-fading memory, but I believe that the attainments of my lifetime are worth recording in the context in which they occurred and I sought to achieve by writing this autobiography.

I started as a player; I became a coach and now I'm mainly a rapporteur. I used to be more formidable but now I am more reflective. I still wish to see better days, or at least the beginning of better days, but my capacity to influence those future days is now almost non-existent.

The current world bears little resemblance to that I was confident we were entering in the 1960s and 1970s. In many respects mine was a lucky generation. No substantial wars, a feeling of optimism as I was growing up, and a belief as a young adult that we as a generation could make a difference; that we could engender change for the better.

What went wrong? We underestimated the power of money and selfishness. We wanted to see a society emerge where a tiny class of property owners no longer determined the fate of the whole human race. In that, of course, we failed dismally. Capital, and especially neoliberal capital, has a skill for addressing threats to its order and converting them to selling points. Most of the high hopes of our early days have been demolished. But the ideals are not completely lost and will re-emerge in the new generations. My niece Felicity once commented to me that my generation is still grappling with the concept of same-sex marriage, further elaborating, 'The attitude of this generation is that if you love someone, celebrate it. My kids are walking into high schools, which have pride weeks and all manner of clubs for all situations.'

For all the foolishness of politics and the rapid spread of ultra-conservatism, I have faith that those who follow will achieve great things. If they do, they will have to cope with power, greed, climate change, over-population, dictators, the Murdochs of the future, Lilliputian political leadership, money, lack of compassion and arrogance.

My creed was 'Do you want to make a point, or do you want to make a difference?', and inevitably that led me into many difficult situations over my long life of public service. Mostly, I have sought adequacy rather than perfection. One thing I know with certainty is that I have none of the feelings of a man who looks back on his life as a time not well spent. I have attempted to make the most of the opportunities that were created or came along. I believe I was ahead of the times, a claim which can now be judged against history. I was perpetually indignant at the unfairness of life for many citizens – people living in circumstances that could have been dramatically improved with some relatively small political changes.

I spent half of my working life in parliamentary politics, which, as I see it, is concerned with helping people. Generally, I loved doing it. For me, it was never about the journey. It was about the outcomes and not about the credits, and that is the measure upon which I will be happy to be judged. Throughout my political career I didn't much worry about popularity at large. I was never a leader in terms of the structures, but I was happy to lead when it came to ideas. Inevitably, I made some mistakes, but if you're not prepared to be wrong, you'll never come up with anything original.

I sincerely believe that I took the lead when it came to formulating, adopting or implementing good policy during my political life. When the Homosexual Law Reform Bill became law, fewer than 25 per cent of the electorate supported the reform. Presumably, the rest were unhappy with me as its author. Of course, now about 70 per cent support sexual equality before the law. Most unfortunately, politics is no longer mainly about disagreeing on issues. It now seems to be about being in entirely separate conversations.

From as early as my 20s, it had always been my intention to retire from parliament in my early 40s. It was my desire to stay in South Australian state politics and to continue to be the Attorney-General in a Labor Government led by D.A. Dunstan. I saw my role as getting the job done and leaving Don to provide the public support or political coverage. It was a great honour and privilege to serve in Dunstan's Government and one of the many sorrows of my life was to see him finally smashed by the dishonourable forces arrayed against him, not just members of the Adelaide establishment but also individuals from the Labor Party.

So what does this career of a quarter of a century in Australian politics amount to? While the comparison may be viewed as arrogant, I feel that, like song writers who produce their best work before they're 35, I did the same, and that is clearly the story told by the record. When I look back at that record, I am contented knowing that justice has been achieved for a great number of Australians, and particularly for South Australians, who would otherwise have suffered grave injustices.

I was involved in all the great social and political issues of my generation, from opposition to the Vietnam War and conscription, to action on global warming. In between, I was involved in the struggles for women's rights – including abortion rights – and rights for Aboriginal people. I supported campaigns to reduce smoking in the community and removed the criminal law applying to homosexual activity. I protected judicial freedom, supported prison reform, opposed institutionalised paedophilia and promoted rights to euthanasia. I have already detailed my role in saving the

Franklin River. Without hubris or arrogance, I think in response to the question: What did my political career amount to?

I am entitled to answer, 'A significant amount'.

Politicians are generally maligned, but those emerging in the 1970s were largely a fair reflection of the community. Mostly, they were honourable, and the best were courageous and inspired. Of course, there were exceptions. When I was in my 30s, I believed that we were on a path to a better, fairer, more democratic and diverse world. If I had been told that in my 70s I would witness truth ignored and science scorned, the demonisation of dissent and the collapse of the mass media, I would have laughed. How naive I was. I have always had a great deal to say about media bias, particularly from Adelaide's *Advertiser*. However, such criticism should not be misunderstood or misinterpreted. In my view, a healthy media is essential for democracy to function effectively.

Labor governments either try to reform society or manage it. Unfortunately, in the past 40 odd years, the managerialists have held sway. They could just as easily have left it to the Liberals. Of course, in the South Australian context, having me around as a symbol of what was once achieved did not suit the managerialists. Recently, at a lunch of former political operatives in Adelaide, somebody reported that I was coping well with Parkinson's Disease. The response from another participant in the lunch was: 'Will nothing kill off the old codger?' I wear that comment with pride.

I have always wondered why the punters would vote for Jay Weatherill and his nuclear dump when there is a perfectly good Liberal Party ready to step up and undertake the politics of financial desperation, which is now all that is on offer.

Once the managerialists had dispersed most of the state-owned businesses and assets, it was inevitable that SA would be reduced to a point where the government no longer had the resources for its effective management: the State Government Insurance Commission (SGIC), the State Bank, the Housing Trust (much diminished), ETSA, ports, land bank, State forests, Lotteries Commission, Samcor and the list goes on. All sold off to keep the current account from deficit. I saw a figure indicating that the state used to own 40 per cent of the state economy and that the equivalent figure is now less than 10 per cent. What is left consists mainly of land, hospitals and schools.

I have been engaged in politics for more than half a century – approaching 60 years. During that time, I have, of course, had some long-held aspirations and desires that might loosely be described as a 'bucket list'. I hope that I will live long enough to see some of these achieved. The list could have been much longer and some are crucial for the world or for Australia; others are personally important. Underpinning them all is the urgent need for action on global warming. Without action to address global warming, the other issues become irrelevant. The following, not in order of importance, are the issues dear to me: a united Ireland, in honour of my Irish heritage; an Australian Republic; the elimination of racism in Australia and equality for Indigenous people; an AFL team for Tasmania; real action on banning nuclear weapons; and a South Australian election conducted without the negative influence of Murdoch's printed Adelaide *Advertiser*.

When I first compiled my list it contained a couple of aspirations that have since been achieved: a census that reflects the secular nature of Australian society and the election of Anthony Albanese as Prime Minister of Australia. A couple of perhaps more light-hearted aspirations are being able to get to know any children Georgia and Jack might have (already achieved with the birth of grandson Hamilton) and for me to own the first electric car in Lombok – the latter may be in my power to achieve.

# Timeline: Peter Duncan

1945 Peter John Keith Alan Duncan born 1 January in Melbourne
1965 Enrolled in Law at the University of Adelaide; joined the University Labor Club and the Labor Party; met Don Dunstan
1966 Holiday job with Commonwealth Railways; consequently joined the Australian Workers Union
1967 Elected to Adelaide University Student Representative Council
1968 Became co-editor of the student newspaper *On Dit*; took up articles with law firm Bruce Roberts and Brebner
1969 Graduated; invited by friend Chris Cocks to become partner in an existing legal firm, renaming it Cocks, Duncan & Co.
1970s Undertakes a substantial amount of work for the Miscellaneous Workers Union
1971 Marries Sally Morton
1973 Elected to the South Australian House of Assembly for the electorate of Elizabeth in the 1973 South Australian election, aged 28
1973 Introduced a Private Member's Bill to parliament to decriminalise homosexual acts between consenting adults in private
1975 Retains his seat of Elizabeth in the 1975 election, the only Labor member of the House of Assembly to achieve a swing to Labor
1975 Sworn in as Attorney-General and Minister for Prices and Consumer Affairs in Dunstan Labor Government
1975 *Criminal Law (Sexual Offences) Amendment Act 1975* passed
1975–78 As Attorney-General oversees reformist legislation, including:
- abolition of capital punishment
- abolition of public drunkenness as a crime
- criminalisation of rape in marriage
- reform of procedures for rape and other sexual offences trials
- abolition of legal consequences of illegitimacy

- appointment of the first Commissioner for Equal Opportunity
- recognition of de facto couples
- discrimination on the grounds of race criminalised
- members of parliament (disclosure of interests) legislation
- establishment of the Legal Services Commission, the Office of Crime Statistics, the Corporate Affairs Commission and Regulations Review Unit for the purposes of consolidation of regulations under Acts
- set up the Bright Committee into the Rights of Handicapped Persons
- consolidation of South Australian statutes
- prices and consumer affairs reform
- rationalisation of credit union industry with protection for depositors
- consumer protection amendments to the *Land and Business Agents Act*
- *Residential Tenancy Act*
- consumer protection amendments to the *Second-Hand Motor Vehicles Act*
- amendments to the *Builders Licensing Act*
- changes to the operation and remit of the Public Trustee

1978 First marriage ends
1979 Don Dunstan resigns as premier
1979 Appointed Minister of Health and Corporate Affairs by new South Australian Premier, Des Corcoran
1979 Marries Tasmanian Julie Badcock
1979 At snap SA election, retains his seat of Elizabeth, but with a reduced majority
1981 Allocated Transport portfolio in state Labor Shadow Cabinet, under Opposition Leader John Bannon
1981 Bannon hijacks Duncan's election as a South Australian delegate to the ALP National Executive
1981 Deciding he could no longer work under John Bannon, resigns from SA Shadow Ministry
1982 Drafts a resolution to save the Franklin River, which was passed by the Elizabeth ALP sub-branch; the resolution ultimately became the basis for the Hawke Labor Government's successful move to prohibit the building of the proposed Franklin River Dam
1984 Elected to the National Executive by the ALP Convention

1984 Resigned from SA Parliament to contest the newly created federal seat of Makin in Hawke Labor Government, a seat he held at every election until defeated when Labor lost office federally in 1996; one of the very few who had served as a minister in both a state government and the Australian Government

1987 Re-elected Member for Makin, with an increased majority; appointed Minister for Land Transport and Infrastructure Support

1987 Amman Aviation affair; opposed Hawke and Evans's decision to terminate the Amman Aviation contract, leading to Duncan's disillusionment with Prime Minister Bob Hawke

1988 Appointed Minister for Employment and Education Services in Hawke Labor Government

1989 Organises successful fundraiser: 'A Night with the Dunstan Government', held in the Renaissance Tower, Adelaide

1990 Re-elected to Commonwealth Parliament but denied a ministry

1991 Supports the ousting of Hawke and the appointment of Paul Keating as Prime Minister

1991 Appointed parliamentary secretary to the Attorney-General, Michael Lavarch

1992 Works on the development of a Disability Discrimination Bill, with legislation passing that year; regards 'this reform is my most positive achievement during my time in the Australian Parliament and the one of which I am most proud'

1993 Wins Makin again in federal election but, due to the influence of the Right faction, is not appointed to the ministry

1994 Is campaign manager for Robyn Geraghty, who is ALP candidate in Torrens by-election; Geraghty wins, with Labor's vote increasing by 12 per cent

1996 Defeated in federal election, decides to leave politics and flies to Spain for a holiday

1997 Becomes involved in Overseas Pharmaceutical Aid for Life (OPAL), as chairperson

1997 Establishes large outdoor dining precinct in Victoria Square, with support from the Adelaide City Council, but the project fails the following year, with investors losing their money

1997 Runs the campaign in Florey for the ALP candidate Frances Bedford, who won with a 12.3 per cent swing to Labor

1998 Meets Malcolm Barnes; travels to East Timor to re-establish the central pharmaceutical facility for the Australian Government, under the auspices of Opal Return Unwanted Medicines

1998 Agrees to invest and become a director in plastic-waste recycling company Omnipol

2002 Omnipol collapses and liquidators appointed

2002 Suffers a breakdown and travels to Bali, later, to Lombok, to recover

2003 Julie and daughter Georgia visit Duncan in Lombok

2003 Julie diagnosed with cancer

2004 Federal police interview Duncan and Julie in Hobart over their involvement in Omnipol

2004 Suicide attempt fails

2005 Julie dies

2006 Meets Puspa

2007 Travels to Hobart for Georgia's birthday; met at the airport by the Australian Federal Police and is issued with a summons; travels to Adelaide, appears in the Magistrates Court, where he is granted bail

2008 Jury acquits Duncan of all charges

2008–11 Works on case of Scott Rush, one of the 'Bali 9', with his assistance resulting in Rush's death penalty being quashed, to be replaced by life imprisonment

2013 Diagnosed with Parkinson's Disease by a doctor in Lombok

2014 Duncan and Puspa's hotel commenced construction around Taman Restaurant and Deli, and it and the rooftop pool survives the 2018 earthquakes

2015 Turns 70

2018 Major earthquakes strike Lombok

2019 Parkinson's diagnosis confirmed by Sydney neurologist

2019 Bob Hawke dies and Duncan travels to his memorial at the Sydney Opera House to catch up with old friends and colleagues

# Legislative and Attempted Reforms at a Glance

This section covers reforms from 1975 until early 1979 – a mere four years – when I was as South Australia's Attorney-General to the visionary South Australian Premier Don Dunstan.

**Abolition of capital punishment**
Although the Liberals were mostly opposed to the Bill, it was passed. Labor Party members were bound by party policy, so eventually a reform that was longstanding Labor policy was achieved.

**Abolition of public drunkenness as a crime**
This law reform was long overdue. My general philosophy is that laws should be relaxed where they impinge on individuals and the way they live their lives. The previous law had been seriously misused by the police. The anecdote involving John Bray, QC, outlined in this autobiography, is an exemplar of why public drunkenness as a crime simply had no place in a modern world.

**Criminalisation of rape in marriage**
A Bill was drafted and taken to Cabinet to simply abolish the protection afforded by the criminal law to husbands who raped their wives. This was the first time in the English-speaking world that rape in marriage had been outlawed. Amazingly, it met with some resistance in Cabinet before being adopted, with some Cabinet members believing that the measure would meet with opposition from established church groups. Similar laws have now been adopted Australia-wide.

**Reform of procedures for rape and other sexual offences trials**
The Criminal Law and Penal Methods Reform Committee, chaired by Dame Roma Mitchell between 1970 and 1981, had recommended the reform of rape and sexual offence trials and pre-trial procedures to ensure that the victims were treated as humanely as possible. When these

recommendations were adopted and passed into law, the stress of the criminal trial for a victim was greatly ameliorated.

### Abolition of legal consequences of illegitimacy
Prior to this legislation, illegitimate children, through no fault of their own, were discriminated against by both society and the law. Changing society's attitudes required education; the legal consequences of illegitimacy required an Act of parliament. The requisite Bill was drafted and passed with little opposition. Now all children in SA have equal status before the law.

### Appointed the first Commissioner for Equal Opportunity
In 1976 administrative arrangements associated with the Sex Discrimination Act were set up, with Mary Beasley appointed as the first Commissioner for Equal Opportunity. An issue of abiding interest to me was sex discrimination, which was still institutionalised in 1970s society. These reforms were among the first in Australia and helped to lead to the revolutionary change in the status of women in Australian society over the past 40 years

### Contracts Review Bill
A Bill was prepared to allow courts to review terms of small or consumer contracts and to void unfair terms. This met with a great deal of opposition from the Law Society, judges and the business community. A fundamental principle of the common law governing commercial or business activity is the inviolability of contracts. Although I was removed as Attorney-General before the legislation passed the parliament, I had a minor success in that my friend, Frank Walker, then the NSW Attorney-General, took up my draft Bill and had it passed into law by the NSW Parliament. After the law had operated for some time in NSW, it was legislated into law in SA.

### Recognition of de facto couples
I could see absolutely no reason in the modern world why de facto couples should be treated any differently under the law from married couples. This issue, however, engendered considerable opposition from the churches. When the Bill was eventually passed, it was a first in Australia and has since been copied nationwide.

### Criminalised discrimination on the ground of race
The *Race Discrimination Act 1976*, outlawing acts of racial discrimination, was passed into law and has had an enormous impact on changing racist attitudes and behaviour over the intervening years.

### Members of parliament (disclosure of interests) legislation
Ongoing community concern about propriety in the parliament resulted in the Members of Parliament (Disclosure of Interests) legislation, and when subsequently passed, it became the template for such legislation across the nation.

### Established the Legal Services Commission: legal aid for all in need
Laws can only be applied effectively and fairly if people have access to the law, regardless of their means. Legislation was passed to establish the Legal Services Commission, whose role was to ensure that legal aid was available to all in need. Under its first chair, David Wilson, either private or in-house legal services were to be made available to needy clients. I proposed that the money to fund these services should come from interest on the large funds in solicitors' trust accounts. The banks and the Law Society were understandably appalled. Eventually, the government won the day, and now legal aid is funded by interest from trust account funds. This reform was again adopted across the nation. Decentralised Legal Service Commission offices were established throughout the state.

### Established the Office of Crime Statistics
After a review by the consultant Dr Greg Woods, an Office of Crime Statistics was established, headed by an American criminologist, Peter Grabosky. Prior to this, the only crime figures available in SA had been provided to the media by the police and these statistics were widely seen as self-serving. The Office of Crime Statistics figures were gathered from the courts, at all levels, and from the Community Welfare department, in the case of juveniles. The Crime Statistics Office numbers were seen as credible and accurate. The quarterly reports issued by the Attorney-General provided an opportunity for more balanced discussion in the media and elsewhere and also limited the capacity of the police to run political campaigns based on shock horror crime wave dramas.

### Extra resources for the Land Titles Office
The Torrens title registration system was introduced in South Australia in 1857, a world-first, and is now the standard system for land title registration across the world. When I became Attorney-General, the process of converting land titles from the old General Registry system had still not been completed, more than 100 years later. A modest increase in resources was provided to enable this task to be completed.

### Freedom of information
Freedom of information laws were drafted but not enacted. It was always my view that government should cheaply and conveniently make as much information as possible available to the public, with obvious exceptions, such as ministerial papers and Cabinet documents. I think a person should have the right to go to court and seek information held by government and which is being withheld.

### Established the Corporate Affairs Commission
Prior to legislation to establish a Corporate Affairs Commission, the administration of various corporate bodies had been spread across several government departments. The commission brings the registration and administration of all corporate bodies in SA under one administration.

### Government Investigation Section
A special office had been established by Dunstan to concentrate on investigating suspect companies and individuals in the corporate field and, where necessary, to launch prosecutions. We expanded the section to include lawyers, accountants and police officers who were specialists in dealing with matters involving company and commercial frauds and malpractices.

### Reduced formality in SA's lower courts and encouraged abandonment of the wearing of regalia in the District Court
I wanted to see District Court judges cease wearing wigs, although this became a struggle between the more enlightened and the more conservative or traditional judges. Eventually a compromise was reached, with the bench wearing full wigs and gowns in criminal trials and only gowns in civil trials, a practice which I understand continues.

### Regulations Review Unit
This unit was established with the aim of methodically reviewing all of the regulations in SA to ensure that they were consistent and up to date in terms of technology and did not conflict with other regulations, rules and Acts etc. The unit achieved a consolidation of the regulations under each Act, ensuring their ready availability to the public. This was before access to information via the internet.

### Consolidation of the statutes
Len King, as Attorney-General, had contracted the former Parliamentary Counsel, Edward Ludovici, to consolidate the South Australian statutes, a task which had last been undertaken in the 1930s. I completed this process

by arranging the printing and publication of the consolidation by the Government Printer.

**Sun light (solar) rights**

As Attorney-General, I established a departmental committee to report on law reform to ensure 'sun light rights', or solar rights for property owners who had or wished to install solar panels. I was concerned that without a right to solar light, a property owner might install a solar system only to have a neighbour construct a building blocking the direct sunlight required by the solar system. Sadly, this initiative was not followed through by later holders of the Attorney-General's office.

**Drug law reform**

Often, over the past few years, I have been asked why the Dunstan Government had done nothing about drug reform. In fact Dunstan and I had wanted to reform drug laws. With some opposition in the Cabinet, Don decided to proceed cautiously by appointing Professor Ron Sackville as a Royal Commissioner to report and make recommendations on how to proceed. Sadly, by the time of his report, Don had resigned, and I was no longer Attorney-General. The report and its recommendations for action were shelved.

**Bright Committee into the Rights of Handicapped Persons**

The 1978 enquiry into the rights of handicapped persons was chaired by retired Mr Justice Bright and represented the first attempt in Australia to tackle discrimination against people with disabilities. Although we didn't have the opportunity to implement the committee's findings, its report pointed the way forward in dealing with such discrimination. When I was parliamentary secretary to the Attorney-General in the Keating Government, I was able to resurrect this matter and was instrumental in the passing of the *Disability Discrimination Act 1992*.

**Tort of privacy**

Privacy as a concept is somewhat indefinable. It means something to everyone and may mean different things to each of us. I was enthusiastic about exploring the introduction of the tort of privacy to protect the privacy of individual South Australians. Legislation to create a right to privacy had been introduced by Len King but had been vigorously opposed in the community and was withdrawn. I asked the Solicitor-General Brian Cox to form a small departmental committee to investigate privacy law and to report. The report was completed after Brian Cox was appointed to the Supreme Court in late 1978 and no action was taken before I was removed as Attorney-General.

**Associations Incorporations Act**
With the aim of providing a framework for democracy in associations incorporated under the existing Associations Incorporations Act, I decided to seek to amend the Act. It was not unreasonable in my view that, if associations were obtaining the benefits under the Act, their constitutions should reflect proper democratic values. Apart from small associations, local sporting clubs, large and powerful groups such as the Royal Automobile Club and the Red Cross were covered by that Act. The Bill provided for the election of worker and community directors. Cabinet approved the Bill, and it was introduced to an avalanche of opposition. In this instance, there had not been adequate consultation and community support had not been gained for the Bill and it had to be withdrawn.

**Spent Convictions Bill**
My initial intention had been to abolish records of convictions for homosexual behaviour between consenting adult males, behaviour that I had removed from the criminal law. It was subsequently pointed out that, as we had abolished the offence of drunkenness, the Bill should also apply to convictions for public drunkenness to ensure fairness and consistency. Subsequently, the internal debate widened to include the removal of the conviction records of people convicted of minor offences who hadn't re-offended for some years. No further progress had been made before I was removed as Attorney-General.

**Prices and Consumer Affairs reform**
On being sworn in, I launched a war on consumer injustice, which was widespread. A good rule of thumb is that there's a spiv lying in wait on every corner. It used to be called *caveat emptor*. Price setting does function as a limiter in consumer society and was useful in that role in the 1970s, but there's no room for out and out gouging. My policy was to use the legislation to give the administration a deal of power and that's exactly what we did. Following that, I encouraged the administrators to use the law to its fullest. My attitude was, where there was evidence of a breach of law, that the matter should be taken to the courts. The number of prosecutions doubled in the first year I was minister.

**Rationalised credit union industry with protection for depositors**
Credit union legislation was introduced that enabled credit unions to compete with the banks more effectively. The banks had the same low standing in the community then as now. More effective supervision of credit unions was introduced and a system of guarantees for depositors was implemented.

**Consumer protection amendments to the *Land and Business Agents Act 1974***
The activities of a small element of land agents were always of concern to the Consumer Affairs Commissioner. Major consumer protection amendments to the *Land and Business Agents Act 1974* were introduced, including proscribing agents' buying and selling on their own account.

*Residential Tenancy Act 1978*
Prior to this legislation, landlords of residential properties could conduct their business virtually without interference from the law. The *Residential Tenancy Act 1978* involved the establishment of an inexpensive and quick resolution tribunal, a major advance for tenants' rights. All residential tenancy bonds were required to be paid into the tribunal and the interest from the bond account paid for the tribunal's administrative costs. The system developed in SA was soon adopted in other jurisdictions.

**Major consumer protection amendments to the Second-Hand Motor Vehicles Act**
Major consumer protection amendments to the Second-Hand Motor Vehicles Act introduced greater protection for vulnerable consumers.

**Insurance Contracts Bill**
Early on in my term as minister, the Commissioner of Consumer Affairs brought to my attention the high level of consumer complaints involving insurance contracts. I arranged for the parliamentary counsel to draft a Bill to, in effect, introduce a code of good conduct for the industry and for consumers. The government-owned SGIC was opposed to the legislation, based on the conservative legal argument that the existing law had been subject to hundreds of court judgements, over generations of legal development, which had been subsequently reflected into the drafting of insurance contracts. Any reform of the law was going to require the recasting of all insurance contracts. The law was not proceeded with, but subsequent Australian Government legislation was enacted to similar effect.

**Amendments to the *Builders Licensing Act 1967***
Amendments were introduced to tighten up the law related to builders' licences, ensuring sub-contractors were included under the Act and in the trust account arrangements in order to protect consumers from defaulting builders and sub-contractors.

**Public Trustee**
Prior to my time as a minister, the two private executor companies in the state – Elders Trustee and the Executor Trustee and Agency Company – were protected from competition by the Public Trustee in much of the work that they undertook. I removed this protection and allowed the Public Trustee to compete unreservedly. I encouraged the Public Trustee to establish and extend a free will-making service for the public.

# Acknowledgements

This book would not have been written had it not been for the COVID-19 pandemic. If the dramatic interruption to the tourist industry in Lombok hadn't occurred, I'm confident it would never have seen the light of day. Even then, the original manuscript was a crude version of what is now published, and began with my childhood and ended in 2020. To say that the book now published in my name is a team effort is a gross understatement. My friend, and Julie Duncan's former work colleague, Peter Baker, read the original manuscript and, apparently liking what he had read, set about a style edit.

Following that, Gabrielle (Gay) Walsh became involved and it is again an understatement to say that, without her involvement and hundreds of hours of work, this book would not have been published. Guiding, directing, challenging, encouraging and loving, she drove the project to fulfilment. I can never adequately express my appreciation of the hours and effort she put into the project. She taught me that critical thinking and accessible storytelling can go hand in hand.

It was on her suggestion that the History Trust of South Australia became involved and with enthusiastic support from the Chair, Elizabeth Ho, and CEO Greg Mackie, the History Trust's involvement led to the decision by Michael Bollen, publisher at Wakefield Press, to publish this autobiography. My special thanks go to Michael and to my editor at Wakefield, Penelope Curtin, for not only their skill but their perseverance and preparedness to put up with Peter Duncan in his dotage. Throughout the saga of getting the manuscript to publication, my friends Don and Annie Neil have been stalwarts, providing emotional and material encouragement. My thanks to Don and Annie.

I recognise that others will have different views on events or individuals I have written about and I hope people will forgive if I have caused unwitting offence or hurt.

When I started this project, I very much still felt that my writing belonged in the '320 Politics' category of the Dewey Decimal classification. I now realise that 900 to 999, History Biography, is where I now belong.

All in all, this publication has been a wonderful team effort and I extend my thanks for their unstinting support and contribution.

Wakefield Press is an independent publishing and
distribution company based in Adelaide, South Australia.
We love good stories and publish beautiful books.
To see our full range of books, please visit our website at
www.wakefieldpress.com.au
where all titles are available for purchase.
To keep up with our latest releases, news and events,
subscribe to our newsletter.

Find us!

Facebook: www.facebook.com/wakefield.press
Twitter: www.twitter.com/wakefieldpress
Instagram: www.instagram.com/wakefieldpress

www.ingramcontent.com/pod-product-compliance
Lightning Source LLC
Chambersburg PA
CBHW040745020526
44114CB00049B/2937